IT HAS COME TO PASS

by

JAMES T. FARRELL

"For as the new heavens and the new earth, which I will make, shall remain before me, saith the Lord, so shall your seed and your name remain."
ISAIAH, 66:22

THEODOR HERZL PRESS

NEW YORK, 1958

Copyright
Theodor Herzl Foundation, Inc.
1958

Printed in the United States of America
NEW YORK, 1958

PREFACE

THIS BOOK of impressions of the State of Israel may seem like a new writing venture for me to readers who only associate me with Chicago and STUDS LONIGAN. But it is not, because I have made it a rule to try to learn something new about any new place I am visiting and the people who live there, and to absorb this material into my creative work. When I went to Israel in June 1956, I had no intention of writing a book about that country. However, after having been there for a while, and particularly after having been gripped by the many fascinating and often poignant stories of the new imigrants, I decided to write this book.

I have deliberately omitted discussing the political situation in Israel, because so much has already been written about it.

As far as the conclusions I have reached are concerned, I am perfectly willing to change any or all of them if I am given adequate facts and convincing reasons. I will do the same if adequate facts lead me to reach different conclusions concerning the Arab countries. I arrived in Israel quite critical of many aspects of the life of that country, as a consequence of my reading. I did not find confirmation of my views and this is why I changed them.

The number of people to whom I am indebted in the writing of this book is such that I cannot possibly give acknowledgment to all of them. I am very deeply indebted to my secretary, Mrs. Luna Wolf, for her editorial assistance and advice. I am indebted to Mrs. Louise Richmond of Braintree Highlands, Massachusetts, who typed the first two drafts of this volume despite the fact that my handwriting is so illegible that I sometimes have difficulty reading it myself. I am indebted to Mr. Hugh V. Hopkins, formerly of the University of Iowa, for reading the manuscript and commenting on it.

Among the many people who helped me in Israel, I wish to make the greatest acknowledgment to Miss Chana Shapiro, Mr. Noah Lucatz and Mr. Uriel Doron. Miss Shapiro is a Chicago-born official of the Israeli Foreign Ministry, and I am grateful for her comments as well as her intelligence in guiding me on the trip through the Negev. Mr. Lucatz, who also acted as my guide, is a Scottish-born Israeli affiliated with Histadrut. My discussions with him clarified many points about Israel and his interpretation and the manner in which he posed my questions to the people I was interviewing were of immeasurable help to me. Working with him and Miss Shapiro enabled me, I hope, to learn much. Mr. Uriel Doron arranged some of my trips or made them more convenient. None of these three Israelis or any other Israelis attempted in any way to influence my judgment, and I was not denied access to any place I wished to visit.

My debt of gratitude to Dr. Raphael Patai, Director of Research of the Theodor Herzl Foundation and one of the most distinguished scholars on the Near East and Israel, is very great. Dr. Patai arranged for the publication of this book, and assisted me in the editing and in the correction of facts and the spelling of names.

Before I arrived in Israel, I had the opportunity to talk to a small group of very intelligent Arabs. Every one of them took an anti-Israel position, but I found them civilized and was able to discuss the Near East as well as the Arab-Israeli questions with them without the rancor which usually pervades these subjects. Through them I was able to look at these problems from a different point of view.

While I make these acknowledgments, I wish to stress that none of these people is responsible for any errors or opinions in this volume.

I hope that this book will be of interest to the reader.

JAMES T. FARRELL

New York
September 1958

CHAPTER ONE

I

I WAS TRAVELING FROM JERUSALEM to Tel Aviv by the *sherut* service, on a warm June morning, and I struck up a conversation with the other passengers, average Israelis or men-in-the-street. They spoke broken English. At first we talked about the trees which had been planted along the route and in other parts of Israel. They were pleased that I, a foreigner, should have noticed the trees, and had seen how Israel was beginning to bloom. But suddenly, one of the passengers, a man of about thirty and in his shirt sleeves, turned to me with concern on his face.

"This is good for one condition."

"What is that?" I asked.

"Peace."

Shortly before I made this trip, a Rumanian born hotel clerk had said to me:

"Believe me, Mr. Farrell, we want peace. Believe me, I was twenty-nine months in a concentration camp. I don't want my son to go through that. I want peace. But if we have to, we'll fight. We'll die. Believe me, I'll die."

In July of that same strange summer in Israel, I was sitting on the veranda of a hotel with a woman who had been born in America, had been raised as a Zionist, and now held a fairly high position in the Israeli government. In the midst of a random personal conversation, she suddenly asked me whether I had just heard anything. All I had heard were the shouts of children and of other bathers in the swimming pool just below us. She asked me had I heard airplanes? Had it come? The sky was hot and blue, silent and full of peace. But a few days previously, while returning from a trip to Tel Aviv by sherut, on a friendly summer morning, her taxi, along with many other cars, had been held up in the Jerusalem corridor for over an hour. She had heard shooting. There had been an infiltration.

Shortly before leaving Israel in August, I had a discussion in Ashkelon with an intelligent, educated group, including a journalist, a Histadrut official and an official of the government. A foreign journalist who had been on both sides of the frontier had voiced to me a suspicion which has often been expressed—that the Israeli government keeps the present tense Arab-Israeli conflict alive because it serves as a spur to greater national unity, as well as a helpful means of increasing the effort to build the country. The Israeli government has frequently been accused of this in America as well as in the Arab world. One of our group remarked with concern that if peace came, there might be disunity and a relaxation of work in Israel. It is quite widely recognized that some of Israel's problems are partially suppressed because of the danger which surrounds her. The government official who was present in Ashkelon denied that the tension was kept alive by the Israel authorities.

The man who had expressed his anxiousness agreed with that statement, but still he feared that peace could disrupt unity in Israel.

"Any government here," said the Histadrut official, "which refused a decent peace offer could not stay in power for twenty-four hours."

Such sentiments and views were widespread in Israel prior to the attack in Sinai. Many Israelis, officials and private citizens alike, believed that they were virtually alone in the world, and that most of the proposals concerning peace with the Arabs which came from outside Israel were of such a character as to weaken them and that these could even lead to the destruction of Israel. We can have little doubt that this conviction was strengthened by the events which followed Israel's withdrawal from Sinai, the Gaza strip and the Gulf of Aqaba, and by many subsequent events in the Near East.

Some observers, journalists and others, believe that Israel is sometimes provocative, and the attack of 1956 has given credence to their claim. They think that if the policy of the Israeli government were softer and more conciliatory, tension would be reduced. However, when I was in Israel, tension was mounting. It was quite evident in June 1956 that an explosion was close at hand. There were almost daily infiltrations! Some of it was for purposes of smuggling, or for robbery. Cattle, sections of irrigation pipe and equipment were either taken or destroyed. Arabs often cross back and forth over the frontier, sometimes to see their relatives, sometimes to smuggle. But in other cases, the infiltration was military, and Israelis were killed. In the summer of 1956, a bomb was hurled into a school house. A young Sabra teacher in the Negev told me a story of how, in her settlement, a bomb was thrown during a wedding reception, killing the groom. On July 4, 1956, a young man and a girl were sitting in a parked car near the Lydda Airport; they were probably necking. Four infiltrators, the Israeli government charged, shot them in the head. Stories like these are commonplace in Israel. Many more incidents occur than are actually mentioned in the newspapers. This was definitely so in the months preceding the Sinai campaign.

In many places along the border, farmers work in the fields with a gun slung over their shoulders. In a wild and rugged part of the Judean hills, a few hundred yards from the Jordanian border, I was being driven along an old and bumpy side road near a military outpost. I saw a pretty dark-haired girl in blue shorts, tending a flock of sheep. She was about seventeen. She also carried a rifle.

I was at a kibbutz in Galilee. The kibbutz children of the fourth form or fourth grade were giving a show in celebration of the end of the school year. There was a big bonfire, and the atmosphere was one of joy and gaiety. A man, carrying a rifle, spoke to a child and then walked off into the night. I asked about this, and was told that the man was a member of the kibbutz, a teacher; he had spoken to his own son, one of the children who was performing. He had told the boy that he couldn't remain to watch because he had to do guard duty that night.

These are but a few of the daily incidents in the life of the Israelis. I could cite similar ones almost endlessly. In fact, the Israelis live in a state of twenty-four hour danger. Prior to the Sinai war, if you took a taxicab between Jerusalem and Tel Aviv after dark, you could not be sure of what would happen to you. People living under these conditions, especially when they feel that they are almost alone, and that the democratic countries of the West have failed to understand their position, their aims and their democratic hopes, will quite naturally develop the attitude that they may have to fight or die for their freedom and their very existence. I know from personal experience that hundreds of Israelis believe that the issue at stake for them is that of survival.

There are many other problems causing the dangerous torment of that vast sub-continent, the Middle East, among them the question of control of the Suez Canal, the problem of Soviet infiltration, the need and the current struggle for unity and power in the Arab world. But insofar as the Arab-Israeli conflict is concerned, the basic question is this—does Israel have the right to exist?

This is the way the Israelis feel. There is considerable evidence to indicate that there are objective grounds for their attitude. The Israelis are convinced that the Arab leaders seek to destroy them, to drive them into the sea.

II

I recall having dinner in Tel Aviv with a young American journalist and an American-born woman, Zionist in upbringing, and now an Israeli citizen. The young journalist asked me did I believe Israel could or should continue its policy of taking in new immigrants on a mass scale.

"Theoretically, no," I answered.

Turning to our companion, he asked her why this policy was continuing, even though it was admittedly a drain and a burden on the country, and was creating so many fresh problems at a time when Israel was already beset with problems and difficulties.

Our companion said that it was necessary for the development of the country and that these people were Jews. She insisted that the new immigrants could be assimilated. The Negev must be populated. But then she burst out:

"It's instinctive."

To an outsider, especially a gentile or a *goy*, the policy of the Israeli government in admitting and giving citizenship to any Jew who returns to Israel can seem bewildering. This is doubly the case if you travel around Israel and consider the many complicated social, personal and psychological problems which mass immigration creates, especially in the case of immigrants from North Africa, the Arab and other Asian countries. Next to the peace problem, that of integration of the new immigrants is, in my opinion as well as that of many Israelis, Israel's biggest and most difficult problem. A number of intelligent Israelis are convinced that the big future issue which they must meet and deal with is this—will Israel remain Westernized or will it become Levantine? Will the weight of the Oriental immigrants overwhelm those with European backgrounds, and, if so, will all of the effort to create a modern and democratic state be in vain?

There are disputes as to how many more immigrants Israel can accept. One Israeli stated that experts had concluded that with continuing development, soil reclamation and conquest of the desert, Israel, within its present boundaries, should be able to sustain a population of 4,000,000. Apparently, this was the population of Palestine in biblical times. Others dispute this claim. When questioned or challenged by outsiders on Israel's immigration policy, some Israelis will state that everything they have so far accomplished seems to have been a miraculous contradiction of the experts. The reclamation of so much acreage which had been but rock, desert sand or malaria infested marshes, the opening up of the Negev, the extended and continuously developing irrigation system, the victory in war over the Arabs—all of this was considered unbelievable by experts or professionals.

Clearly, it is a fair statement to assert that new immigrants have been needed for economic and military reasons. The development of the country required and still requires a larger population than Palestine had. And the frontiers and the Negev desert must be ringed with settlements if the country is to be made defensible. Travel along the frontier parallel to the Gaza strip or in the Negev, and this becomes quickly obvious. The road to Migdal Ashkelon is now dominated by settlements, mostly kibbutzim. An invading army today could—unless it had overwhelming superiority in arms and numbers—meet with greater obstacles than the Egyptian army originally encountered in the 1948 war. Then, it advanced to within ten miles of Tel Aviv before it was surrounded, cut off, and finally defeated in the Faluja pocket.

Similarly, in the Lachish area, a new and truly remarkable development of planned settlement in desert and wilderness, you cannot easily overlook the military as well as the economic significance of what is being done. Kiryat Gat, the planned center of the entire Lachish area, is athwart one of the main roads of Israel. Ringing it are settlements, with new ones constantly springing up.

This aspect of Israeli policy causes concern among the Arabs, and a familiar Arab contention is that Israel's policy of immigration has, as its main aim, the population of the country so that it can become aggressive against them. However, when you consider that Israel is a nation of about 2,000,000, facing 45,000,000 Arabs, this contention obviously contains elements of fantasy. The settlements are being developed to permit people to work the land, to develop industry, to provide the means for a rising standard of living materially and culturally. The military value of settlements is not and cannot be overlooked or left out of account in the present circumstances, but this is different from considering these new settlements merely or solely as preparation for aggressive war.

Further, Israelis, when discussing the new immigration and the problems this has created, stress that they had to take in these new immigrants. In many lands, they were discriminated against or oppressed. A warrant for this contention can be seen in the treatment of Egyptian Jews, after Sinai, the rise of anti-Semitism in Poland, the plight of Hungarian Jews. Like many before them, these Jews have no place to go but Israel. New immigrants themselves often tell you this, or, more importantly, they will reveal it in the answers they give when questioned. Many of them came to Israel poor and diseased. Undernourishment, trachoma, syphilis, tuberculosis ran high among those who came from Asian countries. Babies from North Africa were often pudgy and in infancy had unhealthy swollen faces which made them look like old people while they were still in their mothers' arms. Opportunities for education of the children were slim and in some cases virtually non-existent. In some Arab countries, Jews were definitely oppressed. Since the establishment of the State, there were two counter-migrations—Arabs from Palestine and Jews from Arab countries. Including North Africa, about half a million Jews have immigrated to Israel from countries where the preponderance of the population is Arab or Muslim.

"The ingathering of the exiles"—this is a phrase commonly used in Israel. But there is, on the part of many, faith and emotion involved here. The immigration policy is not dictated merely by economic and military considerations.

I interviewed Prime Minister Ben-Gurion in Jerusalem, and the first thing he said was:

"A Jew cannot become a real Jew unless he's here,"

that is, in Israel. Dr. Yehuda Kohn, until recently an important adviser on foreign policy, and a most erudite legal expert, remarked: "Every nation has persecuted us." The persecution of and discrimination against Jews in many lands, the butcheries of the Nazis, this is but a partial explanation of the faith and emotion underlying the conviction which the Israelis have about their country. You go to Israel and keep talking to people about these questions and attitudes and you come to grasp this unmistakably. You realize that down through the centuries, the hunger, the yearning for a homeland never died. From generation to generation, this deep emotion, this yearning for *Eretz Israel,* the Land of Israel, continued in Jewish hearts all over the world. One may like or dislike it, but again and again one encounters it in Israel, so that one becomes convinced that in many instances it has been and is profound and deep.

In our conversation in Tel Aviv, the American-born Zionist woman offered one of the explanations of this:

"It's instinctive."

An emotional hunger which has been transmitted through centuries and which has survived in the midst of fierce persecutions and pogroms comes to function like an instinct. The feeling in Israel about the ingathering of its exiles is of this character. It is one of the roots of what is modern Israel.

III

There is already a more than considerable history of the return of the Jews to Palestine. It is needless for me to repeat what has already been written. However, a few facts are important, and I shall present them here briefly.

From time to time, Jews returned to Palestine as a consequence of persecution, or because of the desire to die in the Holy Land of Israel. You can meet *sabras* whose forebears returned following the Spanish Inquisition. In the nineteenth century, and especially among Orthodox Jews, some returned to Palestine to die. There was a colony of such Jews in the town of Safed. In the Orthodox section of the New City of Jerusalem, Mea Shearim or the Hundred Gates, some of their descendants can now be seen wearing caftans and fur hats, as they go about with long beards and side-locks. Because of their costume and their fanaticism, they are picturesque. They oppose the State of Israel because they believe that it was founded before the time of the coming of the Messiah. On Sabbath eve, they gather in their *shul* to chant and pray, and their eyes become mad and wild with fanaticism, their heads sway and jerk, their shoulders wiggle, and they are carried away into an emotional trance. They offer a spectacle which matches any of the instances of religious fanaticism in our country. On the outside of their shul they had put up signs in Hebrew which proclaim that Jerusalem is full of harlots going about in short-sleeved dresses. Some of them stone automobiles on the Sabbath, and on one street in their district they built a barricade of stones to prevent cars from passing, and perhaps to give them ready ammunition in case they do spot a car in motion. Their women wear dark dresses with long sleeves and high necks, have their hair cut when married, and are never seen without a kerchief covering their entire head.

They furnish a diverting Friday evening for tourists, and are a source of embarrassment to most Israelis, including pious and observant ones who, while not violating the various rituals of their religion, do not wish to intrude on the lives of others.

Almost no tourist or visitor to Jerusalem misses seeing Mea Shearim. It reveals in the present one of the types of emotion and attitude which stood behind the return to Palestine. However, it is the least important of the reasons for the return, and should not be over-estimated or unduly stressed. Here it is sufficient to recognize it.

In the 1880's, there was the first immigration or *Aliyah*. Immigrants known as the *Biluim* came to work the land. They were early Zionists. Emigrating from Russia, they took their name from their slogan, "O House of Jacob, come, let us go." They dreamed of working in agriculture and realized that the return of the Jews required actual colonization of the country and the application of their labor for its development. They were inexperienced and poor. They met with serious obstacles, faced hunger and disease, and only the intervention of the Baron de Rothschild enabled them to exist at all. Even before the 1880's, however, an agricultural school, Mikve Israel, was founded near Jaffa with aid from the French Alliance Israélite Universelle. Its purpose was to try to teach members of the religious communities of Jerusalem and Safed in Galilee, and to get them to do agricultural work rather than to continue living in a charity-supported community.

The Second Immigration dates from between 1904 and the First World War, but it had been preceded by the founding of Zionism as a world movement. This, as is known, was due largely to the efforts of Theodor Herzl.

Most of those of the Second Aliyah came from Russia and the Slavic areas of Europe. Among them were the youths Ben-Gurion, now the Prime Minister, and Ben-Zvi, now the President, of Israel. Those who went to Israel in the Second Immigration laid the basis for modern Palestine and modern Israel. Many of them were labor Zionists, and strongly socialist in their thinking. As early as 1907, Ben-Gurion applied for admission of the Labor Zionists into the Second Socialist International, but the application was rejected. Their purpose was to reclaim the land by work. They opposed the ideas of Jews hiring Arab labor, and were responsible for the change from Arab to Jewish guards to protect the settlers. Palestine was not the land of milk and honey of biblical times. Its soil had been successively neglected for centuries, under Greek, Roman, Byzantine, Arab and Ottoman rule. Today, if you stand at the top of Mount Zion and gaze about the Judean hills which surround Jerusalem, you can travel, in your imagination, back in history and perhaps gain an added sense of this neglect and of the degree to which there had been soil erosion. Mount Zion is on the Israeli-Jordanian frontier, and in order to visit the basilica and the room alleged to be the one in which the Last Supper was held, you must have a military pass which is checked by an armed Israeli guard.

The hills on the Jordanian side are bare, and, with their pale colors, they stand like naked memories of another era while the unrelieving sun presses steadily upon them. There is a subtle play of colors, and there is rock, the ruins of eroded terraces from early times. On the Israeli side, the trees are blooming. A dark green contrasts with the pale and delicate colors on the Jordanian side. From Mount Zion or along the roads of the Jerusalem corridor, you see new terraces where there are trees, and land newly brought under cultivation by Jewish settlers.

In the early years of this century, Palestine was mostly arid and neglected, and it was such a land to which the Jewish settlers went. Considering themselves exiled, they returned to what they regarded to be their homeland and they set to work courageously reclaiming and restoring it.

They had to learn to work in agriculture. Oppressed by heat, often racked by malaria, weakened and sometimes killed off by other diseases, they lived in tents under the most primitive conditions, cleared away and blasted rocks, drained marshes, were burned by a fierce and brutal sun. They were the shock troops in the re-conquest of the desert. Of those years Ben-Gurion has written:

"For a year I sweated in Judean colonies, but I had more malaria and hunger than work. All three — work, hunger and malaria — were new and full of interest. Was it not for this that I had come to the Homeland? The fever would visit me every fortnight with mathematical precision, linger for five or six days, and then disappear. Hunger, too, was a frequent visitor. It would stay with me for weeks, sometimes for months. During the day I could dismiss it somehow, or at least stop thinking of it. But in the nights—the long racked vigils—the pangs would grow fiercer, wringing the heart, darkening the mind, sucking the very marrow from my bones, demanding and torturing — and departing only with the dawn. Shattered and broken, I would drop off to sleep at last."

However, he also wrote:

"Here I found the environment that I had sought so long. No shopkeepers or speculators, no non-Jewish hirelings, no idlers living on the labor of the others. . . . You follow and guide the plow, turn the sod and open furrow after furrow; and soon the very soil you plowed and planted would clothe itself in green. Before your very eyes it would bring forth its crop. No sooner were the rains over than the grain would ripen, and out you would go to reap the harvest and carry the yield to the threshing-floor. You felt as a partner in the act of creation." *

The Zionist movement, through the establishment of the Jewish National Fund, raised money to be used in buying land. The land purchased was usually marginal,

---

* Quoted from *Sound the Great Trumpet,* by M. Z. Frank, Whittier Books, Inc., 1955, pp. 61, 63.

and high prices were often paid for it. Eliezer Kroll, one of these settlers, told me that he knew of one section of malaria infested marshes which was bought three times. Others tell the same kind of story.

The Jewish settlers were often harassed by Arab marauders and pillagers. During the First and Second Aliyah, Arab watchers or guards were hired. During the Second Aliyah a few of the Jews saw that they must protect themselves. As a consequence, an organization, *Hashomer* (The Watchman), was created, consisting of armed guards who did duty at night as lookouts, protecting the colonies and colonists, and other times guarding them in the fields while they worked. Ben-Gurion was one of these. That is why he is sometimes called "The Old Watchman."

These early settlers were idealists and, as I have indicated, many of them were imbued with socialist and communal ideas. But their ideals and ideas did not alone condition the creation of cooperative and communal institutions and organizations which are so peculiar to Israel and which laid the foundation for the present State of Israel. The conditions of the country called for such institutions. The Jews had to band together in order to work, not only for purposes of protection, but also because there was relatively little work to be found, and this had more or less to be shared. For in the beginning, there were no communal and cooperative institutions. Dagania in Galilee, the first *kvutza*, a fully communalized settlement, was established in 1909.

The settlers worked as day laborers in the fields and as road builders. They lived in colonies, and only gradually could they change from their tents to huts and barracks. Many of them did not have a fixed home. It was with the coming of children that another impetus was given to the development of communalized and cooperative institutions.

In this whole first context, and as an answer to the problems which the settlers faced, Histadrut, the General Federation of Jewish Labor, was formed in 1920. Prior to this, and because of the First World War, there had been a halt to immigration. Many of the Jewish settlers were harried, imprisoned and even deported by the Turks as British agents, or because it was feared that they were pro-British. Ben-Gurion was deported. Also the Jewish Legion was formed, which Ben-Gurion joined in Canada. Others in Palestine enlisted, but they were mostly put to work attending the mules which carried supplies to British soldiers.

Histadrut had to be more than a mere trade union organization. The Jews needed doctors, and by banding together and chipping in, they were able to get doctors. Wages were low and, by joining together, they could get some wage protection. While there were some skilled workers, such as carpenters, most of the settlers did not have one steady occupation. They worked where work was to be found. In consequence, Histadrut was not split up into separate unions based on skills and types of occupation, and this fact has been a conditioning one in its whole later and even fantastic development. Because of the need for medical care, Histadrut took over this function. Such was the basis for its subsidiary institution, Kuppat Holim, which today provides complete medical care for over 1,100,000 Israelis, runs its own hospitals and clinics, and employs its own doctors. And since work had to be created, Histadrut, a few years after its establishment, set up Solel Boneh, a building construction company, so that there would be work for its members and for the new Jewish immigrants.

There was the Third Aliyah of the 1920's, and an enormous one in the 1930's. This latter was, as is known, caused by the rise of Hitlerism in Europe. Hitlerism also produced an intensification of Jewish consciousness.

Sympathetic or unbiased Gentiles had mostly believed that the solution to the so-called Jewish problem was assimilation. A majority of the German Jews believed in assimilation and were virtually assimilated. In fact, assimilation had gone so far that there was resentment in Palestine against some of the German Jews. Furthermore, the views of most Marxists on the Jewish question were anti-Zionist. Marxists generally followed Marx in regarding the Jewish question as economic, and in believing that with economic emancipation and the triumph of socialism and the proletariat, there would be an end to the Jewish question. Added to this was opposition to Zionism on the ground that it was a nationalistic movement.

Many Jews, both those who favored assimilation and those who believed in Judaism as a religion but not in the Zionist movement and its desires for a Jewish homeland, were opposed to Zionism. Dr. Morris Raphael Cohen, for instance, criticized the national aims of Zionism. He thought that these were in violation of the aims of modern liberal democratic thought. While believing that Jews in danger because of Hitlerism should be allowed to emigrate to Palestine, and while also praising the achievements of the Jewish settlers in Palestine, he opposed the idea of a Jewish homeland and saw in it an incompatibility between some of the aims of Zionism and those of modern liberal thinking.

However, the entire question, especially because of the Nazi pogroms, became desperately practical and much more complicated than it would appear if we see it mainly or solely in terms of the pros and cons of polemics and of theory. For once again, the Jews, the most persecuted of peoples, were faced with new and perhaps more terrible persecutions than their forebears had ever experienced. All of their efforts in Germany were destroyed in sadistic pillage and murder which became one of the world's most tragic and gruesome spectacles of butchery and injustice in the history of man. This could only create a freshly intensified consciousness of Jewry. Emancipated Jews suddenly discovered that, in a new sense of the word, they were Jews.

As the Jewish population swelled, there was an improvement of life not only for the Jews in Palestine, but also for the economy of the country as a whole. The British, who had succeeded the Turks, attempted to restrict Jewish immigration; many had to enter the country illegally.

There was much friction between Jews and Arabs prior to 1948. The Jewish immigrants had to protect themselves from marauders and pillage. In 1921, and 1929, and from 1936 to 1939, there was fighting. However, there was also association and commercial relationships. Many Jews and Arabs were friends, and a number of Arabs sold land to Jews. The Jews redeemed the land which the Arabs had neglected; they constantly sought to introduce more modern and rational methods of work in agriculture. They made a contribution in Palestine, and, in fact, in the Near East. And as more immigrants arrived, they sought to increase and create more opportunities for work, that is to expand the economy of Palestine, and, most especially, to reclaim desiccated land and increase agricultural production.

There are many over-simplifications in the usual presentation of the history which led to the establishment of the State of Israel. For instance, it is true that diplomatic help was given the Jews through such means as the Balfour Declaration, but it is, to say the least, a gross overstatement to see the modern State of Israel as a simple product of British imperialism or to regard the Jewish Palestinian immigrants as imperialists. Most of them went to Palestine because of a hunger for their own homeland, or because they had no other place in the world to go. They mainly came from the West and were and are Westerners, but principally in the sense that they sought to apply Western methods and techniques in improving their own conditions and in lifting the level of life in the area. Many also carried with them the democratic and socialist ideas of the West.

After the Second World War, and especially following the establishment of the State, the rising tide of immigration almost overwhelmed the new country. But most of the new immigrants now began to come from Asia, from the Arab countries and from North Africa. The population of Israel has increased threefold since the establishment of the State. The problems of the reception and integration of the new immigrants are among the biggest and most fascinating in Israel today.

CHAPTER TWO

I

BEFORE I WRITE of the more recent newcomers, it seems to me best to introduce the reader to older settlers and established Israelis whom I met. One whom I interviewed was Eliezer Kroll, an old immigrant and guard or watchman from the Second Immigration. Today he is an old *kibbutznik* at Kfar Gileadi, a rich and established kibbutz in the Galilee, near the Syrian frontier.

I arrived at Kfar Gileadi towards the end of a day of hard traveling. I'd seen much, interviewed people and talked or listened to comments and discussions of Israel and its problems. I had also seen a famous old Jew, whose ancestors had never left Palestine, and who lived in a one-room hut in an Arab village. The sun was about to wane. For the members of the kibbutz the day's work was done. It had been like hundreds of previous days in their lives. They live in two-room stone houses grouped around the large communal dining hall, one of the finest to be found in kibbutzim. Before it, there is a large stretch of grass. The relaxed kibbutzniks walked around or sat, wearing clean trousers and white shirts. Some parents played with their children. Kids romped about. The women had put on their print dresses and were enjoying their families. The atmosphere was very peaceful. I sensed among the people, young, middle-aged and old, a feeling of pride and satisfaction at the end of a good day. The Syrian border, so near, with its pale, purple mountains, could just as well have been miles away. You would not have thought that in a few hours, some of the men you saw, seated with their wives, enjoying a period with their children, strolling with the aimlessness of people out walking on a lazy Sunday, would be slinging a rifle over their shoulder to go out and do guard duty, and to peer through the darkness for possible infiltrators who might come carrying murder with them. For at the quiet moments of the day, life at a kibbutz can seem ideal, almost Utopian.

We had come to the kibbutz to speak with an American woman, but she could not be found. At first Kroll could not be located either, but finally he was.

We went to a wooden building in which there was an exhibition of work done by kibbutz children. I saw woodwork, blouses, paintings, furniture, all of it well done; some of it could even be sold commercially. The teacher who showed us the exhibition was herself a member of the kibbutz, and was quite proud of the exhibit. Then we met Kroll and I interviewed him on the porch of this building. He spoke Yiddish and Hebrew, but there were two translators.

Eliezer Kroll is a small, broad, plump man in his sixties who looks patriarchal with his long white beard. His eyes are lively and his broad face has a few red blotches on his cheeks. His manner was one of great assurance. His is the pride of an aging man whose life has been well lived. He wanted to know if I had seen the exhibition, and when I said that I had and was impressed, he seemed quite proud. He spoke of a cemetery close by, where there is the grave of Joseph Trumpeldor, one of the heroes of the Jewish immigration, who died fighting in 1920. Kroll urged me to visit this cemetery.

Then Kroll told of the Shomrim, the Watchmen, declaring that they were the predecessors of Palmach, the commando troops of Haganah, and thus of the modern army. He said that those who had left Russia before him for Palestine knew that they would have to defend themselves. Guards had to stand in the rocky, craggy fields. There was, he went on, no order in Palestine then, when the Turks of the Ottoman Empire were rulers. The Jews could not be sure either of their lives or of their property. When he emigrated to Palestine, he was aware of these conditions, and he planned to become one of those who would defend the settlers. They came, he emphasized, to work, to conquer the desert and, while doing this, to act in self-defense. Some of them immigrated illegally. The Turks were not always too anxious to have many Jews in Palestine.

Officially, Kroll went as a visitor; others did the same. The excuse they used was that they wanted to pray at the Wailing Wall in Old Jerusalem. Also, Kroll said, with twinkling eyes, that he had a Turkish passport and on it, his age was listed as 59. If his passport age were correct, he would now be 96 years old.

It took years to create the movement, The Watchman, called Hashomer in Hebrew.

"We were about a hundred," he said.

He spoke of about four hundred settlers who knew one another. The first group studied how to work in Jerusalem. They had no money. Work had to be found for them. Food was scarce. But then, he added, they were all single men, and their problem was to get on the land, stay there, work it, even though the soil seemed to be so barren. The Arabs, he said, laughed at them. And as I have already mentioned, the same pieces of land could be bought three or four times.

Kroll went on to say that he was one of the founders of Dagania. But even earlier, they had been developing ideas of collectivism. He spoke also of Baron Rothschild having bought 75,000 dunams (about 18,750 acres) and that he and many of his companions had been ready to settle on this land in Hauran, Syria. They were prevented from settling there because of the First World War. During the War, times were hard. The Turks would arrest the Jews, believing them to be spies for the English. Then in 1919 the Arabs and French fought in Syria, and the Jews, caught in the middle, were beleaguered on both sides. They had to leave their settlement. The place was empty; but later, they returned to it.

How did they get along with the Arabs? The Arabs liked their improved conditions, Kroll answered.

He minimized the early struggles and hardships. But having lived to see triumph in a movement for which he worked and fought, he exuded confidence, assurance, satisfaction. Everything about him conveyed the sense that he considered his life useful and that he was proud of what he had done.

Both he and his wife work a full day on the kibbutz. Usually, he is in the carpenter shop, except during the grape season, when he is in the fields. He has two living children on the kibbutz; a son was killed in the War, but his son's widow is also a member of the kibbutz. In all, the Krolls have ten grandchildren. One is a parachutist in the Israeli Army, and, said Kroll, he "is in all the fights."

Kibbutz life satisfies him. His entire family are kibbutzniks. Once he lived in a tent. He guarded poor settlers who also lived in tents, worked the hard-to-win-over, seemingly irresistible, soil. Fighting and danger, gruelling toil, and through it progress, which was slow but steady. Now Kfar Gileadi has 5,000 dunams, or 1,250 acres, of land. It has 350 working people and a kibbutz population of about 1,000. Its total annual sales run to at least 800,000 Israeli pounds. This, his children, his grandchildren, is what a man like Kroll sees as the meaning of his own work and as a core of what Israel means. This is the core and essence of life to him. He clearly feels that Israel is his homeland and that he and his family are integrated into its life. One of his sons died fighting for this way of life. He is ready to see his grandchildren fight, if necessary, as he and his sons have fought. He wants to see them grow up to work as kibbutz members, to carry on the progress made possible by the struggle and sacrifice of early settlers like himself.

It was now twilight. Occasionally, I heard the sound of spoken Hebrew. Otherwise, it was the quiet of a country day peacefully easing into night. Kroll had told us what he remembered. He walked back to the car with us, his figure erect, his gait firm, his beard falling on his chest. Waving goodbye to us, he invited us to return.

We drove on a rocky side road to the cemetery. On the monument for Joseph Trumpeldor, his last words are inscribed in Hebrew. I asked for a translation.

"It is well to die for our country."

There were the graves of the Watchmen. Most of the original group are dead, including Israel Gileadi, after whom Kroll's kibbutz is named. The stone tablets are laid side by side. There were flowers on one for a recently buried Watchman. One of the unmarked slabs covers a vacant grave that waits for Kroll. There are also graves of soldiers who died in the 1948 War.

Looking across from the cemetery, I could see bare Syrian hills with the shadows playing upon them. The scene was wild but filled with an intense, sad quiet.

We left to go on to another kibbutz.

II

It was late, about ten o'clock. The night was dark, but the moon was bright. I had sat around a big bonfire, watching fourth form children on a Galilee kibbutz perform for their parents. This was the last day of their school year. In their classes, they are given a subject, and learn all they can about it. This time, their subject was fire. Wearing improvised costumes, they illustrated the history of fire with pantomime and scenes. They performed with spirit and their acting, if not the setting, suggested a play or show given by children of a progressive school in America. Among the children were dark-skinned Orientals, including a Yemenite girl. She gave a recital of a visit the children had made to Safed, and a couple of the other children interrupted her on questions of detail. A woman translating for me called my attention to a fact which is interesting and, perhaps, somewhat significant. The Yemenite girl described the old and bearded Orthodox Jews of Safed as though they might have been different from all whom she knew, as curiosities. To her, they were of another world, and were even somewhat ridiculous. The other children laughed at the fun which the Yemenite girl poked at the old Jews of Safed. It was here that I noticed the father, a teacher, speak to his son and go off on guard duty.

I sat in a two-room kibbutz home, having tea, asking questions. The home was simply furnished. As in practically all kibbutz homes, there were books. Besides our party of four, there were our hosts, a kibbutz woman who is a teacher, and the daughter of our hosts, a girl of about twelve.

This was the third kibbutz I had visited that day, and the fourth of the kibbutzim I had already seen at that time. This was still my first week in Israel. The questions I asked were mainly critical; not that I was hostile, but rather in order that I might gain a fuller impression of how a kibbutznik thinks and feels.

Why were they opposed to hiring labor? This is a troubling moral problem for the kibbutz. If they employ hired labor, they will be exploiting the work of others, and the idea of non-exploitation is one of their fundamental principles. But some of the kibbutzim must employ labor. Thus the kibbutz Afikim, perhaps the richest in Israel, runs a plywood factory. In order to solve the problem of moral conscience and principle, the kibbutzim established a separate organization which does the hiring of labor.

But these kibbutzniks gave me their answer. To hire labor would violate their principles. Kibbutzim were established on the principle of communal living and cooperation. The kibbutzim, these three believed, can only survive by adhering to principles. Once principles are shunted, the kibbutz might decline. It would lose its moral basis. To hire labor would mean exploitation.

But could not a kibbutz adapt itself to changing conditions? For Israel is changing, and rapidly. City population is growing. With new immigrants having flooded into the country in hundreds of thousands, it is essential that they get employment. Yes, they realized all this, but then insisted that they could not change at the expense of principle. The moral value and the moral example of the kibbutz must remain for Israel. The kibbutzim, as long as they are conducted in accordance with principles, will serve Israel morally. Members of kibbutzim have gone into the Cabinet, the Knesset and government service. They are the carriers of the kibbutz principles. As such, they will be a focal point in opposition to selfishness in the national life. I suggested that there are other ways of serving as a moral example. These new Galileans did not deny the validity of the point. However, they insisted that this was a function of the kibbutzim and they were concerned with the continuation of the kibbutzim. They feared that moral relaxation and a watering down of principle might lead to decline. They admitted that there is an actual danger of decline.

I asked whether it might not be better if children lived with their parents rather than in their own quarters and in common, as is the case in most of the kibbutzim. This is an issue which concerns the kibbutzim today. This, also, she saw as a matter of principle. The children did see their parents, but not in times of strain and stress. When the parents were with their children, they could give them all their time and attention. This was better. And it was better for the women, she added. The mother was not the slave of the kitchen. She could do other work. The teacher, herself a mother, spoke of her own experience. She had been sent by the kibbutz to study. She was able to learn to be a better teacher. She could give full time to her work. Tied down as a mother, this would not have been possible.

Her idealism was firm and genuine. The same can be said of various other kibbutz members with whom I spoke. They were proud that the kibbutzim have made a contribution to Israel and have been successful.

Our host was the man in charge of all the trucking in the kibbutzim of that area. He received no salary for this, and said that he wanted none. He would not change his life for any other kind. He wanted no money, he wanted the kibbutzim to thrive, for Israel to develop, with opportunities for all Israelis to have what he had—food, comfort, recreation, satisfaction in his work, and a sense of participation in a socially creative activity.

However, as we talked, I also watched the twelve-year-old daughter of our hosts. From time to time, she would stare at her parents with a look which seemed both sad and hungering. Most definitely, she did not want to leave to go to her quarters, but it was bedtime. She talked in Hebrew, and finally left. Afterwards, I learned that the girl definitely would have preferred to live with her parents. In the case of other children, it is sometimes different.

III

As is well known, the kibbutzim are not the only form of agricultural settlement in Israel. At the most, about 80,000 live on the kibbutzim and the figure is probably much less than this. Another type of agricultural settlement is the *moshav*. On the moshav, the settlers work their own separate plots of land and determine what they will produce, but market their produce cooperatively. All their bookkeeping is done for them. There are, in addition, plots of ground on the moshavim which are farmed in common and all the farmers share in the profits. Many of the new immigrants are sent from their original transit camp, *maabara*, to moshavim; sometimes now they go directly to moshavim.

The oldest moshav in Israel is Nahalal, in the Valley of Jezreel, on the road from Haifa to Nazareth. It was founded by 75 families of European settlers in 1921. At the time it was originally established, the area, according to one of the moshavniks now living at Nahalal, was "all swamp." Their early experiences were similar to those of so many of the settlers—hard work, primitive living conditions, disease, steady but slow development of the land, trouble with the Arabs, including shooting and bombing, and finally, growth as a result of this laborious toil and of faith and courage.

As a hot afternoon in the Emek was just about to wane, I stopped with a party of four in the home of one of the families at Nahalal. There were clusters of bougainvillea outside the two-story brick building. Inside we found the housewife, a dark-haired stout sabra woman of thirty who had been born on the moshav. Her parents had been among the original settlers. She was taking care of her children. Her home was clean, but with something of the disorder to be found in a home with young children when the children are loved and the home is for them. In the kitchen was a refrigerator, the first and one of the few I saw in Israeli homes.

The house was originally built in 1932, but thanks to prosperity and development, the family was able, out of its earnings, to build on a second story, as well as to buy their household objects and furniture, and even to put in the refrigerator. To own a refrigerator is the hope of many Israelis, although most of them know that this hope will not be fulfilled, at least for many years to come.

This woman and her husband do the planting on their dunams, and her parents, whose permanent home is on the second story, were out on other work. Her father was on loan to the Jewish Agency. He helped new immigrants and, in fact, he discovered some of the Mount Atlas Jews in North Africa who have since been brought to Israel. The woman remarked that those Jews had been living in conditions much like those of Biblical times. Her father spent two years in Morocco, climbed Mount

Atlas, and there found Jews. He said, according to his daughter, "that's his people." Riding on a donkey, "he found one place where they say people lived for two thousand years. They are very, very low, primitive. They know very little about Judaism, about Jewish religion."

The people from this particular settlement, she added, had not yet arrived in Israel.

Her mother was working in a cooperative in Israel. The parents could do this because she is now grown, married, and she and her husband can farm their land. Their home is theirs on the basis of a ninety-nine year lease from the Jewish National Fund, and they were paying an annual rental, as well as improving their home.

But in the past it was, of course, different. This present prosperity was the result of years of labor.

"From the beginning, when it was lots of difficulties and disease. But I don't think it's the same the last twenty years."

The woman would not like to live elsewhere. She would not care to move, for instance, to Tel Aviv. For her children, she wanted the same kind of life she and her husband had, with perhaps some additional improvements, amenities and conveniences.

I spoke of the Arabs. From time to time during the Mandatory period, there had been trouble and violence in the area.

"A man who used to guard the fields, he lived here in these houses, they used to like to kill him. He comes out at night, the watchman, he should have gone through a gate, they shot him. But they didn't shoot him dead."

He lost a leg. Crippled, he became the bookkeeper of the moshav.

Then she spoke of how a boy and his father were killed

when a house was bombed. She lapsed into Hebrew and then said in heavily accented English:

"Twenty years ago, twenty-three years ago, just before the riots, 1936. They thought we are taking their lands. It was all swamp. It was said between the Arabs, 'Who goes through that swamp never comes back alive.'"

She told how in the early days, the settlers lost people who died of malaria.

Also, and having been born on the moshav at Nahalal, she said:

"I never felt it to be without land because I was like that."

She spoke of the problems of the moshav. Some of the children left because there was not enough land for them to work, but things had turned out better in the case of her family. And the moshav was, in her opinion, the kind of a place she wanted to live in, rather than a kibbutz.

"If I am a good mother or bad, I want to raise my children."

At about this point, her little girl, who was about five, became demanding for attention. The mother halted the interview. We sat and I spoke with our chauffeur, a European immigrant who had been in Israel since the 1930's, but who very proudly told us that his wife is a sabra. Our earlier conversation about the Arabs had left an impression on him. Suddenly he said of the Arabs:

"If he get money in the bank [he will fight]. The Arab man never go just for patriotism, he gets five pounds, he will go kill you."

He was referring, of course, to the Arab attacks on people in Nahalal of which the housewife had spoken.

"Perhaps people which are interested, maybe from any power," had organized, directed and paid for such attacks.

And further, the Arab, "his patriotism is paying, you can pay his patriotism."

The husband, in old work clothes, came in from working on their dunams, just outside the house. The housewife sat down and talked more with us. Her memory had been stimulated, and she was less self-conscious about speaking English. She spoke of the school she had gone to as a girl.

"You never saw such a school, it was a small little house, opposite a storage for the cows, food for the cows, it was a wooden one, the house, I think they got it from the Turkish army.

"We lived in wooden houses, which most of them were bought from the Turkish army when they went away."

She and her husband then talked of the manner in which the moshav is run, the various committees to handle community problems, the school and cultural center, a big mixer where the food for the cows and chickens is all mixed, the status of those who work performing services for the community, the children's dance group, Friday night lectures and other details of life at Nahalal. And she emphasized how they "try to work by ourselves."

Then the husband showed me his land in cultivation, and his large chicken house. He said that he had had the most modern chicken house, but that recently his neighbor had been able to install an even more modern one.

We spoke of work. The wife emphasized that life was still hard and the hours of work long.

"Just one person can't do it, even the cows and chickens."

But not only did she repeat that she preferred this way of life to that lived on a kibbutz, but that for her and her husband, this is a good way of life. They both see ahead, and think of improvement and development. Israel to them is home. It is a home built by their parents, continued by their own labor, and to be further built and developed by their children. They believe that they are creating something which will grow and they have some means already of measuring growth and of knowing how there has been change. And this change is not seen solely in the refrigerator in their kitchen. They have a sense of participation in a growing life, a feeling of responsibility for doing their share of the work essential for that continuation. In brief, they believe that they are building a country, a country which is theirs. Mixed in with their feeling for Jewish tradition, their sense of being Jews, there is a social content.

The ideal of integration of the new Oriental immigrants is seen not only in terms of Jewry as an abstract, religious, traditional or emotional concept. The hope is that the new immigrant, and even more so his children, will one day develop as these people are developing, and that one day, the new moshavim of these immigrants will be as Nahalal is today.

In other words, the effort to integrate the newcomers from Africa and Asia is viewed within the perspective of what has been done and in terms of acquired experience and the memories of more than one generation. This, I believe, should be kept in mind if we try to understand a little more of the phenomenon that is Israel. We may agree or disagree concerning Israel, but to sense something of its concrete meanings might, perhaps, at least give us clarity in whatever views we hold and whatever final conclusions we do come to accept.

CHAPTER THREE

I

Speaking of the mass immigration, the ingathering of the exiles, in the Knesset in 1949, Prime Minister Ben-Gurion stated:

"It was for this that the State was established, and it is by virtue of this alone that it will stand."

In 1948, the Jewish population of Israel was 650,000; by 1954, the total had swollen to 1,526,000. Today there are over 1,800,000 Jews in Israel. And as is known, the greater proportion of recent immigrants has come from Asia and Africa. For instance, between 1948 and 1954 Israel took in 370,434 new immigrants from Asian and African countries or from Turkey. By now, the total is nearly a half-million.

The innumerable problems created by such a mass immigration are complicated and more than fascinating humanly. They have resulted in a clash of cultures virtually unparalleled in history. In describing this, Israelis repeatedly remark that if America is a melting pot, then Israel is a pressure cooker.

The great majority of the Oriental immigrants came from backward areas. A few had lived in caves. The

Yemenite Jews had lived in isolation, and it was as though they had been transported overnight from biblical times into the twentieth century. There were immigrants who had never ridden in an automobile or seen motion pictures. Some had heard of inventions like the telephone and radio, others had not. Their customs, manners, habits of living, and values were dramatically different from those with which we are familiar in the West. Immigrants in one group from Mount Atlas in Africa were frightened and fled from their simple huts the first time they saw water come out of a faucet or a tap. They were aware only of the most primitive methods of medicine and of work. Some could only work the land as it had been worked some two thousand years ago. Others did not know how to do agricultural work at all. Some of the immigrants came from Arab cities, where they had earned their living as peddlers. Many did not know how to shoot a gun. There were immigrants who, upon arrival in the tin hut at the maabara, put their few belongings on the bed and slept on the floor. Persian Jews would not take showers inside; their showers had to be built outside their homes. In Israel you can hear almost endless stories and anecdotes concerning the new immigrants, their first reactions, their habits, manners, primitivism and the many early bewilderments following their arrival.

The incidence of illness and disease was high among the newcomers. Children suffered from malnutrition. The aged and infirm came along with their families, but they were welcomed as any other poor Jew. From Arab countries there came polygamous Jews. The ratio of illiteracy was high. In some of the groups wife-beating was a common practice, and women were regarded precisely in the same way as they are among the poorer Arabs.

The majority of these new immigrants came with almost nothing. Some were, in effect, paupers. These people came to Israel for a variety of reasons. When asked, it is surprising how frequently they will answer that they came to Eretz Israel, the holy land of Israel. Many were persecuted. There were virtual pogroms in Tripoli. Others were discriminated against, as Jews have been in almost every country in the world. Mixed with these reasons was the belief that in Israel they would find the land of milk and honey. They believed that they would be taken care of and that their lives would be better and easier. There was also among them a sprinkling of workmen and even some professional people. Usually, the Moroccans and Tunisians, having lived in cities and under French rule, were on a higher cultural level than the other Oriental immigrants. It is not too uncommon for some Tunisians and Moroccans to assert that they came from Paris, rather than from their native country.

The newcomers are brought to Israel by the Jewish Agency. It defrays their expenses with money collected from Jews all over the world, but especially in the United States and South America. In the beginning, their life is hard. Before a number can work, they have to be taught how. They are given jobs of various kinds, working on roads, on construction, and some as agricultural workers if they possess sufficient skill. Others are put into moshavim and begin working their own patch of land almost immediately. Their children are sent to school at once. Since a large majority do not know Hebrew, immediate efforts are made to teach them this language. There are a number of plans for training them. These are being improved and developed, especially in newer settlements such as Kiryat Gat in the Lachish area.

As soon as the new immigrants begin working, and some do on the first or second day of their arrival, they become members of Histadrut. Besides receiving immediate medical attention, they are covered by Kuppat Holim, the medical organization of Histadrut. The Jewish Agency pays for their first six months in Kuppat Holim.

But all of this notwithstanding, the new immigrants do not come to the land of milk and honey. They come to an Eretz Israel where life is hard and dangerous; for them it is often unusually hard. Working on roads, buildings and in fields, they were receiving about five and a half Israeli pounds a day at the time I was in Israel; this was the standard minimum wage. But usually, they have large families and, perhaps a grandfather or grandmother too old to work. Usually they must feed too many mouths on low salaries. It takes time before they can augment their income by working their own land, or by becoming semi-skilled or skilled workers. In addition, a large number of them have had to wait before they can be moved to decent permanent houses.

Immediately after the founding of the State, Israel was swamped by the tide of new immigrants. For a period, it took in something like 17,000 people a month. Mistakes were made. But now the method for receiving new immigrants is more developed and systematized as Israelis are beginning to learn and to correct their mistakes in their efforts to teach and to integrate these new citizens. They are giving serious thought to the numerous and difficult problems which are a consequence of this mass immigration. Dr. Hanokh Reinhold, the educational director of the Youth Aliyah, remarked to me in an interview in Jerusalem that in the beginning they had been fortunate to have handled the problem at all. They could not foresee all of their difficulties, and only recently were they able to develop their understanding. He and many others concerned with the immigration have a flexible attitude as to what should or can be done in integrating these newcomers from non-Western cultures. Also, Israel, from 1948 to 1951, was economically weaker than it is today. It was then suffering from inflation. There were serious food shortages, necessitating rationing. Even now, with all the building done in recent years, housing is inadequate. And still, every day, the new immigrants need food, clothing, shelter, medical care, education and work. It is no exaggeration to state that the new nation could have been overwhelmed and could have gone down in catastrophe under the human flood of alienated and impoverished Jews which it has taken in.

II

In the beginning, the new immigrants were housed in tents. Then, tin and wooden huts were built in the maabarot. Situated close to cities where work was available, some of these transit camps which I saw were eyesores. The new immigrants were living, overcrowded, in one and two room huts, mostly without electricity. Four, five, six and eight would occupy one or two rooms. With big families, new immigrants are not always adequately fed. But even so, a number of them are better off than before they came to Israel. They are receiving medical care, their children are getting an education, the work goes on so that it is possible for them to hope, to look forward to the time when they will have their own homes.

Israel and the new immigrants face trials and adjustments other than those of a physical nature. With a suddenness which can be shattering, some of these people are transported as though across a span of centuries. They are shocked out of their habits and routines of life. Their welcome is often kindly and they are helped as much as possible, but they are nonetheless met by strangers whose skin is of a different color. Between most of them and those strangers, there are insurmountable or almost insurmountable language barriers. Simple and primitive people, they are processed with Western efficiency. Needles are stuck into them, into their women and children. They are driven to new settlements in trucks along dusty, bumpy roads, often in intense heat. Other than knowing that they are in Eretz Israel, they have no way of knowing where they are. Their knowledge of the new country is meager, and in many instances less than that of a two-year-old sabra child. Even we Westerners, when we visit a foreign country where we do not know the language, are quite like children in many ways. Thrust into the Western civilization, the Oriental is a bewildered child. In a sense, the truckloads of new immigrants can be considered as throngs of children. It is impossible for us to know the precise character of the insecurity which many of them must feel. They cannot really know what is expected of them, and they cannot understand their own feelings.

And then, during their first days, they must begin to adjust to new ways, learning new methods of work, and a new language. They must adapt themselves to the ways of Western civilization. This means that their old life, even when it has been miserable and wretched, is torn down. Just as homes for them must be built, so must they build a life on a new foundation. They must do this when they are largely incapable of understanding the concepts of Western civilization. Some cannot even count.

Socially and morally, the new immigrants face troubling and even menacing problems of adjustment. From small details of sanitation to the broader ones involved in the general cultural pattern, they must learn and relearn. While they are Jews, their values and their way of life have been set in a world utterly different from that of Israel. It is almost as though they had come from the moon to this earth. Western ways often constitute a shocking violation of their mores. Thus, the role of women in many of their cultures has been totally different from what it is in the West. Their daughters at the age of eighteen must now go into the Army. Their children, boys and girls alike, are required to attend school; it is often difficult to convince the parents that by keeping their children in school, instead of putting them to work early, the children will have a better future and the family will eventually benefit. In school, the children quickly learn some Western ways, and then they begin to sense a difference between themselves and their parents. The children and the youths begin to know more than the elders. The seeds of a conflict between the generations are planted. As a result, there is estrangement, and, often, a weakening of the ego of the parents, especially the fathers. As time goes on, the wives are affected by the example of the free Israeli women. They change. If their husbands beat them, as has been the custom before the immigration, they protest and run to complain to the social instructor, the anthropologist, the teacher, the doctor. The husband's kingdom, the father's empire, might crumble. And all the while, with difficult adjustments, bewilderments and misunderstandings, there must be hard daily labor before their condition can be materially improved.

Various and different ideas have been and still are held concerning the integration of the new immigrants. In new *shikunim,* that is housing settlements, immigrants from all over were lumped together. A Yemenite, a Moroccan, and an American might be living side by side or across the street from one another. The desire to integrate and to Westernize the new immigrants was so intense that a realization of their own need to retain an ethnic integrity was often forgotten or ignored. Some Western Israelis believed that little could be done with the older immigrants, and that the only hope of Israel was to educate and integrate their children; this attitude has far from died out.

Thrown together with other new immigrants from different Asian and African countries, as well as from the Balkans, Western Europe, America, Great Britian and South Africa, problems, frictions and antipathies developed. In Holon, a Histadrut town, a Bulgarian woman school teacher complained heatedly and bitterly about the Oriental immigrants. She wanted to move. The Orientals would not put lids on their garbage cans and to her the odors were unbearable. Westerners have a clearer sense of what Israel means. They comprehend civic spirit. Many of the Orientals do not. The Orientals are less inclined to mix with neighbors. Sometimes they live in a shikun and scarcely know their next door neighbor.

Today it is being more clearly realized that the culture and ethnic integrity of the new immigrants should be preserved, and the number of Israelis who are learning about many problems of integration is on the increase. Today, whenever possible, new immigrants are placed in established settlements rather than in transit camps. They are now usually being kept together as a group. Mistakes are definitely being corrected.

CHAPTER FOUR

I

THE SPECTACLE of new immigrants disembarking at the port of Haifa affords one of the most moving and humanly interesting experiences which you can have in contemporary Israel. The ships are usually full, containing around four hundred immigrants, including a horde of children. On the boats coming from North Africa, many Moroccan Jews from the cities are mixed in with others who come from villages; some of them look quite like Arabs in their native dress. The women, and occasionally the little girls, are loaded with jewelry: bracelets, rings, brooches, earrings, all shiny and sparkling. The immigrants cannot take out money, and consequently they usually put what they have into jewelry. Bedouin women often do likewise, and in the market place at Beersheba, you can see Arab women, beating goats' hair for tents, their faces covered with a jingling metal veil of coins. The immigrants line the ship rails, move about, are processed by medical and immigration officers, until they are gradually let off the boat. They then come down the gang planks carrying packages, bundles, baskets, babies. The others wait, usually in patience. Most of the immigrants are quiet, but it is not difficult to sense that they are full of bewilderments and anxieties. Family groups will be sitting on the deck, with perhaps a mother nursing a baby. Other children sit or move about. Some of them wander away. Here and there, lines are formed at the tables behind which the customs officials stand. The men buzz around, collecting their families and belongings. An old bearded Jew will sit patiently like an Arab beside a wall. A feeble old man or woman will shake in a chair, attended by a child, a son, a daughter. Little girls, some of them dirty and almost ragged, take care of infants and small children. Many of the babies are pudgy-faced, and look even old and unhealthy in their infancy. Wandering among them, you hear Arabic, French, some Hebrew, and even a little English. Now and then, you might be grabbed, questioned, or show documents. One stout man in a shabby suit collared me aboard a ship, showed me a card and told me in French that he had been an electrician. Others asked for directions.

Gradually, the immigrants go down the gangplank. Entering a narrow room, they are first checked again by officials at a table, and then, at the next table, they get food—coffee, cheese, bread and orange juice. The officials handling them and feeding them are by now experienced, and treat them kindly. They try to give them breakfast as quickly as possible, because then the immigrants will be less likely to become irritable. A few Israeli women, dressed in nurses' uniforms, will be fluttering about, doing what they can to help the immigrants.

After they have been processed and have been given food, the immigrants enter the big hangar-like dock shed. They have been admitted to Israel, and after collecting their baggage, going through customs, and receiving the two Israeli pounds which they get for immediate spending money, they have only to wait until they can board the big trucks which will take them to their new homes. Porters steadily pile luggage on the floor, shouting to people to get out of their way as they move back and forth. The scene is the same as at any dock, when a ship comes into port. But the passengers at Haifa look quite different from tourists, and because of their dress add an Oriental flavor to the scene. Many of the women sit on benches or on the floor. Some of them look old before their time, and their dark faces bear an expression of inscrutable patience. They wait. Others, not having found benches on which to sit, stand, usually near their possessions. A main concern is the luggage, which will consist of barrels, boxes, crates, suitcases (usually old and of inferior quality), baskets and bags. There will also be some crated bicycles and boxed radios. The very nervousness of some of the men as they look through the piles of baggage for their own, reveals worry lest one of the family's possessions be lost. But it is usually found, checked through customs, and put on the right truck.

In a corner, you will see a family group. A son or cousin or other relative is in the uniform of an Israeli soldier. He is talking to the newcomers, explaining. Already he seems different from them. His time in Israel, his experience and training in the army, have affected him. He speaks with assurance. His manner and his walk are cocky. He looks healthy and well-fed. Other relatives have gotten inside the barriers, and they talk with the new arrivals. Men kiss each other on the cheek, in the French style. The old men are kissed by all the children. The children are looked over, stared at, touched. Moroccan city girls, with their jewelry and modern dresses, often tight-fitting, move about. Some of them are so beautiful that you cannot resist casting an eye on them.

A woman or a child will be gnawing on a chunk of bread. A child cries. A little girl screams and her mother comforts her. A man suddenly rushes frantically towards a uniformed customs official; he wants some information. A few buy soft drinks at the stands. Others line up at a cash window for their allowance of two pounds, or else to change some currency. Customs officials, in khaki uniform, move about. They look like soldiers. They walk erectly. Their manner is one of confidence and assurance.

Beyond a wooden fence and gate, a large crowd is pressed right up to the fence. Those are the relatives. Immigrants find them. There are scenes of family reunion across the fence, kisses, talk, the display of children from both sides, more kisses and more talk.

I noticed a bearded old Jew in a long brown coat standing at the fence, gesturing, talking in Hebrew, and nervously trying to get inside. He looked as old as one of the prophets. A large group of immigrants finally found him. He was kissed with homage. He was admitted inside the gate at last, and I followed him. A fat, bald man of about forty-five rushed up to him and kissed him. I asked the younger man who he was; the old Jew was a Rabbi, the younger man his son.

I saw a humpbacked woman, her aged face lined, shaking and shivering. She was so bent that when she stood or walked, with help from a relative, her eyes met the floor. A bench was found for her, and while sitting on it, she shook and trembled. A thin, dark boy wandered by. In answer to my questions, he told me in French that he was Egyptian, that his uncle in Cairo worked for customs, and that he had a relative in the police department at Haifa. Waiting for this relative, he sat on his baggage with Oriental patience. His alert eye was taking in the scene.

There were other groups, including some teenagers of

eighteen or nineteen. Where were they from? They answered surily or curtly. What did they do in Morocco? A number of them refused to answer any question. Did they have relatives in Israel? No. They were afraid that if they revealed something, it might be used against them. They might even be saddled with the support of relatives.

I noticed a plump, well-dressed, bespectacled man of about thirty who was talking to a thin, light-skinned girl in a bright dress. She had three children at her side. I caught the man's eye. He smiled. What did he do in Morocco? He was a bookkeeper. He showed me his papers. Then, with a manner of efficiency and concern, he went about collecting his boxes and suitcases. Against the pile where he found one of his suitcases, a dark-skinned, moustached man sat with folded arms, looking straight ahead. He had on a turban, and wore his white pantaloons like an Arab.

I kept wandering about, looking and watching. More family groups. More men moving and bustling. More children. More women sitting with inexpressible resignation on their faces. Israelis were talking, answering questions, watching the immigrants, processing them. And there were a few other Israelis, who had come merely to see this spectacle. A woman from the Jewish Agency remarked to me on the number of youths on the ship; this meant a good shipload. Another Israeli proudly told me that the immigrants were being well received. A third commented on the variety in the dress, the jewelry, and the luggage.

Outside, at one end of the shed, the trucks were waiting. The truck drivers hung about while porters steadily loaded the trucks. After the immigrants were classified, they were assigned to a truck, their destination having been arranged in advance. In time, the trucks were filled, and the new immigrants were driven off to see Eretz Israel for the first time, and to begin their new lives.

II

I stood outside the big shed, talking idly with several Israelis, waiting for the immigrants going to Kiryat Gat in the Lachish area; I was to ride in the truck with them. After wandering about the ship and the docks for two hours, their faces had become familiar to me. I was half beginning to believe that I knew them. I could see from their Western clothes that most of them came from cities. Time dragged. The sun over Haifa was intense. A few more immigrants found their truck and took seats.

I talked with my translator, a brilliant young man who gave up a promising and possibly lucrative career in England in order to live in Israel. I remarked that unquestionably these immigrants got a better reception than did many of our own in America in the days of large-scale immigration. But how much does this mean? We are living in the twentieth century, and that was in the nineteenth. A young man at our side also commented on the reception given the immigrants. A good many Israelis want to take pride in any achievement of their country, in anything good or creditable which is done in Israel. They are hungry, sometimes touchingly and pathetically so, for Israel to become a success.

As we talked randomly, we became impatient. We wanted to be off. The immigrants also were becoming restless. Time still dragged. A man from the Jewish Agency lost his temper and shouted angrily in Hebrew. A few moments later, he spoke to my translator. He wanted me to know that he hadn't shouted at the immigrants, but rather at one of the porters, and that if I should write about this scene, I should not say that he shouted at the immigrants. We all laughed and agreed that one must sometimes lose one's temper working there. It is a trying job. The immigrants become confused; so do the porters. People get in the way of one another and of the porters. Children get in everyone's way. The immigrants must ask many, many questions, because they know almost nothing of Israel. Some of them are almost inescapably suspicious.

We started walking around inside, and spotted an Orthodox Rabbi in black, standing alone with two suitcases at the counter where tourists, rather than immigrants, must check through customs. He had a rich gray beard. His suitcases were rather battered. We had seen him earlier, and had imagined that he had come with the immigrants; we were surprised to learn that he was a tourist. My translator spoke to the Rabbi, and learned that he had come from New York, was going to Jerusalem, and would stay in Israel if he could find work.

I questioned a few of the new immigrants, and noticed a small proportion of old people. They would be unable to work. Some were feeble or infirm. One such was the old humpbacked woman. A young man helped her into a truck which was now almost filled. She sat at the end, her eyes peering strangely at us; she was the most misshapen human being I had ever seen. But the old and infirm are welcomed just as the young people are, even though they will only be a burden.

A thin man, apparently the son of the humpbacked old woman, fell as he climbed onto the truck. A shudder went through the immigrants. A driver and two others immediately sprang to help the fallen man. Those on the truck began to talk rapidly and nervously in French. The man was quickly on his feet. Not seriously hurt, he stood holding his forehead, drank a glass of water and then continued to hold his forehead. The immigrants stamped their feet, and talked and shouted hysterically. The hump-backed woman sobbed convulsively. This continued for five minutes before they quieted down. The man who had fallen had not been injured, but the outburst seemed to have brought some ease to the immigrants. In another truck, which had just about filled up, the mood was different; there was gay singing to the music of a guitar.

Finally we all got off, driving through the gates and out of Haifa. It was shortly past noon, and the day was very hot. We took the road from Haifa to Tel Aviv, and I looked at the Mediterranean, blue and cool, as we left the city. The road was crowded. Traffic was heavier than usual. Scores of people were going to Tel Aviv to see the soccer game between the teams of Israel and the Soviet Union. Almost the entire country was excited about the game. Traffic would continue to be heavy until we skirted Tel Aviv.

I rode in the truck with the baggage and there were three truckloads of immigrants ahead of us. My driver had come to Israel from Germany in the 1930's; he spoke English very poorly. We talked little on the long and tiring trip. After driving for about an hour-and-a-half to two hours, we stopped. Many of the immigrants got out and bought ice cream. Except for the docks, this was the first time they were putting foot on Israel's soil. They were curious about prices and Hebrew words. Then we went on. Army trucks passed us frequently. There were summer maneuvers, but the passage of soldiers in jeeps and trucks brought home, emphasized the realities of life in Israel today, where there is no peace, and danger can await you almost anywhere in the country and at any time. We passed many settlements, products of so much work and sacrifice. Fields in cultivation, the small white houses, usually grouped together, here and there, people in the fields which lay green in the sun—a country that is growing and developing.

We rode on, going down a side road where the dust rose, and finally we reached the settlement of Kiryat Gat. As we bumped along a sandy, rocky road, past new white cement houses, Moroccans came out and ran after us excitedly. Passing the permanent houses, we reached a section of tin huts, the maabara. At the end of this group of huts, we stopped. The immigrants piled out of the trucks and the luggage was unloaded.

One of the huts was used as a supply room by the Jewish Agency, where the immigrants received blankets and other household equipment, and where they were also told the location of their huts.

The new immigrants formed groups and earlier ones crowded about them and talked. Most of them seemed happy. The humpbacked old woman was placed on a camp chair in the shade of the supply hut. A gray-haired woman began to sing with joy because she was in Israel. A crowd of older inhabitants clustered around her. When she began to sing, the older immigrants laughed, joked, made friendly fun of her. They also sang, but they were laughing at her naiveté as a newcomer.

Another group of earlier immigrants gathered around a woman from a travel agency who had also come along in one of the trucks, merely as an observer. The woman quickly incited an argument in French. A fat Moroccan spoke angrily, complaining of working and housing conditions in the settlement. He said that in the maabara they were poor, conditions were bad, and they were not happy. The woman from the travel agency grew very disputatious, her voice growing loud and raspy. She insisted that they were happy. If they were poor, they could work. The fat man became more excited, and there were murmurs from the small crowd pressed around them. The women standing up around were clad in faded dresses. One of them held up her baby; another called out sharply to the woman from the travel agency. A third said she couldn't work because she had too many children to take care of. The man talked, almost as though he were making a political speech. The woman from the travel agency harangued him and the others. A few of the newly arrived immigrants listened. Others were getting their baggage and lugging it to the huts. The nearby crowd was still singing. The argument continued.

A thin man of thirty or so was listening. He wore a clean white shirt and blue shorts. His appearance was very neat. His skin was light brown. He looked as though he might be an intellectual.

"I speak six languages and I cannot find work," he complained in English.

The woman from the travel agency continued her harangue. There were a few more murmurs. This scene and the woman's conduct suggested how trouble, even riots, can be provoked. Apparently the people from the settlement believed that she was from the Jewish Agency or from the government, and they had wanted to speak of their problems and of the conditions of their life. But the argument ended, The people quieted down.

By this time, all the luggage had been unloaded from the trucks and these had gone off. But a truckload of tomatoes had drawn up. Boxes of tomatoes had been unloaded and the new immigrants came and were given all the tomatoes they could carry in boxes, baskets and bags. These were being distributed by a dark-haired woman in her late thirties. She spoke only Hebrew, but her remarks were translated for me. She was a kibbutznik, and had come to Kiryat Gat as a volunteer to assist the new immigrants. She said that she was keeping a diary and on learning that I was a writer, she told me that her diary would make a very interesting book. There are many women like her in Israel. Willingly they go to new settlements and live with the new immigrants in order to help them and teach them. They want to contribute whatever they can in the many tasks connected with the problems posed by integration.

The inhabitants of the settlement wandered off. The new immigrants also began to go to their huts. A gray-haired man in native dress settled himself in the shade by a hut, crossed his legs, folded his arms, and just sat. He had been in Israel less than one day, but he was sitting as he must have in his native Morocco.

We left to eat and, on returning about an hour later, found the scene almost deserted. The new immigrants were in their huts unpacking, arranging their belongings, or else resting. They had completed one of the most exciting days of their entire lives.

The next morning, I again visited the settlement. It was as though the new immigrants had already become adjusted. The old man I had seen the previous day was back on duty, sitting in the shade of a hut, and nearby, a second man had joined him. A few of the immigrants walked about. In front of one hut, a small flower garden had already been planted. Another man had neatly laid out stones in front of his hut.

We spoke to some of the people. Most of those I questioned said that they like it in Israel and were glad that they had come. They asked many questions about distances, the geography of Israel, the time it would take to go to Tel Aviv, the possible opportunities they might have to go swimming at a beach. A few were quite surprised to learn that they were only about half an hour by car from the bathing beaches at Ashkelon. They had imagined that they would have to go to Tel Aviv to swim, and feared that they would not have an opportunity of doing this. Young men expressed a desire to find work quickly and to help build the land. I spoke to a family of five in one of the huts. The oldest son was an earlier immigrant. Until the day before, he had worked as a shoemaker in Jerusalem and said that he had been earning seven or eight pounds a day. But he had given up his work and would live with his family, seeking new work in the Lachish area, helping them economically, and easing their first period of adjustment in the country. Also, he had done his military service and said that he had liked life in the army.

We were invited into a second hut. There were four cots, a table, a few chairs, The luggage had all been piled up nicely and neatly, and the floor was swept. Two of the members of the family were young men. In Morocco they had been workmen, and the older brother said that it had not been bad, economically. Why, then, had he come to Israel? He did not want to serve in the army. Why? It was not his country. Would he object to serving in the Israeli Army? No. This was his country. He looked forward to serving in the army. And hitting his breast, he added that he would serve.

"*Avec mon coeur!*"

He didn't mind hard work, and had known that in coming to Israel he would have to work very hard. He pulled a cardboard carton from under the bed, opened it and showed us the food which the family had received. There was canned food, coffee, sugar, and other edibles. He was pleased with this gift. The entire family assented when he expressed satisfaction with the manner in which they had been handled on arriving in Israel. He did not like the Arabs, but the French, he said, were not bad. Most of the responses of the other immigrants were similar to those which I have recorded above.

But the bookkeeper with glasses whom I had noticed the day before on the docks was dissatisfied and disgruntled. Noticing us, he smiled and drifted closer as we walked about the settlement. It was clear that he wanted to be recognized and that he wanted to talk. However, I did not have an opportunity to speak to him immediately, and he wandered off. Then, before leaving, I spoke to him and to his wife. Talking French as did the others, he called the settlement a barracks, and he repeated the word several times. He said that in Morocco he had been told that there were houses, not this barracks, that the settlement was already established. Another complaint was that there was supposed to be an Anglo-Saxon group at Kiryat Gat. Actually, this was planned, but at that time the English Jews had not as yet arrived. His wife was as dissatisfied as he was.

Continuing, he said that he had had a good job as an accountant or bookkeeper in Morocco. He could not do hard labor. He was skilled and believed that he deserved a better fate than that of a laborer. Looking at me directly, he also said that French methods of accounting are more difficult than those used in America. In America, he told me there are many machines. A person who was as trained as he merited a decent job and a better living than he and his family could have in this barracks. And his wife was a trained stenographer. She could be useful in the offices of the settlement. It was observed that before either of them could do the work they wanted to, they would have to learn Hebrew. Yes, he agreed to that.

He pointed at the flat sandy land in the distance, declaring that this was not what had been described to him. He had been told that he was going to a settlement near

Jerusalem. Instead he was here in the desert. Actually, the plans for these immigrants had been altered a day before they landed. Tension had been mounting in the area around Jerusalem and there had been an increase of border incidents. More were expected. Because of this, it was decided to send the immigrants to Kiryat Gat, rather than to the Jerusalem corridor. This was motivated not by a desire to trick the immigrants, but rather by a concern for their safety. Because of the sudden increase in danger in the Corridor, no one would willingly travel there at night, unless it was necessary.

Pointing to the interior of his hut, he spoke of how well he had lived in Morocco. How could he live in this tin hut with his family? His wife agreed with him. We looked inside. Their hut was not as neatly arranged as some of the others which we had just seen. Suitcases were piled on a bed; one of them was opened and only partially unpacked. Cartons lay about. The appearance of disorder gave the impression that the hut was dirty, although the stone floor had been swept and was clean.

My translator was an official of the Foreign Ministry. The newcomers would not accept his explanations that Kiryat Gat was still being built up. As quickly as new homes went up, the new immigrants would go into them. The ultimate aims and the significance of operation Lachish in terms of overall Israeli policy were too remote for this man and his wife to impress them. The immediate future and its barren prospects were on their minds on this first day of their new life. They would face many demands for adaptation and adjustment as well as difficult and even depressing work and labor.

After leaving the maabara huts, I saw a Moroccan who had come to Israel earlier. In this manner, I could make at least some comparison. Along the same sandy, rocky road which led to the maabara we drove to a row of newly erected two-room stone houses. These are permanent. The occupants are Moroccan and, like the immigrants with whom I had traveled from Haifa, they also had come in the trucks, and they had lived in the tin huts. They had studied Hebrew, the men had worked at hard labor for the standard Histadrut wages, and their children had started going to school. The new and permanent homes had gone up, and now they were living in them.

There were flowers in front of the standard, low stone house at which we stopped. We walked to the entrance at the side. Pans of sliced tomatoes were drying in the sun and the flies over them were thick. The Moroccans slice their tomatoes, and allow them to dry in the sun. In this way, they are preserved to be eaten in the winter. A gray-haired woman sat on the ledge in front of the door, preparing more tomatoes.

The inside of the home was bright, cheerful and very clean. There were three rooms, including a kitchen, and an inside toilet and shower. The new immigrants had neither inside toilets nor running water; there were outside showers for them. The couple I visited was young and they had one child; the old woman outside was its grandmother. The young husband was in bed, ill, apparently recovering from laryngitis, but we were welcomed. The colors in the home were bright, and there were a few chairs. This, the curtains and drapes, as well as many other household objects and utensils, had been acquired since their arrival in Israel some months previously. The man was thin, short and dark, and had learned to be a mason. He was, he said, earning about ten to twelve pounds a day, extremely high wages for Israel. In fact, he was earning more than a government official who was accompanying me. He had come because he was Jewish and wanted to live in Israel. He thought himself incomparably better off than he had been in Morocco, and did not want to go back.

Most people measure a country or a society in terms of their own fate rather than by broader criteria. In the last analysis, in the long run, people decide on what is happening to them and to their families, and not on the basis of some future achievement and bliss which might become a reality after they are dead. While men do not live by bread alone, they nevertheless want, need and must have their bread. And even though an intense and widespread idealism and spirit of self-sacrifice has led many to contribute, to suffer, to die for the reclamation of the Palestinian desert, and the establishment of the State of Israel as a Jewish homeland, satisfaction or dissatisfaction will largely depend on material conditions.

This, as we shall see perhaps more clearly as we go on, is especially pertinent and to the point in the case of the Oriental immigrants in Israel. While many of them have come because their new country is Eretz Israel, they want to live in a land of milk and honey, and they are much concerned with getting a goodly portion of that milk and honey for themselves.

Satisfaction or dissatisfaction depend on what has been and what is happening to them day by day. The vision and the aims of settlers from the earliest immigrations were influenced by a stronger and more understanding sense of the future than is possible for most of the Oriental immigrants, including those who come from cities in Tunis and Morocco. The majority of the earlier immigrants were poor. But compared to them, immigrants from Mount Atlas, Yemen or Iraq are feebly educated and backward. Many of the earlier immigrants possessed the power of abstraction. It is this power or capacity which is one of the distinguishing differences between East and West. Through abstraction, we can look forward and backward, above and beyond. We are enabled to conceive plans, and to put these into operation. And in addition, many of the Western immigrants know that it can be done, that material progress is possible. In fact, the faith in progress of Israelis is often stronger than in Western Europe and even in some American circles. The courageous pioneers and settlers of the Second Aliyah were young men and women who were stirred, not only by visions of the prophets, but by this faith in progress. Prior to the First World War that faith in progress was a veritable axiom of the Western world.

We must also remember that the new Oriental immigrants are Jews. They came to Israel from lands where they were not fully at home. Besides discrimination and persecution, they felt a sense of difference. The Moroccan Jews were not Arabs, although the culture and the mores of the more backward among them were and often remain Arab. Nor were they French. They speak French. Large numbers of them are from urban centers; they are literate and have some education. But skin color, birth in a colony, and religion or nationality (if we consider Jewishness to be a nationality also) set them more or less apart.

Even under the best and easiest of circumstances, adjustment in a new land, as we know, is difficult. It produces confusion, uncertainty, resentments, anguish—much anguish.

I have here briefly described the new immigrants who went to the Lachish area. If I speak briefly of Operation Lachish, this might help us to see the problems involved more broadly. For while it is true that the new immigrants live in primitive conditions and can only gain some alleviation by suffering and hard labor, we should see what aims for the future are here involved and we should gain at least a passing awareness of what is being planned and done in the effort to make that dream a reality rather than a mere promise. We may agree or disagree with these aims, but at least if we disagree and criticize, we can then, perhaps, do so in a more rational manner and not out of scorn or because of fixed clichés, prejudices or mere offhand conceit.

CHAPTER FIVE

THE LACHISH REGION is one of the world's oldest battlefields. It guards the approach to Jerusalem and lies astride the ancient trade route from Egypt to Mesopotamia. The scene of battles in ancient times, the area is today one in which there are many ruins of fortified towns. In this area Canaanites, Egyptians, Jews or Israelites and Philistines fought. There Samson carried on most of his exploits. After the Roman conquest, this region was neglected. In 638 C.E., the Arabs swooped into Palestine and the Lachish area was captured. After thirteen centuries, it was barren, but its strategic importance remained and it was the scene of one of the decisive maneuvers of the Israeli Army in the 1948 War of Liberation. The Egyptian Army had crossed the Negev, and established supply lines running from Gara to Jerusalem. The settlements of the Negev were isolated. The Israeli High Command planned Operation Ten Plagues, a double movement, intended to split the link between the armies of Egypt and Trans-Jordan, and to end the isolation of the Negev. Beersheba was captured in November 1948 by Israeli forces. The Egyptian lines were pierced in a surprise attack launched along the Migdal-Faluja Road, and a junction was effected with Israeli forces in the Negev. This cleared the way for the subsequent capture of Elath on the Red Sea. Israel gained more territory than had been originally assigned to it in the U. N. partition plan. This region is now one of contention and concern to Israel. If she should accede to demands for a restoration of the intended partition boundaries she would lose part of this vital strategic area. The sacrifices which went into achieving victory were heavy. Thought and attention were given to the northern and more developed and fertile areas of Israel. The Negev was a desert of wilderness. It was then that the conquest of the Negev was conceived.

The reasons for this were evident. The desolated wilderness was a weak, a dangerously weak link in Israel's defenses. It needed to be settled in order to provide greater security. A network of settlements would have great value for purposes of military defense.

To reclaim the soil of this desert also would mean a big stride forward in Israel's struggle to attain self-sufficiency. And the settlements would provide homes for the flood of new immigrants. The conquest of the desert, the irrigation and cultivation of the Negev, would provide work for the new immigrants and would increase the food supply as well as the industrial productivity of the nation.

Prior to the establishment of the State of Israel, and the armistice, it was not possible to plan settlements to the degree that Operation Lachish has been. Land had been acquired wherever it was available. And then with the rising tide of immigrants, they had to be taken care of as well as could be done. Thousands poured into Israel during a period of food shortages and inflation. The new State was suffering from the wounds of war. Every day there were more mouths to feed, more families needing a roof. But with improvement, planning was possible. And as I have already pointed out, it was essential that the Negev be settled. This appears to be the rationale, then, of Operation Lachish. One of its main motivations and aims is that of handling the problem of new immigration and integration more rationally. The maabara or transit camp was only a stopgap means of receiving the immigrants, and it produced many new problems. I have already made it clear that thousands of the new immigrants came from backgrounds and cultures totally different from that of the West. Many were "primitive." [1] Yemenites living in walls of seclusion existed virtually on the level of Biblical times. They and many other immigrants could not do skilled labor. They had to be taught the most rudimentary skills as these are known in the West. Jobs had to be made for them. And at first, a number of them were not even capable of working at these made jobs. Before they could farm, they had to be taught. Most of those who had had experience, as for instance some immigrants from Mount Atlas in Africa or from Yemen, knew only the most primitive methods of agricultural labor. In such circumstances, thousands of immigrants had to be cared for and this produced the consequence of a number becoming dependent. They wanted as much help as they could receive, as much from the Jewish Agency as they could get. This dependency was demoralizing, and there were, I understand, a number, sufficient to be disturbing, who preferred to remain living in the tin or

---

[1] I put the word "primitive" in quotes here in order to remind my readers that we can easily fall into habits of Western conceit. It is very easy for Westerners, and especially for Americans, to assume that the values of Western civilization are *totally, absolutely* superior to those of any other culture. Today, there is a strong tendency, on the part of many, to regard these values in terms of technological advance alone. From the standpoint of Western conceptions of progress, we can use the word "primitive." But if one thinks of values and cultures, we cannot always be certain about what we would call "primitive" and what is merely "different."

wooden huts of the maabara rather than to get houses and better jobs. Along with the development of this dependency, there were other demoralizing features to prolonged life in the maabarot. Living conditions were overcrowded. It was hard, confusing, and even dangerous for the children. The danger of delinquency and of many of the girls being ruined were quite real.

With observation and the accumulation of experience, there was developing awareness of mistakes which had been made, and of the number and complexity of the problems. An effort was made to eliminate maabarot. And of all substitutes, the most rationally worked out is the Lachish project. In this brief account of it, the reader should be able to grasp how the immigrant question and the problems of integration interlock and tie in with the other major problems of the country.

Operation Lachish is an example of coordinated regional planning which has already evoked the interest and even extravagant enthusiasm of a wide variety of foreign visitors. In a pamphlet, *Operation Lachish,* published in Jerusalem by Keren Hayesod-United Israel Appeal, the basis of this project is explained as an effort at a "complete, coordinated, functional stage-by-stage planning and implementation based on experience gained through trial and error in past mass settlement projects in many different parts of Israel, under many highly varied local conditions."

The entire project is divided into three types of centers which are planned in accordance with their functional role in the general or over-all plan.

"Center A" is the primary unit. It consists of existent types of settlements such as the kibbutz or the moshav as well as such new types of settlements based on local conditions and varying degrees of cooperative farming as may be evolved. In these centers, there will be houses and only such buildings as are necessary for day-to-day use. These would include barns, livestock sheds, a small cooperative store, a kindergarten and any other buildings required for daily living.

"Center B" is a rural community center servicing four to six A Centers. In it will be buildings and facilities needed once or twice a week or on a weekly basis by the A Centers which it services. Also it would include buildings and facilities which can be shared by more than one center. Among these are a school, clinic, tractor station.

"Center C" will be located in the geographical center of the region or roughly so, and will be like a market town providing the services such a town furnishes for villages in an agricultural area. Through Center C, economic coordination between town and country can be established. The farmers are not to be left at the mercy of urban price fluctuations. Each village will participate in the cooperative ownership of the main processing plants located in Center C. Production and crop rotation can be rationalized. The villages also share in the ownership of marketing organizations, stores and so on. It will also provide a technical high school, a hospital, administrative centers, municipal offices and factories for processing raw materials from the region. A large proportion of the crops in the Negev are industrial crops, such as cotton, ground nuts and beet sugar. This is the master plan and it provides for many autonomous and semi-autonomous units. It is going ahead steadily, and houses are springing up in centers, factories are under construction or soon will be, stores, clinics, and synagogues are being built. And Kiryat Gat is the center of the region. It was to Kiryat Gat, as I have stated, that we went with the new immigrants. And they are to fit into this plan, work and share in it. These particular immigrants with whom I traveled were to become workers rather than farmers, although they may plant small gardens once they are estabished and fitted into the life of the newly evolving community.

The maabara huts in which they were housed on arrival are only the first stage of their new life in Israel. However, the signs are that this will be a briefer first stage than was the transit period of earlier immigrants. Some of these had lived in the maabarot for a year or more, and I spoke with a woman who was the last among her friends still in a maabara. It takes about three months to put up houses. In three to six months from the time when these particular immigrants arrived, they had a chance to be settled in permanent and adequate houses.

Immigrant housing is financed by the Jewish Agency. It is usually paid off at cost price in 15 years, sometimes in twenty. The Agency thus recovers money for further housing, and the immigrant buys his house at cost and in easy payments amounting to about ten dollars a month or twenty at most. The immigrant gains a stake in the country. This is in contrast to private housing for old-timers which is financed for building at a profit. Agency funds are available only for immigrants and land settlers. In addition to this form of housing or luxury housing, the main form is housing financed by the government through the Ministry of Labor for worker veterans, that is nonimmigrants. This is also at cost and on easy payment terms. Free enterprise and the profit motive would be a bad substitute in low cost Israeli housing. It would slow up the process of integration, increase the difficulties of new immigrants, and probably condemn a number of them to live disgruntled in poverty, all in order to uphold the sacred principles of private profit.[1]

They, or some of them, may remain disappointed or disgruntled, but whatever they see or feel, whether this be joy and elation or disappointment and even bitterness—this is only an initial reaction. They were beginning a new life in a new settlement. They went to a city in the process of being built in this one-time desert and on this historic land where the course of the earlier history of Palestine was settled by fighting armies. Near to them, twenty minutes by car, is Ashkelon, an ancient city of the Philistines. It is another planned and new city, about six miles from the Gaza border, and on the shores of the Mediterranean.

The progress of this extensive and planned settlement is so remarkable the question of its successful completion, barring disastrous and destructive war, is now beyond doubt. And it is here that many of the new immigrants have gone and others will go. Progress of this kind, however, does not mean automatically that there will be good or perfect adjustment. To adjust to a new and evolving life such as one finds in Israel is very difficult. The desire and the capacity to adjust is important in this effort. And here human nature, itself, is tested. But the indications that adjustment is possible are clear. Besides the mason I visited there were others. Leaving Kiryat Gat and returning to Jerusalem, we drove through other settlements and stopped at two. There we found settlements or villages beginning to thrive. Fields were green, thanks to labor and the irrigation pipes. Moroccan immigrants who

---

[1] Some Americans have advocated free enterprise as a so-called system for new and under-industrialized countries, in ignorance of prevailing conditions and without showing any concern for masses of people who cannot possibly look forward to any betterment through the functioning of an uncontrolled system of free enterprise.

had been in Israel for some time were working the reclaimed land, commencing to prosper as a consequence of this planning and their own labor. Flowers blooming in front of pink houses, more attractive than most of the low, white houses of Israeli settlements, the green fields in the sun, a new life beginning to root itself in this soil, so much has already been accomplished. Will or will not the immigrants with whom I traveled fit into this life and find their place in it? The question can only be answered in time. The chance, the opportunity are there, and there are enough people with skills, intelligence and the will to build the area and the country so that they have a chance. That much is self-evident.

But Lachish is only part of Israel, in a sense the newest part, the product of past experience and also past mistakes. Only a fraction of the newer immigrants are in the Lachish region. Others have been flung all over Israel. There were many more whom I saw, watched, met and talked with, and I shall, following this partial digression, continue on this subject.

CHAPTER SIX

I

INASMUCH AS SO MANY of the new immigrants are from backward areas and countries, as well as because of the fact that a number have a different skin color, it is easy to lump them all together into one category and to think of them as one homogeneous group. Not only do tourists and foreigners slip unconsciously into this easy error: Israelis themselves sometimes do. In conversation, they will thus speak of the Oriental immigrants as though they were one group. While it appears that a large majority of Israelis favor the government's immigration policy, and while you keep meeting idealistic Israelis who live with the new immigrants in order to teach, to guide and to help them in many ways, you also find dislike, resentment and even fear among others. Of this, I shall write further on.

The new immigrants are backward, different, and it would seem that they might even swamp the Western Israelis and especially the sabras. An old revolutionist here in America, who is strongly anti-Zionist, told me, almost with glee, that this would happen. There are many Israelis who are not opposed to the immigration policy;

in fact, they want it to be successful and are aware of its great value for both the possible defense and development of the country. But they tend to categorize the immigrants in the same fashion and for the same reason.

This, may I add, is "normal" in ordinary thinking, and should cause neither surprise, shock nor indignation. The vast majority of Americans, for instance, continue to see Asians as one enormous and indistinguishable mass. Thus, we observe in the United States habits of mind, emotional attitudes and reactions which can also be found in other countries. Until we know peoples and groups at least a little, if not intimately, we fail to think in terms of differences; rather we fasten on common denominators that are usually over-simplified. There was a time in America, for instance, when almost all foreigners were seen as one group; in addition, many considered them an undesirable group. Today, in Chicago, the "hillbillies" are thus regarded. And two classical illustrations of this same habit of (a) thinking in clichés and *en bloc* about peoples, and, (b) thinking in derogatory clichés, are about the Negro and the Jew. This same habit is often turned against Americans abroad. It is necessary, then, to hammer home the obvious and to remind the reader of a truism—there are many inner differences among Israel's new Oriental immigrants. These differences are observable in language, familial relationships, attitudes towards work, the role of women and in many other ways. Yemenite immigrants are better workers than some others; they are more ready to work than recent immigrants from Cochin or Bombay. The Mount Atlas immigrants grasp the need for defense and learn to shoot more quickly and accurately than the Indian Jews. As I have already suggested, the Moroccans and Tunisians are generally more used to Western ways, and in that sense more "advanced" than the other Orientals. These differences suggest then that Israel's problem of assimilating and integrating its new immigrants is not at all simple. Inasmuch as we in America have had problems of integrating immigrants, we might too easily draw literal parallels between our experiences and those of the Israelis. There are two points of difference between American and Israeli experience which can be stated.

1. The rivalries and national antipathies in Israel are probably less than they were in America because practically all the immigrants are Jews. Thousands of the new immigrants do not come to Israel with the national antipathies so often found among Europeans. Yemenites knew nothing about Moroccans, or probably did not know that there was a Mount Atlas, let alone Mount Atlas Jews. However, among European immigrants, the sense of rivalry and antipathy is similar (though possibly less violent) than that in America in the 19th century. The Rumanian Jews brought with them the prejudices of Rumanians against Hungarians; German Jews, called *Yekes,* were for long disliked in Israel. This attitude towards Yekes has not completely died out.

2. There is a common religion, a sense of Jewishness, of being a Jew, which creates a feeling of common identity.

The tasks of integration are actually producing adjustments on a two-way, not a one-way, street. When some Western or sabra Israelis discuss these problems with you —although usually not those who are working directly in this field—they see integration as though it were a one-way adjustment. They do not always appear to perceive that the Westerners are also becoming adjusted and are changing. Their lives are being affected by the new immigrants and in more than a material or economic manner. Originally, most Israelis appear to have viewed integration as more or less of a melting pot. This idea is changing. Increasingly Westerners are coming to understand that the Oriental ethnic groups have a culture of their own, and that they have values to contribute to Israel as well as labor power and sons and daughters. In many cases, for instance, Asians—and we must realize that a number of these new immigrants are Asians as well as Jews—are highly and often extremely and acutely sensitive. This sensibility can be seen in the handicraft work, for instance, of the Yemenites. But more broadly, the contacts with Orientals, the problems engendered by their having come to Israel in such numbers, the efforts to teach them, the difficulties encountered in guiding them, the questions, doubts, suspicions, the singular and peculiar psychological traits of the Orientals, all this has the effect of putting to constant and daily test the values which we would roughly or broadly term Western. Israelis must think differently about the Western tradition and its values than we do, because they are in the process of applying and implementing this tradition and these values in building a nation; they must teach, convince and show by example to thousands from other traditions and cultures that Western traditions and values, Western ways of doing things, are viable and worthy of imitation.

It is apparent that complications or complex situations can be interpreted in many different ways. Where a situation is complex, there is not one but many problems. The immigration-integration situation in Israel involves many problems which are being lived through, solved, partially solved, or which are pressing for solution. Once we begin to gain small or partial insights into this situation, we can quickly see that it is anthropology in the raw. Here East and West are meeting in terms of living together. Here past and present are thrown one into the other. Here science meets custom, tradition and superstition. Here the raw material for a new life is being molded. Values are tested. Reason is being applied extensively in order that one of the most singular situations in the world can be dealt with.

It is difficult for us to see a problem, an issue, a situation from more than one standpoint. However, unless we learn to try and do this, our understanding will always be limited, grossly distorted and even dangerously biased. And considering the immigration-integration situation in Israel, we should try to keep looking at it as though we were on a revolving platform. To change the metaphor, we should try to make two eyes serve as though they were at least five or six eyes.

II

The new immigrants are now scattered all over Israel, in town and city, in the country, on the frontier. You see brown-skinned policemen, workers, soldiers. Europeans and Orientals walk side by side, live side by side, work side by side, and intermarry. In the schools and on the kibbutzim, children from Israel and from Iraq or Persia or India or Tunis play, learn and work in gardens. In the children's villages or institutions, the children who are orphans or "social cases" come from all over the world. They are educated as Israelis in a spirit of equality. In hotels, Moroccan-born waiters and waitresses are employed alongside of Rumanians. In the factories, a similar situation prevails. The newer immigrants and their children are penetrating through the life of the country. Even though it remains true that the majority of leaders are Westerners, there are cases of Orientals who have risen to the top of Israeli society. For instance, an acquaintance of mine, Captain Yeruham Cohen, a Yemenite, was Chief of Staff of General Yigal Allon in the battle at the Faluja Gap in 1948; he participated in the secret armistice talks in the Negev, and also served on the mixed Israeli-Egyptian Armistice Commission. It is very likely that a number of the children of Oriental immigrants will play an important role in the future artistic life of the country. At the present time, there is daily contact of every variety, from the most superficial to the most intimate. The problems which have evolved and have been engendered, then, are in essence problems in living. In some cases, these are individual; in others, they are of a group or social character. Some of the new immigrants have been thrown fully into the life and activity of the country and are living individually in cities or in settlements where ethnic groups have been mixed together; others are among their own kind in colonies or settlements where they preserve many of their customs. Some have prospered in at least a relative sense, or else they are beginning to prosper. Others are depressed, poor, overburdened with children, and their life is a daily struggle to feed six, or eight or even more mouths. This complex of problems is part of the living, on-going, day-by-day process of a new society in its initial stages of growth; the new immigrants are living in Israel, minute-by-minute, day-by-day, month-by-month. The situation is fluid. In many ways, the Orientals are set apart from Westerners; in others, they are not. But they are definitely involved in the life of Israel. Like the Westerners, they are now Israelis, though they live in a state of flux. They are in flux, inside of themselves, in their own minds. More is happening to them than they are usually aware of. Some of them change much more than they are capable of realizing, articulating and expressing. At the same time, and while conscious and planned efforts are made to remold them and their children, they are also consciously resistant. We see the contradiction—they want to change and become Westernized, and they also want to remain as they were.

But what is all this like in the concrete, in terms of persons, situations, activities, in terms of living? I can only offer a few glimpses, because after all, I was merely able to get glimpses myself. But for what these may be worth, I shall present some of them.

CHAPTER SEVEN

I

CASTEL is a promontory dominating a side road which connects with the main one from Jerusalem to Tel Aviv. Its name comes from the Latin for castle or fort. During the war in 1948, it was the scene of bitter fighting until it was finally taken by Israeli forces. Even today, it is the scene of many incidents and is a danger point close to the Israel-Jordanian frontier.

Some years ago, there was a mass immigration of Kurdistani Jews to Israel. Some of them are at Castel. The settlement is in the process of transformation. It includes a maabara and shikun or permanent housing settlement. Nearby, there is a quarry providing stone with which people build their own houses. Along with the Kurdistanis, you will find Iraqi Jews who came in the newer immigration, the aliyah following the establishment of the State. While building provides work in addition to agricultural jobs, there is unemployment from time to time.

Accompanied by a guide who also served as my translator, I entered a tin hut. I was glad to get away from the merciless sun. Inside the hut, there was an old blind woman. Never again would she see Iraq, where she was born; never would she see Eretz Israel. She was one of the old people brought to Israel who must be cared for and who had come, in effect if not by intent, to die in the Holy Land. She had one son, who had his own children; on his wages as an unskilled worker, eight people had to be supported. Toothless, the old woman faced you with her unseeing eyes; her round face was brown and her gray hair was slovenly. She was barefooted, and her cotton dress was worn and dirty. Suffering seemed not merely to have cowed her: it had infiltrated her being, her mind and her body. Her gestures were meek, and her voice was meek, pitifully appealing in its monotonous pathos. Since it was summer, school was not in session, and there were small children in the hut. The son was away at work, in the village, she told us. Her daughter-in-law was also in the hut, a small, brown woman with straight black hair and with that pervasive weariness of the women of the poor beginning to alter her features. There was a sadness about her, the world-wide sadness of women who work and bear children and grow old before their time while their men earn pittances. Here one could find the material to write perhaps the simplest of all those "simple annals of the poor." The life and surroundings of the settlement were harsh. The unrelieved light of the Judean sun glared outside on rocks which were scattered about as though nature had carelessly flung them there as a boy might fling tin cans about a vacant lot. The huts were spaced on the hilly ground. As we entered the settlement and walked to this hut, we saw a few women walking in the field, and here and there a child. But because of the heat, the settlement seemed largely deserted.

I asked questions which were interpreted. Slowly I was able to glean a few facts about the life of this family.

There was then no electricity in Castel. The family had been in Israel for six months. Another of the old woman's sons had lived with them, but he had gone to live in a new housing project. The old woman did not know her age. There were four synagogues in the settlement.

As we talked, a neighbor woman entered. She was about thirty, and said that she had five children. Her face was clean and light brown. Her print dress was worn but clean.

A question. Would they care to go back to Iraq?

No, no, the blind woman did not want to go back.

The neighbor spoke. When her husband worked, he earned eight pounds a day, "but no matter what he earns, it is not enough." The direct quotation here is from the words of my translator, who was a government official. On that day, the neighbor's husband was working in the stone quarry.

I asked whether, considering this poverty and hardness of life, it is better in Israel than it was in Iraq. Yes, they answered, it is better.

Why is it better?

The daughter-in-law answered that in Israel, a woman can have her babies in a hospital. There is care for women in Israel. In Iraq, she added, no one cared.

Why did they come to Israel?

"God brought us."

And then again:

"Here, it is much better."

In Iraq, they said, one who spoke of Jerusalem and the Holy Land endangered his own freedom. He could go to jail. He could die. The neighbor said that her father and brother had been in jail for five years because they had mentioned the word "Zionism."

How did they come to Israel?

By airplane.

And how was the trip?

It was very nice. They weren't afraid. They "flew like a bird." The Yemenites usually say that they "flew on the wings of eagles."

Before coming to Israel, had they ridden an automobile?

Yes, in buses, and they had seen small cars.

The government in Iraq knew in general that people were leaving for Israel, and tried to get them to stay. They weren't, however, forcibly prevented from leaving.

What were the opportunities for the education of their children in Iraq? The answer was that only the boys received religious education. And doctors? There had to be payment for doctors, and they of course were poor people. Then the blind woman's daughter-in-law added that millionaires in Iraq wouldn't give a cent for a poor person.

The neighbor woman said that in Iraq, her husband had worked cleaning tracks, and he had earned about five pounds a month. Here, too, she had troubles. She had no house. But it would be better in a few years, and even at the beginning, she believed it was better.

She went to the cinema in Israel, but had also seen motion pictures in Iraq.

Her main reason for considering life in Israel better was because of her children. This was a comment made by many of the new immigrants from almost all of the Asian and African regions. The woman said that not only her own children, but all of the children get on in Israel. One of her girls was twelve, and went to school.

What did this girl want to do when she grew up?

"Whatever the Lord will decide."

I asked the women did they like to vote? The question merely confused and bewildered them. I had been with them for almost an hour, and could see that they were wearying of the questions. Although these had been put simply, the mental exertion of answering troubled them. I looked around the hut. There were several cots and an old table. Simple household things were scattered here and there in some disorder. There was a primus stove on a ledge.

I rose. The women looked at me with saddened faces. We thanked them and left. They came to the door and stared as we tramped off, over rocks and uneven ground. The glare of the sun brought tears to my eyes. A few children walked in front of us. I saw other huts spaced out all around us. In front of one, washing was hung out on a line. Ahead, a dark man walked slowly off with a shovel slung over his shoulder like a rifle.

II

After seeing the Kurdistani woman, we visited a thirty-year old Persian woman who also lived in a maabara tin hut. The mother of six children, she had already been in Israel for three years. She was both depressed and apologetic, as she explained that her husband was over fifty and that he was now working on road building. She said that she was ashamed. All of her friends and all those who had immigrated with her from Persia and had been in these huts were gone. They now lived in permanent homes. She and her husband were trying to save money for the deposit in order that they, likewise, might be able to have their own home instead of having to continue living where they were, overcrowded and in poverty. Again she said that she was ashamed. For in their three years in Israel, she and her husband had been unable to save any money. The reason was—their family. There had been illness. Her little boy had had a throat infection and the doctor had operated on him.

I asked her that since this was the case, was it still better for her and her family in Israel than it had been in Persia? She answered that it was "if there isn't war."

One reason why she considered herself better off despite her poverty and her shame was that expressed by so many of these simple and unlettered Oriental women—"the children."

All of her children were in school. One of her girls had reached the fourth grade. And she liked the schools in Israel for her children. Especially, she liked the festivals and the processions.

Then she contradicted herself and said that it had been better in Persia. Originally she had lived in a wooden hut, and then the family had come here to this tin hut. It was going to be better, though, when they were in the shikun.

Had she voted in Israel? Yes, she had taken part in the last election. What did she think of Ben-Gurion? The translator, after listening to her answer, told me that she hadn't understood. As he spoke, she was watching as though she were struggling to grasp something of what he was telling me in English. She spoke in Hebrew. If he, that is Ben-Gurion, is the government, then he is good, he is all right.

Occasionally, I asked the new immigrants what they thought of or knew about America. What did they think it was like? In response to these questions, the Persian woman answered that she did not know, she had never been there.

Here, I had met an immigrant family which appeared to be encountering greater difficulties than those with whom they had immigrated. In order to get a house in a shikun, a deposit of 500 pounds was needed. Loans were granted for this. But she and her husband still had nothing. In this respect, they were almost in the same condition as new arrivals. She was sensitive about her poverty. She did not like it. She had come to learn that life could be different from what she had known it to be for her and for her kind. Her shame at still living in the maabara appeared to embody a sense of failure, but also an aspiration to live differently. She had learned that in Israel this was possible for a family like hers.

How do we interpret stories such as this woman's? Do we use them as an example to prove or disprove a bias, a pre-conception? If we are anti-Zionist, or anti-Israel, should we cite this case as an instance of exploitation of the immigrants? If we are sympathetic to Israel and its aims and wish to see it survive, succeed and flourish, should we extract crumbs of hope, and emphasize that there are small advances and benefits, such as schooling for the children, better medical care?

Is it not simpler to think of people such as those I have sketched as members of Asian humanity in a rapidly changing world? And with this can we not see that here is the root meaning of the aspirations which can stir simple people, not only in Israel, but on the entire continent of Asia? If we do, we have a better chance to retain greater sobriety of judgment.

With all this in mind, let us now catch a few more camera shots of other members of this vast Asian humanity.

III

The Yemenite border settlement called Eshtaol is located in the Jerusalem Corridor. The homes, spread on uneven ground, are permanent, low, flat two-room structures with showers and toilet facilities. On a blazing summer morning in July, I visited this settlement of 67 families. Nearby is the birthplace of Samson, or at least this is what is believed.

At Eshtaol, I spoke with a thirty-year old Yemenite who served in the border police and was responsible for the security of the small community. He took us into his house, which was clean and orderly. He met me with an air of assurance and with a willingness to answer questions, to explain to me anything he could about the life of the settlement and of his own people. He had no complaints, and while not a rich man, he was suffering neither hardship nor poverty. He gave the impression of a man who believed himself settled for life, and sure of his place in society. Besides his work in the border police, he had three dunams of land which he cultivated. The other Yemenite families in the settlement have six dunams, but since he had other work and another source of income, he had less land.

He said that he had come to Israel because:

"We dreamt about it for a long time when we were waiting for it, a long time. When we can have it, we agree. It is our country, and we are all the time waiting for the time to come to go back to it and work on it and depend [on it]."

And the Arabs, a problem with which he must live daily?

"No fear. We were always surrounded by Arabs. They didn't use to be friendly." He spoke, too, of the Arabs in Israel. He had met some at the village of Abu Gosh near Jerusalem. In his opinion, they are different from the Arabs in Yemen. He went on to say that they are the same Arabs, but in Israel, they work. "There (that is, in Yemen) everybody works for his own." He added that in Israel, people can work for others. This was important to him.

He had been in Israel for six years, and for five of these he had served in the border police. Before emigrating, he had worked in the manufacture of explosives. His income is better in Israel, but "over there," everything was so cheap that he could make a good living. Nonetheless, he declared firmly once again that by all means, living conditions were better in Israel. He stressed that this was so, especially for the children, and said that there had been no facilities, or at least no adequate ones, for health and education in Yemen.

"The country [Yemen] didn't give the children a thing when they were sick.

"There were no doctors, no possibility to get a doctor."

But he wanted me to know that this was not the only reason for his emigration. Before leaving Yemen, he and his people had heard that "when we come to Israel, we might have one," a radio. Now he owns one and it is "very nice." And he "never heard of electricity." Also, there is running water in every house at Eshtaol. This had not been the case in Yemen.

However, he told me that in his former country, there had been no persecution of the Jews until the "War of Liberation." Then, the Arabs began to talk of the necessity for the Jew to fight the Arab.

He came to Israel by airplane, the first time he had flown, and he is happy to be among his own people who have a state of their own. Furthermore, on coming to Israel, he believed that he was in a different world from what he had previously known. This belief was not based on technical advances, but because he found himself "among his own people." This sentiment, obviously, is one which he feels strongly. He mentioned it repeatedly.

On arriving, he was put in a maabara. After two months, he was sent to Eshtaol, to work on the soil, but his wife and two children remained in the camp. Now his home is his own and he is still paying on it, but he receives extra pay because he watches after the security of the settlement. He is an Oriental immigrant who is doing well in Israel and finds himself in relatively good circumstances. He bought his own furniture, beds, tables, chairs, pots and pans, and, also, his radio. I asked him how his standard of living compared with that of the other Yemenites in the settlement; he answered that it was the same. This can be taken as truth. The Yemenites are hard-working and thrifty. This particular group is settled in a developing moshav and the market in Israel for all agricultural produce, or almost all of it, is steady. These people are over the hump.

We sat at his table, smoking, discussing; I asked more questions. Voting in Yemen does not exist. The first time he voted in Israel, he knew nothing about it, and "he had to be told what the whole thing is about." But now, he votes and he has come to see that it is "a thing of importance." He also said that he was happy that his wife could vote and had the same rights as he himself had. In Yemen, his wife couldn't read; now, she has learned to read "fairly."

His children come from school and tell their parents what they have learned. There are festivals quite often, and they all like these. In Yemen, he said, there were only the Jewish festivals. Quite obviously, the festivals in Israel are also Jewish; but here I am telling precisely what he said.

The Yemenites are highly religious, and usually they are strictly observant. Many of them wear sidelocks, but this police officer did not. Their family life is closely knit and they are reported to show opposition to and dismay in the face of Western ways. Such reactions have developed especially in relationship to girls. Our conversation now switched to these questions. What did this particular Yemenite think about these matters?

There is a difference in Israel, he said, from what there had been in Yemen. People are talking of this. But in his settlement, there are no signs of the breakup of families. Personally, he was not worried or disturbed as were many of his fellow settlers. Even about the girls going away and into the army, his views were the same. He had gone a considerable distance mentally and emotionally since coming to Israel. In Western methods, he saw the means for improving the lot of his own people, for creating a better future for children. Emotionally, he had come to accept the ideas of progress as good. Most specifically he considered them good for his own people.

Since he had served so long in the border police, he has more contacts than most of the other Yemenites in Eshtaol. But in addition, he and the others had come in contact with other immigrant groups in the maabara. For instance, he had met Moroccans. And yes, they get along, the Yemenites and Moroccans—"except when they get into a temper." When this happens both Yemenites and Moroccans quarrel. "You are a Moroccan!"—"You are a Yemenite!" When the Moroccans are truly worked up and angry, they use what he called strong expressions. They would claim that, "These Yemenites all like to kill us." He hastened to explain that the word "kill" wasn't literally intended. What they meant was that the Yemenites intended to do them harm. But he took no serious view of such episodes.

Some Israelis had told me that the Yemenites from the Second Aliyah in the early 1900's had been standoffish, embarrassed by and disinclined to help the Yemenites who had come more recently. If this be so, and it probably has varied with individuals, it did not come within this man's experience. The settled immigrants helped him and his group. They explained how life might be in Israel, spoke of how there would be difficulties and hardships in the beginning and warned them to be prepared for these. This, he said, had been most helpful.

I changed the subject and asked him what he thought of America. He said he doesn't know. A moment later he had more to say. America he thought of as a big rich country, a country very much advanced in science. And what of Russia? He told my translator—"They are out to slaughter the world."

Could he save any money? Absolutely. He must, because he might not earn enough some day. But he, his family and others in the settlement have enough to eat. They have meat, vegetables, rice and he buys margarine and jam. But at one time he couldn't buy bread. They would make bread from grain.

In this settlement, the Yemenites manage their own affairs through an elected Secretariat. They have two telephones. Pipes were being laid to bring water for the religious bath of the women. Sixteen of the children had been sent off to a kibbutz. The rest of the children were under the care of a volunteer Israeli worker of European origin. She brought her own blond little girl to play with the Yemenite children. They play, sing holding hands, receive a hot lunch which is being prepared and served by other Israeli workers.

Trees are springing up among the rocks, and the land is being cultivated. As it is, the Yemenites are slowly progressing materially. Their children are learning, and health conditions not only for them but also for the adults are described as being much better than they were in Yemen. Although this is a border settlement, there had not been any incidents for months. Six months before, Arab infiltrators had stolen some mules. The women work at home or in the gardens. The men work their dunams and the ground which is held in common for all in this moshav. Day by day, a simple life goes on here. The old beliefs and traditions are clung to, while gradually work is being modernized and the fruits of technology are being brought to this small settlement—irrigation pipes, telephones, showers. The children are receiving outside or out of the home guidance along the lines of modern ideas of child guidance and education. You walk around and look off at the hills in the hot, silent sun. The quiet surrounds you. A Yemenite woman, in black, or in a colorful native dress walks by with a bundle. A little boy wearing sun glasses passes along. Here is a garden in front of a low stone house. There are young trees. The rocks are white, pale and they shine from their long and continual bleaching. The heat presses on you. You continue staring off at nearby hills. There Samson was reputed to have been born. This means much to the Yemenites. They have come from Samson's world towards what is something of our own world. Old and new are entangled on these rocky hillsides, close to the Arab border. And this land, those rocks and hills, is for the Yemenites their own land.

The children played and sang on the porch of the community center. The little boys wore sidelocks. Some were dirty from play. They were ushered, with small disorders, into the bare dining hall. And they shouted. A fat woman served them at their benches. One boy didn't eat. The fat woman helped him and he ate. They talked and shouted.

Then we left this small spot of Israel to go on and to see others, to speak and question in other settlements.

IV

Maslul is a settlement near Beersheba and on the way from there to Ashkelon on the Mediterranean. The inhabitants are about three-fourths Persians and the others are Kurdish Jews. Electricity and telephones were brought to the settlement about 1954. Of course there are no telephones in the individual homes. That is a long, long way off. In fact, it is still difficult to get telephones in Tel Aviv and Jerusalem. The inhabitants of Maslul individually work about twenty dunams of land per family, and eventually this might be raised to thirty-five. Also they have vineyards which are worked in common. There are radios in practically all of the homes and, in some, there are ice boxes and electric irons. The Kurdish Jews, like many of the other Oriental immigrants, will not plant gardens. The insides of the homes are usually disorderly, although this varies more from individual to individual than among groups. In one home there were five children and, in addition to the man and wife, an old grandmother. A fat, plump but pudgy-faced baby boy was lying on a cot with a bright red blanket under him; young children sat on the floor. The small house was thick with buzzing flies which kept landing on and crawling over the face of the sleeping baby. Now and then, the grandmother swished them away but only for an instant. They returned. As we talked it was disconcerting to see the numerous flies crawling on the baby's nose, lips, chin, cheeks and over his closed eyes. There is a fly problem throughout Israel. When I asked about this, I was told that the flies were immune to DDT.

The head of the family was a thin, small man and he

was at home that afternoon. When I asked why they had come to Israel, he answered: Because of the Bible.

"We have been waiting for two thousand years," my translator told me that he had said.

They had been in Israel for six years, but the man declared that living was easier when they had come than at present. The older he gets, he also said, the more mouths he has to feed. But still he would rather be in Israel. There are tractors for farming, and in Israel "they know how to work much better" than in his homeland. The children are very pleased. They come home and tell stories about school. They tell what happened, and what others have said. When the family sits together, they tell the stories.

The flies were still crawling all over the face of the sleeping child.

The children go to kindergarten, he said. He meant all of the children in the settlement, not only his own. Did he want his children to go to school? I asked. Like some of the Arabs, many of the Oriental parents do not want to keep their children in school and this creates many difficulties for teachers and social instructors in the maabarot and other settlements.

"Even if you kill the children, they'll stay in school," the man told me; he seemed bitter.

Also, he told me that he and his wife had voted. But he showed neither great interest nor enthusiasm in answering questions. He considered me an intruder and it seemed best to cut the interview short.

After visiting this family, we went through the treeless settlement to the home of a Persian. A garden—exceptional in the settlement—bloomed in the yard. A teacher who was guiding me had told me in advance that this family was modern and really somewhat exceptional among immigrants. The man works in the stockroom on the moshav—a job which requires some training and education. His home was neat, clean and contained good furniture. The colors were bright and gay. In a corner stood a radio, an expensive one for an Israeli. Also, there was an ice box and an indoor bathroom which the man had put in from his earnings.

He was a tall, middle-aged man with a moustache. He was not only pleased but also proud for me to visit him in his home. He answered questions more readily than many of the immigrants, and he knew quite well what he thought. Yes, it was better in Israel than in Persia. One reason was because of the Muslims. He had been fed up with them. It had been terrible with the Muslims. Schools, too, were better. "All teachers were Muslims and they didn't care about Jews." But there had been no active discrimination, and the Persians, he said, were better than the Arabs.

He had come to Israel because he wanted to. He had signed up with the Jewish Agency. And he was more than glad that he had, because "here, everybody is equal." And the homes were better. He had space. In the oil center where he had lived in Persia, he had been "walled in a house. Everything is closed." In Israel, he felt more secure.

Back in Persia, women didn't vote, but "No, it was unimportant there. It's important here." And the doctors there charged too much money. Also, he accused them of prolonging treatments in order to collect added fees. The best prospect for a Jew in Persia had been to be a small merchant. He had worked as a jeweler. In Israel, he claimed you could earn 20%, 25% more. Then he said 100%. His income in Persia had ranged from 300 to 500 Israeli pounds per year. On this point, he was unclear, but I guess that he meant this sum as an annual figure.

On leaving Iran, he and the other Persian Jews had not been allowed to take any belongings except clothes. They had to sell everything they had, and, he added, they were robbed. They waited for two months after signing up to emigrate, and then they had to come to Israel by plane. He had not been afraid. What about his wife?

She answered:

"I died on the way." (She meant that she had fainted.)

V

At the moshav, Mesilat Zion in the Jerusalem Corridor, there are Jews from Bombay and from Cochin on the Malabar coast of India. Like practically all of the settlements in the Judean hills, the houses are on rocky land. Looking down, you can see the fields which are in cultivation. The people at Mesilat Zion are dark, and some of them are black; most of them are young. When the Cochin Jews came to Israel about four years ago, many of them suffered from eye diseases and malnutrition. They were among the poorest of the immigrants. They, as well as the Indian Jews, are usually phlegmatic. The men, unlike those from Mount Atlas, for instance, do not learn to shoot easily and readily. They work less well than some of the other Oriental immigrants, most notably the Yemenites.

With a translator, I was admitted to the home of a dark, twenty-two year old girl from Bombay. She had one child, and after fourteen months in Israel, her husband had become a frontier policeman. He was on duty at the time of our visit. They had come to Israel because they were Jews, but she said that in Bombay there had been no prejudice against Jews. They had come in a plane but this had not frightened her. And having lived in a city, she had been familiar with automobiles and with the features of urban life in general. She did not believe that she had been badly off in Bombay. This, however, is a relative matter, since the poverty, overcrowding and malnutrition there are still widespread, and are unmatched anywhere in the United States.

On their arrival, the Bombay and Cochin Jews did not know how to work the land. They had to be taught patiently. But, the girl said, they could stand work in agriculture after having been instructed. However, it takes them two to three years before they can work the community land of the moshav and at the time of my visit they were still not as yet ready to do it. This I was told by their agricultural instructor. On their arrival they began to work gardens under supervision. However, they were anxious to learn and asked questions. When they saw something they did not understand, they would even wake up the instructor at night to find out about it. They raised chickens and made some money from this by selling the poultry in Jerusalem. On the whole, the difficulties of teaching them were very considerable. It was taking longer to instruct them than was the case with most of the other groups of Oriental immigrants. And the young housewife from Bombay said that yes, they were happy because they were better cared for than they had been in India. In the moshav there were about five old people. They got light work and were paid for it. This impressed the immigrants. Many of them were not even-tempered. They could change in a half hour. Their opinions were not firm or clear. It was difficult to find out from them what they really thought. When there would be a rise in border tensions, many of them would run for news, either to get newspapers to read or else to have these read to them. Not all these immigrants can read.

The children were required to behave strictly at home, and in school the stress on language was heavy. Linguistic problems were significant in this moshav. The parents said that in Israel they wanted their children to be made "like sabras." But the parents generally only stayed in contact with Indian Jews. They felt better when they did. Many went to agricultural schools themselves. Like their children, they were still learning. The pregnant women at first resisted going to hospitals. Then they wanted to, not only because of the care, but also because they know that if they do go to hospitals, they will receive fifty pounds. The changes in the adults have been small, and mainly in lesser matters of details. There was a committee in the moshav to manage its internal affairs and the secretary was paid. Its decisions were always accepted. However, it had to be dissolved, because the people did not understand its working.

The 230 Indians in this moshav were all relatives, coming from two families. There seemed to be hope that a few of them would develop and form a more workable committee than the previous one. At first, they had to go to social instructors when ill. This changed later. The husbands would then rush to the community telephone and call about illness themselves. The men did guard duty to protect the settlement voluntarily and by rotation. But they were afraid. They are traditional in religion, but not strictly observant as are the Yemenite, the Mount Atlas and some of the other immigrants. They have their own rabbi.

This, then, was roughly the condition and situation of the Indian Jews when I visited Mesilat Zion. These few snapshots demonstrate the considerable difference and variety among Oriental immigrants. We shall see more of it in the following chapters.

CHAPTER EIGHT

I

I WENT TO KATAMON, a shikun in the Jerusalem area. With me was Dr. Eva Landsberg, a naturalized American woman, a doctor who has specialized in pediatrics. I had known her in America, where she had had much experience working in the New York City Department of Health. An American woman interested in social work and a South African woman and social worker stationed in Katamon were also in our small party. At Katamon, there are about 1,500 families. The Iraqi Jews predominate, but there are many North Africans also. Four or five families a week were being moved in, and it was hoped to fill the shikun as fast as possible. At Katamon, the new immigrants have not been settled in ethnic groups. Rather, they are jumbled together. Many of the men work as day laborers and earn about five pounds a day, but they do not work every day. There was unemployment among them when I was there, and living conditions were hard for some of the inhabitants, especially because so many of them have such big families. In fact, about one third of the families were welfare or social cases, and in this group, many were virtually classifiable as unemployables. Perhaps the number of welfare cases was higher because in the shikunim the immigrants are less protected than in the moshavim. In the former, the new immigrants are not guaranteed twelve days' work per month, as they are in the moshavim. They own their own houses, on which they have to pay a deposit and a low rental or monthly installment; they pay water taxes, also.

Since the inhabitants are not divided into ethnic groups, one of the problems at Katamon has been of stimulating and developing more community spirit, more neighborliness, and even of trying to get the inhabitants acquainted with one another. They do not mix easily, and the idea of civic and community spirit in the sense in which we know it in the West is foreign to their cultural pattern and outside their past experiences. This is broadly the case among the Oriental immigrants, and it imposes one of the many and serious problems which the Israelis must resolve in their many-sided efforts at integration.

Katamon is an enormous shikun, a small city. Some of the houses are arranged on small streets, and each home has two and a half rooms. Others are two stories high. There are many vegetable or flower gardens in the settlement.

We first went to the house of a poor Iraqi woman. The moment she became aware that we were Americans, as three of us were, she imagined that we had come to help her, and to give her money. She was a small, dark woman, looking drab in her old print dress; there was something pitiful, beaten, in her voice. She said that it was the same for her in the shikun as it had been in the maabara. She had three children, and with her was the old grandmother, who joined in the conversation. The grandmother told us that she was hungry, and had nothing to eat. The father was away, temporarily serving in the Army. The young woman did not know her age, but said that she thought she was twenty years old. And she said that she had immigrated because:

"My whole family came to Israel, so I came."

She did not want to return to Iraq, and said she couldn't return there because of the Arabs. She was quite confused because of her simplicity and her lack of education. But she was like many of the new immigrants. She was far, far away from many of the simple things which we in America take for granted.

After leaving the Iraqi woman, we went to a home on the second floor of a stone building. There, the young Moroccan mother was faring better than the Iraqi woman. On entering, we spotted a baby carriage. The home was clean, fully furnished, and there was showy glassware around. The family had a radio. The rug on the living room floor was very bright. The young woman was plump but pretty; her cheeks were round, her hair was dark, and she was wearing a gay printed dress.

The South African woman with us had been attempting to form small groups of women in each block of houses. Our hostess was in one of these groups. There were four or five women in each group, and they sewed, or were taught to sew. In this manner, an effort was made to stimulate neighborliness and to get the immigrants acquainted with each other. Those who participated in this group, would, it was hoped, then influence their neighbors. In this way, progress at integration and in instruction might be achieved.

The young mother whom we were visiting immediately got three other young Moroccan wives, all of them belonging to the same small group. They said they liked this activity and believed that they were learning things. Having come from cities, these young women were more advanced and aware of urban life than the poor Iraqi woman or than many of the other women in Katamon. Six of these groups had already been formed when I visited the settlement. This included only thirty women, a small number if one considers how many families had already been settled there.

Among the subjects we discussed was that of breast feeding. Dr. Landsberg was professionally interested in this question. She had noticed how many of the infants brought from North Africa were pudgy. Their faces were fat and looked swollen and unhealthy. After they had been in Israel for a short while, their physiognomies changed; they began to look like normal, healthy babies who received the proper nutrition.

Dr. Landsberg asked if there was a lack of food among the Moroccan Jews.

No, there had been plenty of food, our hostess explained in French. Vegetables and fish, she told us, were cheap in Morocco. She knew about vitamins, also, and then she added that chickens were plentiful.

In Israel, the pregnant mothers worked in the home and did not get any rest. In her case, she said, she gets up at four in the morning and works and has no milk. In Morocco, the pregnant mothers were well fed and they had milk. The other young mothers assented to these statements.

But why, if the mothers were well nourished, did the babies look so unhealthy? We were told that the mothers gave milk. After a few more questions, this statement was clarified. The babies were fed solely or almost so on the mother's milk, and they were breast fed for two or three years. The young women said that they believed that so long as they breast-fed their children, they would not become pregnant. This is an ancient superstition, held among many simple women. I told them, for instance, that my own mother, who had fifteen children, had believed in and had followed a similar custom. In Israel, through clinics, nurses, social instructors and doctors, the women are convinced to give children a balanced diet in accordance with contemporary views on nutrition. Thus the change in the babies.

A sabra girl named Sarah was brought in to join us. Thin and shy, she had big, beautiful eyes and silky black hair. She sat without speaking until we encouraged her. Then she talked with spirit, enthusiasm and idealism. Not knowing French, she had to speak Hebrew, and her story was translated for me.

Sarah worked with the immigrant women in one of the small groups, teaching and instructing them. Her group of five was less advanced than the ones with whom we were talking. Her account, given with a certain amount of breathlessness, interested the Moroccan girls as much as it did us, the visitors.

Sarah said that the immigrant women wanted to learn sewing so that they could make dresses and other articles of clothing. But in order to do this, it was necessary to know how to use a tape measure, and they could not count. While Sarah's account was translated, she watched us closely, with pride; she was eager to go on. She wanted us very much to know her story. The translation was slow because the South African social worker's Hebrew was uncertain. This made Sarah more impatient. Finally, she continued her tale, but suddenly she stopped and looked around with quick dark eyes. She spoke to our hostess, who gave her several paper napkins. Then, talking on, she laid one paper napkin on the table. What she had done was to take such a napkin, place it on a table as she had just done, and explain to the women of her group that it represented one. She wrote one out for them ten times. Taking a second napkin, she placed it on the table, and said that this had been her next step in teaching the women. One and one make two, she explained to them. She wrote two down ten times. She continued up to ten in this fashion during her first lesson. Then she told the women to go home and write from one to ten, ten times. They followed her instructions. In three meetings they had learned to count to one hundred. Encouraged by this simple and elementary learning, the women told Sarah that they wanted to learn how to write their names. When they made their monthly installment payments on the houses in which they lived, they wanted to be able to write their names instead of continuing to make a mark with their thumbs. Sarah had been successful in teaching them to write their names. She was planning to proceed further in giving them these simple instructions; in addition she was going to organize a second group to teach them in this same fashion.

When we left this home, the social worker asked me, did I not want to see a new immigrant at Katamon who was dissatisfied. I had been thinking precisely of this at that moment, and told her that I did.

We were taken to see an Egyptian Jew whom I will name Sholem. He lived in a one-story, two-room house with a fenced-in, well kept garden for a front yard. Sholem is big and plump with soft fat on his body. His face is round and also fat and he sports a moustache. He was seated in front of his door, and wearing a good pair of dark trousers and a clean white shirt. As we approached, he rose and met us with geniality. He began talking in broken English and invited us into his home. The social worker asked him if things were improved since she had last spoken with him. He said no, and she asked him if he would tell us about all his complaints and dissatisfactions. He launched into this instantly and with pleasure. His problem was money; he could not get enough money. For himself, he said, he did not care. It was for the others that he wanted the money. If he could not get the money, he could not do the things he wanted to do. There had to be more money, but they, that is the Jewish Agency and the government, would not provide it.

"Nobody has lived here for two thousand years," he said, seated opposite me at the table in a clean small room. "It's not agreed to live in this condition."

And, he said, he had written to the Prime Minister and told him just this. The shikun needed many things for the people. But where was the money for them? He wanted to get these things, fight for them. He wanted to do things for the people. But there wasn't the money. So, he was going to do nothing. Two other people here felt just as he did. One was a Rumanian. He could do nothing. And this was discouraging, he told us energetically.

But even so it had been worse in 1953. Then there had been no bus to take the people to work. He complained and in two weeks, they had gotten bus service.

His own difficulties were many and he was not as well off in Israel as he had been in Cairo, where, he said, he had been a manager in a chocolate factory.

"Life is very hard here. The people, they start from zero. In Egypt, it is very civilized there."

Why, then, had he come to Israel?

"You must have something in the blood. Zionism is in the blood."

He said that he had many troubles, but then shrugged

his shoulders in a gesture of pathos. He remarked that he speaks languages and added:

"I am a civilized man."

But he is not faring well. He is not a healthy man. Yes, he is in Histadrut and through Kuppat Holim, the medical insurance organization of Histadrut, he had been helped very much. He goes to a clinic. He also spoke very favorably of Hadassah. His baby can be put in a nursery and one of his children is in the kindergarten. But when he came to Israel, the situation had been different.

"We did all this," he told me, meaning mainly himself.

But, he went on, what was still needed was considerable; this was on his mind.

"More what we need," he explained, "it's a place for a library, books, a library—a place for all pupils. But money, without money, we can't move."

And he repeated again, the money is not being given.

"I work without friends to make money."

This was no use.

Then he said that he suffered from a chronic kidney ailment which permitted him to do only light work.

"I stay fourteen months in my home. My daughter gives us bread every day." (He meant that he had been confined by illness.)

She is a factory worker and after my questioning, he estimated that her take-home pay was about 172 to 174 Israeli pounds a month. He does light work for about six hours a day as a janitor in a school. He did everything. He whitewashed the floors, cleaned, worked as a clerk, managed the school. But the school should be bigger. And in the midst of this explanation, he repeated to me:

"I'm a civilized man."

He goes to a small night school, and:

"What I know as Hebrew, I know better than people who live here thirty months."

Then he said the Katamon needed a theater. But again, there was no money.

And he was faced with his own financial problems. In eight years, his home would be paid for. But it contains only two rooms for five people. He must pay his debts, "altogether slowly." The total debt on his house had been, he said, two thousand pounds. Recently he had borrowed two hundred pounds from the Immigrants Bank, and he had to repay this at an interest of 9%.

With his income, what could he buy? Prices were high. How could he and his family have much? They can buy a small quantity of meat per month at low prices, as can everyone in Israel. If they wanted more meat, it had to be bought in the free market at not less than three to four *Liras* (pounds) for one pound of meat.

No, it was bad. There was not much hope. But he would continue to do his best. Only he insisted he couldn't do things, get things, without money.

Sholem wanted to speak with me at more length, and to show me the school where he worked. But here, as in most other cases, I had to go on. By and large my visit to Israel was one of interrupted conversations. Sholem urged me to come and see him any time. I was unable, however, to return to Katamon.

II

I visited Taanakh. It was a partially completed moshav settlement near Afula in Galilee. Its land is cultivated right up to the Jordanian border. Families from Tunis and Morocco, including Mount Atlas, live there. Many of the immigrants were only getting started and they were not sufficiently trained to work the fields well. The atmosphere was that of newness, of a beginning, with some of the immigrants in their first stages of adjustment. They were generally poor and have not yet had time to accumulate, to buy themselves many new household articles. Electricity had not as yet been installed either when I was there in June, 1956.

The social instructor was a man of thirty-one, Russian born and happy in his work. He learned about agriculture after having come to Israel, and told me that his first days in the country were much harder than those of the new immigrants in the settlement whom he was then instructing. He spoke German and all of his other comments and answers to my questions were translated to me.

We sat in the car on a rocky road in front of the new stone houses where Moroccan and Tunisian Jews lived; I began to question him. What, I asked, were the problems faced by the immigrants? There are many. One is that of language. The new settlers speak different languages and when some of them try to communicate with one another, they require translators. The Mount Atlas immigrants speak a peculiar dialect which is not Arabic, and among them, the language problem is most difficult. But immigrants want to learn Hebrew and are quickly acquiring some acquaintance with it.

How did they respond to instruction? It was the instructor's opinion that they responded very well and when they did not understand, they would ask questions. The whole approach to work of the Mount Atlas immigrants had been very trying at first and was still difficult when I spoke to the instructor. It was taking time to train them. In the beginning, he said, they "approached work like an animal." They had no idea of how to work in a steady, rational or organized manner. They would run about, do a little work, and then take it easy. One of his main tasks in teaching was to pace their work; he was still teaching them to do this. But, he insisted and repeated, they are very observant. He liked them exceedingly, more than he did the Tunisians and Moroccans who lived in the same settlement.

In religion, they are very observant, but never had a real congregation. They have one head or leader of their group who also is the rabbi. They eat kosher food. It is unwise even to raise the question of religion with them. The way the instructor put this to me was, "You can't touch the subject."

The Mount Atlas people all work for themselves. They have meetings and a committee which runs local affairs, and they had been able to organize the rotation guard duty at night, since there must be guards to watch for infiltrators; their land runs right up to the Jordanian frontier. At meetings they put questions relating to their problems and their life together. They also ask questions about education. When they arrived in Israel, the children were mostly illiterate, but some had learned a little Hebrew from their own people. Now, the parents are pleased that there is a kindergarten and school for their children.

On the arrival of these immigrants, many of the children were ill. Injections frightened them so much that in the first days they ran away to escape them. But they have since come to know that injections are given them for their own good; they submit to the needle. When they saw water coming out of a faucet for the first time, they fled in terror. Likewise during their first days in Israel they tried to keep doctors out of their houses and above all else, they would not permit doctors to examine the women. A child couldn't be touched. Many of the children had eczema on the head and other illnesses. Quite a few died during their initial period as newcomers. The Mount Atlas people showed intense resistance whenever efforts were made to take sick children to a hospital. The children, weak as they were, ran out of the house. In one instance two sick little children were placed on a bed and covered with blankets so that they would be concealed from the visiting nurse. But so many blankets were put on top of the children that they died of suffocation. The head of the community, that is the leader and rabbi, had been stricken while working in a field. He required hospitalization, but in order to take him, force had to be applied. The diagnosis called for an operation, but he refused to grant permission for it.

At the time I visited the settlement, the attitudes of the Mount Atlas Jews were just beginning to change. They would see doctors, and accepted care by both men and women doctors. The use of a woman doctor had helped significantly in dissipating their suspicion and puncturing their resistance to the reception of medical care. Children sent to the hospital wanted to remain there instead of returning home. After six months, the Mount Atlas people began to want their sick children taken to the hospital, and also, they had come to accept the idea of the women giving birth in hospitals or clinics. Their acceptance of hospital deliveries, of course, was made all the easier because of the money the women receive as a form of aid. All this, they had come to regard as just wonderful.

The committee meetings are run democratically, but they always do what their leader says and vote in elections as he wishes them to. Two of the main subjects taken up at meetings are work and their circumstances of living. They want to live side by side and everybody wants work near his own home. They dislike working any distance from the settlement. They get various kinds of work, such as planting trees in the main center of the Taanakh community, and since the center is obviously close to home, they all like to get this employment. Finally, they decided to rotate the more desired types of work and successfully managed this by themselves. The instructor told me more about the quality of their work. He repeated that they had to be taught everything, and that those who had worked on the land, in their native villages, had done so by hand. But one of the younger Mount Atlas immigrants had already learned to drive a tractor, which he now did. They were proud of him; he had become an important person in the community. The first time a tractor had come to the settlement, they had all turned out to see it. They had never seen one before. They regarded the tractor as one of the wonders and marvels of Israel.

At night after dark they pray and then go to bed. Every day, they kiss the land. Some of them began working on their day of arrival, and now have vegetable gardens which they can care for themselves, without having to be watched or supervised. Also in the beginning they didn't understand movies, but now they all attend and like movies very much. They like anything they see; in the theater they sit very quietly as they watch.

At Taanakh, as I have stated, there are also Tunisians and Moroccans. The Tunisians are the most advanced of these groups and look down upon the others, specifically the Mount Atlas Jews. The groups do not understand one another. A committee representing all groups functions in community affairs. One of the major issues which they consider is what and how much they can get from the Jewish Agency. Mostly, they are not satisfied with what has been given them, an attitude which seems to have been fairly general among newer immigrants in Israel. Candidates for the committees are elected by secret ballot; they are listed according to number. The age qualification for voting is eighteen years. The immigrants, of course, know one another in their own ethnic groups. In the local political life of the community, those who are more aware and have more understanding explain to the other immigrants. This is especially true of the Tunisians; they can speak better on issues and this enables them to get influence. But customs and traditions from their past and their native habitats also influence local settlement politics. Thus a son will not interfere as long as his father lives but will bow to the latter's view. The respect for the father is enormous and, hence, age is honored. An older man will always be elected as against a younger one. The Tunisian women vote in the community elections, but not those from Mount Atlas. One Tunisian girl, whom I interviewed and will describe below, was elected to the committee, but in a subsequent election she lost out. She was not defeated, the social instructor insisted, because she was a woman. Rather, her own people believed that she was not working sufficiently hard to get them more benefits from the Jewish Agency. To the contrary, they believed, rightly or wrongly, that she was buttering up the representatives from the Agency, and trying to get favors only for herself and her family. This revealed the main core of dissatisfaction among the immigrants at Taanakh. The Tunisians had even written to the Jewish Agency asking for the removal of the social instructress who had been assigned to help the women.

Concerning the elections, the instructor said that they could have new ones any time the entire community wanted them. They were only learning the practices of democracy and of self-responsibility in a democratic society. This is true among the new immigrants as a whole and it is one of the major problems and most fascinating aspects of the question of the integration situation in Israel. We know that democracy does not come to people by instinct but rather by teaching and as a consequence of experience. Obviously most of the immigrants have had no experience in democracy. Those who have, such as some of the North Africans, have not known democracy in a society or setting where full political and civic responsibility was placed on them. They were both colonials and Jews. And in Israel, the issue of democracy among the new immigrants must be seen in the simplest day-by-day matters. They can all vote in elections for the Knesset. I was told that during election time all of the parties come to the settlements and try to outbid each other in the promises they make to the new immigrants. What the new immigrants get or are promised appears more important in determining their votes than any issue. This is not unusual; even in advanced democracies, a great majority of people vote and make political decisions on the basis of how they are personally affected. In any democratic country, it is only a small minority which votes out of any dispassionate or objective concern for the fate of society as a whole, or in terms of the merits of the issues. In the case of the new immigrants, many of them don't know for whom they are voting, but democracy comes much closer to home, is down to earth. Local democracy must be established; this is very difficult to do. In some settlements, the committees had to be disbanded because they could not function—one instance of this was the Indian committee at Mesilat Zion which I have mentioned previously. The practice of local democracy is uneven and varying. But civic responsibility must be inculcated in the new immigrants if the Israelis are to succeed in their task of integration. Democracy cannot merely be explained to them: it must be lived. And many of the new immigrants are, in the main, learning something of democracy as a child learns to walk. They are in a toddling stage of democracy. Furthermore, and as I have already noted, in Israel there is not one big or major contrast between the Western or European Jews and the Eastern or Oriental ones. This contrast exists in a broad or gross sense. But within it, there are many other contrasts or sub-contrasts, differences in culture, advancement, religious views, the level of awareness, and so on. I have read many statements in America that the Westernized or European Jews look down at the Oriental Jews with contempt. There are instances of this, perhaps too many. But there are also instances of some of the newer immigrants possessing this same attitude toward other of the Oriental immigrants. Contempt for others is a common characteristic when there are pronounced cultural differences. It is not a peculiarity of Israel, and those who over-emphasize it as a means of polemical argument are only dealing in distortions and confusions. Listen to a Parisian intellectual tell you that the French peasants live like animals. Listen to the English and the Welsh, when they let their hair down about one another. Listen to some American urban dwellers talk about the farmer. Something of the same contempt has been found among many light-skinned Negroes, who feel socially superior to dark-skinned ones.* Also, we are now beginning to realize that many Negroes look down on Puerto Ricans. This kind of contempt is often the result of the fear of more

---

* Some of the poorest Negroes from the South, as well as poor whites, "hillbillies," are scarcely more advanced than a large number of Israel's Oriental immigrants.

educated and cultured people that their values will be drowned out by those who are more backward. In a larger number of instances, it is a defense reaction of those who are socially or culturally in an inferior position. The real problem is that of difference, difference not only in education and levels of advancement, but also in attitudes, in mores, in habits. The problem here is actually worldwide. Today in Australia, where about one million immigrants have been received since the War, we can see something of a parallel problem and with it a development of the same kind of contempt. Here we have one of the really important problems which democracy must face and handle. In Israel, the contrasts of East and West, of old and new, of the modern and the medieval, and even the biblical, are so wide that we can observe this problem in an unexposed setting.

III

There is a thirty-year old Moroccan woman at Taanakh. Into her there has seeped some of the weariness of women of the people, the weariness of gesture and with it the sad mask which you see on the many faces in Asia, in the Karl Marx apartments in Vienna, on the streets of Paris, in the villages of Italy and Spain, along the Irish countryside or outside the mosques of Smyrna. There are many such women among Israel's new immigrants. They become worn out with work and with childbearing. In Asia, the lot of the women of the people is more harsh than in Europe. This thirty-year old Moroccan woman at Taanakh was one of them.

The loan necessary to acquire this woman's house in the moshav was 900 Israeli pounds. Her eyes were bad. She had seven children. She said that she was not happy. For many other questions, she had no answers. Even though they were simple, she did not understand them. It was a cause of bewilderment to her that anyone from a far-off foreign country should be interested enough to visit her and ask her questions about her life. I found out, however, that in Morocco, her husband had had a little fish shop. In Israel, he became a laborer and was learning to work on the land. Her children went to school. This was a part of the Israel in evolution. It was one item of the long list of items which go to build the question of democracy into a huge sum of differences. It was something we should understand because of our American past. It was something that had parallels with a life that was known on the East Side of New York and on the West Side of Chicago. Here was the issue of democracy, progress, advance and social justice to be seen in its nuclear form. Here was part of the story of humanity which, even to the present, has been too little told.

And another woman. She said that there was "no work" in Morocco. Her husband had been a peddler. In Israel, he was working in a vegetable garden. In Morocco, she said, her husband earned just enough to be fed on, only little, she repeated. No, there had not been many vegetables for her and her family to eat. No, he had not earned enough to live on. In Israel, they had a house, but it was difficult with the children. The oldest was fifteen. The others were small. They expected to have a vegetable garden near their home. One boy had gone to school for a year in Morocco. The girls never went to school. Did they in Israel? Her face lit up. It was wonderful. The children liked to go to school. In Morocco, they hadn't had money, so their home was not good. They had four rooms, but couldn't keep the roof fixed.

One of this woman's neighbors was the young Tunisian

wife who had been on the committee which I mentioned in the previous section.

She was slender, and her brown skin had a fine texture. In New York, she would be taken for a very attractive mulatto girl. The men might whistle as she walked down the street. When we visited her, we saw that her home was clean and orderly, with bright and cheerful curtains and table cloth. Unlike a considerable number of the immigrant women, she had found a place for all of her household objects. Her home seemed larger than those of the Mount Atlas people in this same settlement, merely because she had put it in order. She wore a light print dress which revealed a shapely figure.

She told me in French that in Tunis, her husband, a watchmaker, had been employed in a big shop. She said he had been a director, but this was probably an exaggeration. Many of the new immigrants exaggerate about their lives, status and income before having come to Israel. In the case of this woman, the social instructor later told me, he believed that her husband had been a foreman. She said that she had taught in a school. She was a seamstress, and at the same time, she also cultivated a small vegetable garden outside her home. In Tunis, she had been better off and had had a bigger house. In Israel, her husband worked in the fields, and their monthly income was about 220 pounds. Her one child, just out of infancy, was sleeping at the time of our visit. Life would, she knew, be hard for twenty years. It would be less hard for her child.

She had come to Israel from Tunis in a group of forty-eight immigrants. After this, two other groups of sixty had arrived. But since she had been better off in Tunis, why had she come? She told me that she had been a Zionist since she was a little girl and had been in a Zionist organization for girls. She had made a special trip to Israel to see what life was like, and had brought back a clod of Palestinian earth. After her visit, she had decided to immigrate, and she had recommended to her people that they go to Israel. They had come with little luggage and knowing that their life would be difficult.

This young wife, who talked spiritedly, read books and could well have seemed like a Parisian midinette, was both glad that she came and dissatisfied. She resented having been deposed from the committee and criticized her fellow Tunisians. They wanted too much for themselves, she said. She decided to take less interest in community affairs. The social instructor interpreted it differently. It was his view that she was disgruntled for having been frustrated in her personal ambitions. The Tunisians, so much more advanced than their Mount Atlas neighbors, wanted and demanded more. Dissatisfaction with the Jewish Agency was rife among many of them. This girl said that they wanted too much for themselves and not enough for everybody.

I asked her about the Mount Atlas immigrants. She didn't at all like them. There was no way of getting along with them in an understanding and a community manner. You couldn't understand their language. They were two hundred years behind. They were two centuries behind, she repeated. They were like her great grandfather, and for her, this was past. It did not interest her.

Then, too, she said that they were too religious. She was a Jew, but not that kind of a Jew. They prayed every night. Could she go pray in one of their houses? If she visited them and became friends, she would have to pray. That would be all that she could do with them, pray. They wouldn't allow her in their village on the Sabbath. Girls in shorts shocked their religious sense. She, and some of the other young Tunisian women did wear shorts.

The Mount Atlas Jews had a fear of women being spirited, and acting like the Tunisian women do. And their own young girls were different. They refused to change because of conditions. They were behind, but perhaps in twenty years, the next generation would change.

But then she said that she had enough to do not to worry. After twenty years of sacrifice, her life would be better. She showed us her sleeping child, her garden, and asked us to eat a tomato grown in it. She said that she would expand her garden and would also grow flowers. She repeated that she would work hard.

IV

After visiting her, I went across to the Mount Atlas settlement in Taanakh. The same kind of stone houses were spaced along a rocky road. In front were gardens, thick and green, and, as I have indicated, they extended right up to the Jordanian frontier which was only about three or four hundred yards ahead.

We met the leader. He was tall, handsome, very black, and he wore a full beard. He was dressed like an Arab. To be leader of the group, he had also to be the rabbi. He invited me into his home, and also brought in four of his neighbors. His wife looked like a girl of thirteen, but she was eighteen. She was his niece. The kitchen room was disorderly with things spread about the floor. There were four little children and an old grandmother. The wife cooked on the floor, as she had done back home. In all of these settlements, I might add, the immigrants have a primus stove. The day is probably still far off when they will have gas stoves. In many instances, they also have ice boxes.

Our young hostess was pretty, and of a lighter skin than her husband. Her hair was half-combed and one tooth was missing from the center of her mouth. She was barefoot. She greeted us with meekness and spoke no more. She was not allowed into the other room where we talked, except to bring us glasses of tea flavored with peppermint. We were not allowed to question her or the grandmother, and had we been, I should have gleaned nothing. The girl would not have understood. To have questioned her about details of her life would have overwhelmed her into a frightened and awed silence.

There were four others besides the head of the settlement sitting in the room with me and my party. I asked many questions and the answers were translated to me from the Hebrew. Before coming to Israel, some of these Mount Atlas men had lived on the land and worked it in a primitive fashion. Others had been peddlers. What had they sold? Sugar, nuts, grain. The bearded leader said that he had made shoes and had then peddled them. How many shoes had he made? His answer was about twenty-five a day, but this quite clearly was incorrect. Only four or five among their people had earned more than the merest pittance. However, it was not clear what they meant by earning money. Most of them had been very poor. They had worked for Arabs who got part of the crop which they produced.

How had they been treated by the Arabs? "Good," the leader replied. The Arabs hadn't wanted them to leave because then there would not be any skilled working people. Skill here is obviously very relative, for the Mount Atlas immigrants were not skilled in Israeli or Western terms. They had come in a group. Some, the leader said, had had land. One had had fifty dunams, and a few had had twenty. But here again there was confusion. Apparently, from what I could make out, the situation was this. The Arabs owned the land and the Jews provided the labor. Then the produce was split fifty-fifty. The Mount Atlas Jews had thought that they owned this land. They had raised wheat, barley and maize, all by hand labor. The cutting was done by hand, not by machines, the leader explained. He had become aware of machines only since coming to Israel.

At the time when I met him, he and his group had been in Israel for about half a year.

"Does he like it here?" I asked.

"Yes."

"Why does he like it?"

"This is our land," the translator gave me his words literally. "It is ours, our country."

Then he used the phrase, Eretz Israel, and one of his countrymen repeated it.

Continuing, he said that they had come to Israel "all at once." They were told by a representative from the Jewish Agency that Israel was their land.

How long had they felt or believed that Israel was their land?

They learned this from the Torah. They learned of the promised land. "Until five years ago, they didn't know that a modern Israel existed," the translator said after the bearded leader had spoken further. But they heard of Israel and learned that they could go to it. They had applied at government offices to get a permit. Then they were convinced that what they had heard was true: they were given the permit. The leader had gone to Casablanca. He had walked two days before he could get any transportation by bus. And in Casablanca, he had gotten a letter from the Jewish Agency, specifying or saying that he should get his people together and bring them to Israel. All had wanted to go, but ten people had been left behind. This was because they had been ill.

They had come by plane. In Israel, he said, it was different. In their old country, there had been no roads as in Israel. And tractors? No. The leader himself had ridden in an automobile, a bus. Others of his people hadn't before embarking on their journey. And in Israel, he added, the children went to school. He and the other adults were getting used to this now. He thought it was "very good" for the children to be in school. They come home and tell all of the things they do, the songs they are taught, and they try to show off. All of them speak of the plays. Soon, the leader also said, the children will be telling them what to do. In Israel, that was the way it was going to be.

This man was the one who had been stricken in the field and whom I mentioned above. He spoke of this experience. He had been lying unconscious and knew that he had been saved by the doctors. He knew he needed an operation. He told the doctors or the people who can read and write that he would not give his consent for the performance of the operation. He knew that if he had not been taken to the hospital, he should have died. But he hadn't allowed the surgery because he was afraid. He was still afraid, even though he understood that he required the operation. The doctors, they are good, they save people. But he repeated that he was afraid. Then he said that the doctor came to their settlement to look after the children. All that, he liked, as he did the food they ate in Israel. There was more for them than there had been at Mount Atlas.

I asked him what he thought was going to happen to them now that they were in Israel. This was a matter of "what God will give." And the children? They will "do what they want." Then he added:

"I don't know if they will stay with us or go away."

He recognized the difference between Israel and Mount Atlas and the fact that the children would be affected by customs and attitudes different from their own. Already, and in only six months, the children were commencing to come home from school and tell them what to do. His son now could ride a bicycle. He was quite proud of his son's accomplishment.

He liked the fact that they voted and could be represented. Fifty-nine out of sixty of his people voted. This was all new and surprising to him, but it was "very good." They had come with nothing much, a blanket, a few things. They will have their land to work on and for the rest, they were in the hands of God. They had left everything behind to come here—to Eretz Israel. I repeat this phrase because it meant so much to these simple people. For to them, Israel is truly a holy land.

I asked some other questions quickly. He had seen one motion picture and liked it. He, and the others in the room, all thought of America as a place full of rich Jews who sent money to them.

After leaving the leader's home, and walking back to our automobile, the social instructor told me that he liked the Mount Atlas people. They were easy to work with and quick to learn simple things. He said the Tunisians were different. They did not understand life in Israel and were more European than African or Israeli. They were half Europeans and would rather be living in Paris and that this, in his opinion, was the main reason for friction between them and the Mount Atlas immigrants.

Also, he told me how, even though he was not an observant Jew, he had gained a big reputation among the Mount Atlas people. They had come to him and asked that a proper cemetery be laid out in the settlement. They believed that in every Jewish settlement or place, there must be a cemetery. He had been able to get them the cemetery they wanted because of their piety and belief. And this had not only strengthened the reputation and influence of the social instructor among them: it had also aided them in their adjustment and reinforced their belief that Israel was their land, the holy land. They always told him that he was a better Jew than they, despite his lack of orthodoxy.

We paused a moment before getting into the car. Ahead was irregularly and carelessly cultivated land stretching off towards a distant mountain. No one was in sight on this land. It was the land of Jordan. And at night, the Mount Atlas men took turns at guard duty, rifle in hand, looking at that land, dark and silent.

In the Lachish area I saw a settlement of Mount Atlas Jews who had been in Israel several years. The land was rich, the houses were surrounded by fenced-in flower gardens, and the settlement looked like other developed and prosperous ones in the area. A bearded old man came out from his house and asked us if we needed directions. He was settled and content. In a few years, he and his people had become as though part of the land and the country. Day by day, these newer Mount Atlas men with whom I spoke were working towards that end. Their children went to school and learned things their parents had never dreamed of. This is part of the Israel I saw.

CHAPTER NINE

I

ONE AFTERNOON I came to a settlement, a moshav, on the frontier, which borders on the Arab Triangle. In this region there are Arab villages and from the Jordanian border to the Mediterranean, the distance is about nine miles: this is the narrowest part of Israel. The flat land was under cultivation; the settlement looked like many others in Israel. The houses are off the road, spaced out in groups. Beyond them are the fields, marked off, green and thick in vegetation: they stretched to the frontier about five hundred yards away. In the distance the bare mountains were purple, and wrapped in a haze of sunlight. I had with me a chauffeur and translator. We walked towards the frontier, which was merely an unseen line ahead of us. Across it there was no sign of life. There were merely patches of earth which had been cultivated by Arabs. But somewhere off, unseen by us, there was or could have been men with rifles or machine guns which could have been pointed at us. At any moment there could have been a zing of bullets singing past us in the hot and immobile summer air. At this point of the frontier, there was occasional sniping. The inhabitants, all of them from Morocco, work the fields in constant danger. To stand in these fields, to walk ahead, rouses anxieties. You have no control over what can happen to you. You do not know at what second the bullets will come. Days and months can go by and no bullets will wing past you or hit you; and then, one minute they come, singing a threat of instant death.

To work or even to walk in such fields can be a deadening experience. There are different kinds of danger. Some dangers can be exhilarating, exciting and can stimulate your faculties so that you are keen, alert and you become so highly concentrated that you know no fear. Fear is then irrelevant. For instance, with another chauffeur and translator, I was driven along a road in barren, rocky and deserted land and mountain. The border was very close. On our right were bleached rocks rising up, and beyond them, the ever-menacing frontier. The entire route could be an infiltrator's or a sniper's dream. The road was bumpy and it ran straight on ahead into Jordan. Travel in the automobile was very slow. We were three of us in a world of silence save for the sound of our voices and the noise of the motor. Silent rocks. Bleached weeds. Stones. White promontories. A deserted world that man had abandoned, a world not for man where the rocks had been burned by the sun of centuries. A world that man would not and could not want except to view as the bare, awesome fascination of a forlorn and desolated nature. A world which had been a plaything of winds for thousands of years. Here was the untamed beauty of desolation.

We proceeded very slowly, our car bumping. We stopped talking. Every few seconds our chauffeur gave a quick stabbing glance to right and to left. My translator, an official, had taken an automatic from his brief case. It lay at his side on the seat. He was a gentle man, but very loquacious about the achievements of Israel; he was even enthusiastic to the point of unimaginative naiveté. He was pious and strictly observant but not a fanatic. His orthodoxy was a matter of his own belief. He did not seek to impose it on anyone else. His dream was to see the desert bloom. Every tomato, each onion in a field of Israel, excited him. He did not love violence and death. But there was the gun. He kept darting his eyes to the right at that rising promontory of pale and gray mountain rock.

We were tense but not afraid. We knew what we were doing and where we were going. We were alert for danger. We went on slowly. The road became worse, rockier than any back country road of America on which I have ever ridden. We passed a group of army jeeps in a cove off the road. There had either been maneuvers or else a patrol was out searching the deserted land inch by inch. We came to a place where there was barbed wire along the road and a sign in Hebrew. It contained a warning not to go further because there was danger beyond the point of the sign. In spite of this we drove on towards the border.

Here, let me repeat, we faced a different kind of danger. We were not standing in a peaceful field which men had cultivated, a field full of growing things which gave a livelihood to pioneer farmers. Whomever we would meet in this forlorn border area was there because of the danger. It would be a soldier or a policeman. Those who work the fields in this area are pre-military age boys and girls who have volunteered to do this work and at the same time to receive military training prior to their induction into the army at eighteen. In fact they are already soldiers. They live the life of both a kibbutznik and a young soldier. We were picked up by a patrol of two boys and a girl in khaki uniform. They carried sub-machine guns. On previous patrols they had been fired at but nothing had occurred on this particular afternoon.

This is a military area. No one goes into it without knowing where he is going. We ventured without military passes, and took our chances. To have been afraid under these circumstances would have been vulgar in one's own eyes. And my feelings were different from when I stood in those moshav fields, gazing ahead at rows of melons, tomatoes, potatoes, of big green leaves, and beyond to the silent purplish mountains which were so softly and so eternally gloomy in the distance. For there, in that field near the Triangle, men who had come from afar were working with hard patience to find, to have, to earn a new life for themselves with the effort of their own backs and muscles and by their own sweat. There they go out to dig, plant, weed, and out of this, to earn a living which most of us in America would call poor. Their children might go with them, or walk and run along the sandy road between the marked off dunams. Their children might run in barefoot play. And that unseen bullet can bring sudden death, striking at an unexpected moment of peaceful labor or happy play.

Here I was afraid. More than fear, I was hurt by a sense of what should not be. Given the conflict which exists, it is different in a security area near a military post where the houses are surrounded by sand-bagged trenches, and where the boys and girls have volunteered knowing what risks they are assuming. But on that field in the Triangle there was a peaceful settlement of immigrants who had been poor peddlers, little merchants, in another land, a land which they had never felt was truly their own. It was also a land torn with struggle and killing. Some of them had left because of this very fact. And they were peacefully working the land. They were surrounded by Arabs, not only across the frontier, but also inside of Israel. All about them were Arab villages. They had little relations with the Arabs in Israel, but no trouble. Some of them had been in the nearby Arab villages. A few of the Arabs, at least, had been to see the moshav.

On both sides of the imaginary line which designates the frontier, simple people of little education work these ancient fields. The hot sun bakes the fields, and they look lonely. On the Arab side, no one was to be seen. On the Israeli side, only a few of the Moroccan Jews could be seen. We walked ahead, slowly and lazily, toward that invisible frontier. A small brown man was throwing cucumbers into a sack. He wore old blue jeans, and a dirty white shirt. He warned us in French that we should not go any further alone. It was dangerous. He offered to go with us. There was no need to walk ahead for a few more hundreds of yards and to see what we were already looking at. And fortunately we had come on a day when there was no sniping. We asked him if there had been any recent incidents in this settlement. He answered that there had been none. When they had first settled there, there had been shooting. Now, they—the Arabs—saw that the settlers were not afraid and so there was no trouble. There could be at any moment, but there hadn't been so far. We asked if he were afraid. No, he said.

He offered us some of his cucumbers and we ate them with relish. How long had he been in Israel? A couple of years. How was he doing? He was doing well. He was happy, and liked it. He was living better than he had in Morocco.

We accompanied him to his home, another two-room stone house, plain and standardized. The interior was orderly and clean. We met his wife, his sister, his parents. The mother was a stout, spirited woman of fifty, with gray hair, a round face. She exuded energy. It was she who did most of the talking and she spoke French. None of them, except the daughter, knew much Hebrew.

Her husband, a thin, dispirited man, stood against a wall, saying little. His shoulders drooped and he was beginning to show the signs of age. Merely to look at him was sufficient to sense that here was a man who had probably been broken.

The twenty-year old daughter wore blue jeans and a dirty white shirt which hung outside her pants. She was well formed, with fine firm breasts under her shirt, black hair, and beautiful dark eyes. Her face was not only beautiful, but mobile and lively.

"She looks like Gina Lollobrigida," my guide and interpreter told me in English.

The man's wife was thin, quiet, rather nondescript, and unnoticeable. She served us tea. For the rest, she sat and did not speak.

The family said that they would all answer any question I cared to ask.

Now it was good here, the stout, gray-haired woman told me. But at first, she had not liked it. There had not been enough of her family to do the work. The work itself had been too hard. She had wanted to go back. But when her children had joined them, there were more to do the work. She no longer wanted to return to Morocco. But, pointing to her husband, she said that he did not like it. He wanted to go back. I was struck by the tone of her voice when she referred to him as he, *"il";* she did not say *"mon mari."* Turning to the old man,

I asked him if he liked it in Israel. Meekly, he said he didn't. Yes, he did want to go back. It was too hard in Israel. The work was too hard.

The son, the man whom he had picked up in the field, also spoke. It was good here. He had enough to eat. They were better off than in Morocco. In Morocco it would have been all right with the French. They liked the French. But not the Arabs. They had left because of the Arabs. Here, he could have children, and they would go to school and have food. They could grow up. Here it was good for the family. He had three children. He was going to have more, six, seven.

"Bravo," my interpreter said.

The grandmother beamed with pride and shook her head in agreement. Then I observed to the grandmother that clearly everyone except her husband thought that life was better for them in Israel than it had been in Morocco. The grandmother then spoke energetically, and with a tone of criticism that appeared to border on contempt. She said that you can live well in Morocco if you have money. You can have a good life in Israel if you have money. It can be good for you everywhere if you are a millionaire. Everything depends on work. You have to work or you have nothing.

Did she like to work?

Now, yes, but as she had said, she had not liked it at first. There had been illness in the family, and there had been too few of them. Now that the family was together in Israel, it was good. The old man leaned against the wall, crushed in his silence.

The beautiful young daughter spoke, spiritedly, so rapidly that I had to try and slow her down, and, at points, I had to ask my interpreter to translate for me. Her fluent, excited flow of French was too swift for me.

She said that her sister had just been married. She herself had but recently come out of the army. Did she like the army? Yes. Which would she like most, being in the army or getting married? She had liked being in the army. And she would like being married. Did she intend to marry? Yes, she would. And the work? She worked in the fields with her brother. She liked that, too. She could help and they were eating, and were going to save money. Like her mother, she insisted that in order to get anything, you had to work. Her eyes shone. Her face became most expressively mobile. She spoke with an enthusiastic sincerity. She wanted to go on working as she had. She did not want to go and live in Jerusalem or Tel Aviv, but rather she wanted to stay here, do what she was doing, then get married and continue living the same kind of life. No, she would never go back to Morocco. She had learned Hebrew. She had learned to farm. She could work well. If she had to go back in the army, she would go.

They did not speak of Eretz Israel. They had come to Israel, they said, because in Morocco there was nothing more for them. They repeated that it was because of the Arabs. They did not have open hostility toward the Arabs, or at least they did not voice it. But they thought, for them Morocco was finished. In Israel, they were beginning. They were now beyond their first days of hardship. They had their home, their fields, and they wanted only to continue working there and to live better than they had in the past. They were convinced that they could and were doing this. I turned to the father and asked what he thought. No, he didn't like it. He said no more. His wife had developed in Israel. His daughter was a lively girl, virtually like a sabra. She was independent and was learning constantly. His son had land and was ginning to realize that this attitude is dangerous. There is at least a slow shifting away from this over-simplified point of view. Thus, while you still frequently hear Israelis say, "all for the children," we can expect that there will be an increase of effort to further the adjustment of the adults. The Israelis are beginning to learn from mistakes, and to alter their points of view on the basis of experience. Those who are directly concerned in the area of integration must constantly deal with and help the adults as well as the children. Even if the attitude of "all for the children" were to be continued, it would deeply involve the adult new immigrants as well as the children.

All of this became quite clear to me when I visited the moshav Maslul, which is situated near Beersheba. At Maslul I met and had a long interview with a sabra girl of twenty-two who was completing two years of teaching for which she had volunteered. As I have already mentioned, three-fourths of the inhabitants at Maslul are Persian, and the others, except for a few teachers or social instructors are from Kurdistan. This girl was bright, intelligent, brave and confident as the young sabras are. To volunteer for work as a teacher at a settlement such as Maslul is an indication of dedication as well as courage. It is near the frontier and danger of injury or death from infiltrators is correspondingly greater than it would be in Tel Aviv where this sabra girl's family lives. Her people were either first generation or immigrant Americans, and she herself spent some time here. She spoke English quite well.

As a result of her experience at the settlement, she had concluded that one important change in immigrant attitudes since coming to Israel concerned the children. Gradually the older immigrants had come to interfere less and less with the education of the children. They would tell her, "the children are yours." She also spoke of the problem of women as teachers. At Maslul, the parents accepted woman teachers but at a neighboring moshav, the Kurdish Jews did not accept them. The parents want the children to study, but in the beginning, there had been a serious problem of work. The parents also wanted the children to work, and they were good workers in the fields. Consistent persuasion and effort had to be made to bring the parents around to the idea of allowing the children to continue their education. She said that she had to try to get to know the parents, to visit them and to win their confidence at least partially. In doing this, she had to tread carefully in any matters which would touch their religious prejudices. They were almost all strictly observant. The parents, she said, had no understanding of teaching. To them, schooling meant the three R's, on the most simple or elementary level. Even at the end of the two years, there were still two Kurdish families who were stubborn and would not send the children to school when there was work to be done.

Speaking of the children, she said that, yes, a number of them were disturbed. This was in answer to a question of mine, I might add. She couldn't give me a specific number of those who might be disturbed; the question of disturbance is relative, especially in the case of the children of new immigrants where there are cultural differences and clashes, as well as problems of assimilation in a new country and with it, the need of so many to learn Hebrew.

In this situation, she said, the children were in the middle. Many of them are neglected. Most of them come from large families. There are so many brothers and sisters, that usually an individual child does not count too much. The parents, themselves, I reflected, have not counted much, so how can they believe that the children count. The mothers become worn out with work, and the children are burdens until they can help at home and by working.

It had been my impression that many of the new immigrant mothers were happy about the fact that their children could get schooling, or at least better schooling in Israel than in their home countries, and also that the health conditions for the kids were better. However, many who work intimately or closely with the immigrants told me that a great many of the mothers don't care. They did not completely agree with the correctness of my impression. The young teacher was of this opinion. I wondered about this and thought that possibly they themselves were changing in a new environment, even though it is difficult to measure the degree of this change. Most clearly the various immigrant mothers gave me the impression of caring, of being pleased with the fact that their children have better prospects in Israel. However, my impression was a passing one, whereas those of the young teacher were based on solid day by day contact. To continue, many of the children have foster mothers, and because of home neglect, they often will draw close to the teacher. When they are angry at their father, they curse him, calling him "a dog." But in school and in the settlement, they are exposed to and instructed in Western values. They live in a world where there are radios and newspapers. There is a Persian newspaper in Maslul. The teachers must help the children, as well as the adults, in understanding the newspapers, and the radio, better, and must also assist them in gaining understanding of the new technical world which they have come into. Further, both adults and children must be made to know that they are in Israel. The teacher makes an effort to educate the children in a love of Israel, as Zionists, and as patriots. She further tries to teach or to get them to love their classroom and their settlement, Maslul. All of this, she said, is part of the effort to educate them in a love of Israel and in the feeling that Israel is "not like any place else." With this, she spoke of the great emphasis on the Bible, and on the entire Jewish heritage. The Bible is treated, not always solely as a sacred work, but also as an historical one, telling the history of the Jews and the geography of Palestine in ancient times. She further added that she, and another girl like her who had spent two years as a volunteer teacher at Maslul, had tried to teach the children not to hate.

"That's not constructive," she added.

Among many, she had observed a negative attitude about working on the land. Some of the immigrants had not even recognized tomatoes as such when they had first seen them "lying on the ground." This is suggestive of the setting in which the children first come to school.

The teacher also said that in general, it was evident that there was a conflict of Western and Eastern values. She considered this to be one of the most important facts in the educational life of the children. In her view, the Western values were gradually beginning to prevail. Those of sixteen and seventeen, she went on, know about Greece, Hebrew, history, mathematics, and also basketball. A number of them seem to her "like sabras." Of course she was referring to those who had already spent some time in Israel. They see movies, and are most fond of Westerns; a number of the children walked out on *Pinocchio*. The children know more than they did in Persia, and are beginning to know much more than their parents. However, many of the adults, and some of the children, say that in Persia everything was wonderful. Many families left Maslul and went to live in Tel Aviv, but they were beginning to return to the settlement. They had gotten to like showers, and some families bought boilers for hot water. The children spoke of home often, and were happy when they could tell of a pleasant occasion, such as a visitor, something which gave them joy; they acted differently when the father had beaten the mother, for instance, and then said little. Apparently, there still was considerable wife beating among the new immigrants at Maslul. On the whole, this girl thought that integration was working. Teaching the children was, in her own eyes, a most gratifying experience, even though she was glad that she was returning to Tel Aviv. I had come to her settlement on the last day of her two years.

The school year was over. Many of the children were in the cultural center, preparing for a festival and busily engaged in fixing decorations. They were healthy, dark-faced little boys and girls, quietly absorbed and well behaved. A number of little Persian girls were making festoons. Celebrations have become an important part of the educational and social life of the children. The Oriental children take to this more easily than to some of their formal studies. They seemed far advanced from what they had been in the beginning, when they had to be taught to brush their teeth as well as many other simple things. As I stood watching them, they paid little attention to me and went on with their activities.

It was mid-afternoon and hot. As I left the quiet community, you would not have thought that it was so close to a dangerous frontier and that its inhabitants go about their peaceful work, some developing, others not, day by day, never knowing when danger will strike. But this is part of Israel. And Israel's future depends much on what happens in such settlements, and on how successful the volunteer teachers, such as the girl I interviewed at Maslul, are.

Having a cup of coffee at Kiryat Shmone, a settlement near the Huleh Project in Galilee, I met a similar girl. Kiryat Shmone had, let me add, unexpectedly mushroomed into a town. Along the side of the road, there were the maabara huts. Only gradually were the inhabitants being removed from them into more permanent housing units. At the end of the day, they would gather in front of their huts, or walk around the small settlement. They were dark-skinned, and some of them wore Oriental clothes. The scene was very colorful, and unless you reminded yourself that you were in Israel, you might have believed that you were in Morocco. Children were swarming everywhere; men gathered in groups and talked. It was a living picture of a teeming existence.

A number of the inhabitants were working on state-run farms which have been laid out on land reclaimed by the draining of the marshes, a result of the engineering feat which controls the sources of the Jordan River. In the schools, there is a mixture of Oriental and Western children, but most of them are of the former group. A twenty-one year old girl told us about this, but since she knew no English, her remarks had to be translated for me from the Hebrew. Her story was much the same as that of the girl at Maslul. She spoke of difficulties with the parents, possibly more serious than at Maslul, since so many still lived in the huts. They were poorer than the Maslul settlers. The children, she told us, were eager to learn, but she constantly had to see and talk to the parents, because they needed to be convinced and reassured. This was a slow process, but she was devoted to her work, and believed firmly and definitely that she was doing something for Israel's future. She had no doubt that the effort at integration would be successful.

There are many intangibles in the situation of the Oriental children. Success or failure in the efforts to Westernize them can only be finally gauged by the observable results, many years from now. One of the intangible factors is psychological. The children receive attention from teachers, nurses, even cooks at their communal meals. This they did not get before they were brought to Israel. In many ways, they are treated as important citizens of the future. Also, and even though they study the Bible, the education of most of them is more secular than religious. They are not growing up as observant as their parents. Obviously, what all this will mean cannot be determined now. However—and this was the final conclusion of the Maslul teacher—what is most important is that the children and even many of the adults are beginning to realize that for the first time in their lives, someone cares about them.

II

Ben Shemen, near Tel Aviv, is a children's village, set in natural beauty, surrounded by fertile country and close to some Arab villages. It pre-dates the establishment of the State, and has attracted the interest and support of many foreigners. The late Dr. Albert Einstein maintained a lively and enthusiastic interest in Ben Shemen, corresponded with its director, the late Dr. Lehman, and sent, as a gift, some of his instruments which he used during the early days of this century, when he was developing his Theory of Relativity. Ben Shemen is supported by Hadassah's Youth Aliyah, and has become something of a show place of Israel. In fact, the children, among themselves, make fun of and mimic tourists. The grounds are spacious.

There is a farm connected with the village and school, and the children learn agriculture while they pursue their formal studies in the usual Israeli curriculum. The director, Dr. Lehman, was a revered man. Unfortunately, when I visited Ben Shemen, Dr. Lehman was leaving for a conference in Switzerland, and I was unable to see him. I talked with his assistant, a slender, gentle man in his thirties, who spoke English with a pronounced Yiddish accent.

Most of the children at Ben Shemen come from families which are social cases, and they are from mixed and varied origins. They are not, in other words, exclusively Oriental. A minority are sent to live and be educated at Ben Shemen because the parents want them to go there, and wherever possible, the parents pay tuition, but this is decided according to means and income. A number of the children have parents who can afford little or nothing, and some of the children are orphans. Parents must give their consent for the children to be educated at Ben Shemen, and at times an effort at persuasion is necessary in order to get this consent. After the children are at Ben Shemen, the authorities must sometimes re-convince the parents to allow them to remain. A number come in a state of emotional disturbance. A child can be considered to be a social case either because he or she is emotionally disturbed or because he or she comes from a family too poor to support it. Inasmuch as many of the Orientals have such large families, some of the Oriental children are sent to Ben Shemen, where they will not be a drain on the wage earner.

The children live together in rows of barrack-like rooms, with usually two to a room. They are housed according to age and sex, rather than background. Thus, they are freely mixed and there is no discrimination on the basis of background and origin. Sabbath is observed with ceremonies and candles, and the children are taught the Bible and Jewish tradition, but the institution should be considered as more secular than religious. As the slender and idealistic assistant to Dr. Lehman guided me around, he explained this and much else about the institution, speaking of its routines, procedures and aims. Again and again, he repeated that they all try to inculcate "spiritual values" in the life of the children. "Spiritual values," which he did not define, are important, and without them, he insisted, Ben Shemen would not be what it is. However, it became clear to me that by spiritual values he meant what amounts to a genuine religious emotion that need not be precisely defined; he also meant a respect for and appreciation of culture, and especially of music, and, in addition, patriotism, love of country and a realization that work itself can have a spiritual value or consequence. The director and the teachers try to convince as many of the children as they can to join kibbutzim when they leave Ben Shemen at the age of eighteen. But, shaking his head regretfully, he admitted to me that they were not too successful in this respect; they did, he added, convince only about forty percent of their children to go to the kibbutzim.

The children are from seven or eight to seventeen years of age. I visited Ben Shemen late in the day. Classes were over. Many of the children walked about, others read, or were grouped together in rooms, where they were having bull sessions. Boys and girls were talking together in various of the rooms we visited, some of them squatting on the floor while others sat on the beds or on chairs. Here I would find two girls talking; there a girl sleeping. An Oriental boy of fourteen sat in the empty dining room, reading. A small boy of about ten was drawing a horse with a plough behind it. Two other boys watched him. A group of girls of about ten to twelve stood near a row of houses in a dormitory block. Most of them wore blue shorts with blouses or shirts of varying colors. Among them was a tall, thin Chinese girl. She said hello in English. Asked where she had learned English, she answered in China. Angrily, she told me that China is better than Israel. She wanted to go back there. Speaking of her parents, she said:

"*They* live in Haifa."

There was hatred in the pronunciation of the word *they*. We continued our brief conversation. During it she repeatedly referred to her parents as *they*, pronouncing the word with the same intense hatred.

"*They* make art."

One of her parents was an artist. Her father and mother got along badly, and both were disturbed people. The girl herself was hostile, unfriendly. The director's assistant told me that she had been very slow to learn, was unhappy at Ben Shemen, and he admitted that they did not know what to do in order to help her. She was resisting help, and the man thought that she might have to go elsewhere. He further stated that after two years at Ben Shemen, she had not progressed or fitted into the life of the children there. But her parents wanted her at Ben Shemen; at least, they did not want her at home. She stood watching me with her glowering hostility.

We moved on, and found more children talking, playing, seemingly contented and acting as though they felt themselves to be completely at home. Many of them were in groups. There were well-formed teen-age girls standing by a door. One came from Yemen, a second from Persia, a third from Rumania. Another was Moroccan. With little boys and girls, it was the same. Many of the children smiled at us. A few asked where we were from. They looked up from talk and play and watched us with curiosity. Then they went on with their games. From time to time, the assistant director apologized because destruction from the 1948 war was still evident on the grounds. The physical facilities of Ben Shemen were not what he wished them to be, although they appeared adequate to me, especially considering the conditions in Israel. But after his apologies, he insisted again that what was important about Ben Shemen was its spirit and its effort to inculcate "spiritual values." The children all acted respectful, but at their ease, with the assistant director—that is, all except the Chinese Jewish girl. A number of them paid no attention to us unless we spoke first.

There was a Yemenite girl of about eight. Several times, she asked why European chickens laid bigger eggs than did other chickens. She spent much of her time in the poultry yard. Every night, she wrote a letter to her parents. Normally, in the first few weeks, a child will write three or four letters to its parents, and then, as the child becomes adjusted to and begins to feel at home at Ben Shemen, the letters decrease. If a child keeps writing too many letters home, this usually indicates that it is unhappy or dissatisfied. This does not conform with the normal or average conduct and practice of the children at Ben Shemen. After six months or so, during which time the little Yemenite girl kept writing home so frequently, the authorities became concerned. They worried about the child and feared that she was unhappy, although she seemed quite adjusted and contented. They did not know what the trouble was. But then they learned what was in most of her letters. She kept writing over and over again, trying to explain to her parents and to teach them how to raise chickens which would lay eggs as big as those laid by "European chickens."

III

Ramat Hadassah Szold, named after Henrietta Szold, one of Israel's social heroines, is an institution where disturbed children and the offspring of families listed as social cases are sent temporarily. They are tested and observed, and after staying there for a short period, usually a few months, they are sent to the school, the institution, the kibbutz or other place where it is believed they will fare either best or, at least, satisfactorily. Supported by Hadassah, this institution is spread out in a beautiful setting near Haifa. It is like many Israeli institutions, with small offices in wooden structures, rows of dormitories, a cultural center, a big mess hall and kitchen. You see the boys and girls mostly in shorts. They are of different ages and of varying shades of skin; like all children, they are occupying themselves with things that interest them. On visiting it, you practically must, out of politeness, see everything, and view the entire physical layout. This is the same wherever you go in Israel; the Israelis are so proud of what they have, what they have built, that they cannot resist showing you everything, kitchens, showers, rooms, bathrooms, and, most especially, the rooms or buildings set aside for cultural activities.

I spoke with one of the men directing Ramat Hadassah Szold, a large man in his late thirties or early forties. He talked English with a Yiddish accent. He patiently explained the purposes, functions and character of the institution. From his manner of speaking, I became more than convinced that he believed in his work and had real affection for the children who came to this institution. He was certain that they were being helped, and that much good was being done for them and for Israel. He was a sympathetic man. However, the first information he gave me was that intelligence and other tests had demonstrated overwhelmingly and conclusively that children from Western backgrounds, European and Israeli, were superior to those from African and Asian countries. This information seemed to make him a little sad; he wished it were otherwise, but he made it clear that this was the conclusion to be drawn, not only from his own direct experience with children, but also from the results of many tests which had been taken. However, discussion and questioning clearly revealed that the measuring and testing of children is done on the basis of Western conceptions and Western educational standards, methods and levels of knowledge. Everything else he had to say concerning the successful results of his work was based upon faith in Western standards of progress. In other words, he measured success among the children in terms of the degree to which they would become Westernized. This man and other Israelis seem to have since recognized the inadequacy of these Western tests for Oriental children from a different culture, and I was told that they are now attempting to perfect more adequate and nonverbal tests.

One of the problems which must be faced at Ramat Hadassah Szold is that of discipline and orderliness. As I have suggested, a number of the children coming to this institution have emotional problems. At the present time, many of the children are from Oriental backgrounds, especially North African. The fact that they have been sent to this institution in itself indicates that they need help and direction, and that in their home experiences they have not been given much incentive to be orderly, to have ambition, and even to love life. As children, they cannot possess the same passion or dream of living in Eretz Israel which stirs within some of the adult Oriental immigrants, no matter how primitive the latter may be. Usually these children have been neglected, even severely. In many cases, their background and history is one of emotional disturbances which have preceded their arrival in Israel. The files of case histories of the children show this. The children must live together as a group and there is no chance that they will receive individual psychiatric attention and guidance. One of the purposes and tasks of Ramat Hadassah Szold is to prepare the children so that they will fit into and be prepared for training and education in one or another school or institution which already exists in Israel. The guiding social ideals of these institutions and of the dream and vision of Israel in all of them is Western. I repeat this for emphasis. Concerning the children, the things they must first be taught are simple—matters of hygiene, brushing one's teeth, keeping oneself clean, making one's bed and so on. The teaching of these tasks, as well as other instruction, is quite complicated by the factor of language. Most of the children do not come to Israel with a knowledge of Hebrew. They must learn Hebrew and some, when they go to this institution, are still in the process of learning it. Quite obviously, the language factor complicates all the problems of the children and all the efforts which the adults and authorities must make to help them. How much do we know concerning the relation between language and emotional disturbance? What weight does this very factor of the new language have upon the problems of these children? These are questions which call for careful thought and observation.

I raised such questions during my conversation with the authority with whom I was speaking at Ramat Hadassah

Szold. He granted that they had validity, but nevertheless felt that there was definite progress among the children in the process of Westernization. However, this seemed to include changes in hygienic and social habits, rather than in the area of psychology. This, to me, seems to be one of the roots of Israel's problems with the new immigrants. It seems likely that these problems will be solved in a relative sense, as such mass problems involving human beings are solved. However, problems of this character are ones which are really solved only over a course of generations. Superficially at least, success is being attained at Ramat Hadassah Szold. The habits of new immigrant children are being changed. This is only the first step in making Israelis out of them, rather than immigrants. What this means will be known in any truly verifiable sense only years from now.

Most of the children who go to Ramat Hadassah Szold are ready, after a few months, or six months at most, to be sent elsewhere. The great majority of them are not sent back to Ramat Hadassah Szold. If they would not fit in elsewhere, they would be returned. Hence we can conclude that the work at Ramat Hadassah Szold is successful.

While at Ramat Hadassah Szold, they live together much as do the children at Ben Shemen and other institutions and children's villages. There are classes at which the children receive much the same instruction as do their peers elsewhere in Israel. The children are treated as normal, but they are observed and records are kept of them. They receive as much thought and attention as is possible, considering the fact that this is not a psychiatric institution where individual care and attention can be given. The whole idea of Ramat Hadassah Szold is to integrate in a socially normal sense. The aim thus is not treatment but fitting them into a suitable and harmonious environment somewhere in Israel.

There was one boy of about fourteen. He had been sent to a kibbutz but he had not fitted in and then he was returned to Ramat Hadassah Szold. At this institution, he did very well; elsewhere, he was a problem. I read the boy's history. He was the second oldest of about six children and the family had been in Israel for about four or five years. The oldest brother had been in Nahal, and seemed to be quite adjusted. The boy's father sold dope, I believe hashish, and he also was something of a pimp. He bragged of this in front of the family, especially when he was drunk. They lived near Tel Aviv. Once, when drunk, the father had forced all of the children to watch him have sexual intercourse with the mother. The father also beat this boy. There appears to be, I should add, considerable beating of children among the Oriental immigrants. This is one of the problems which the teachers, the social instructors and others, attempt to cope with. But this is a practice not easily checked or stopped.

After the boy had been originally admitted to Ramat Hadassah Szold, he did very well in school, and his progress was most encouraging. His aggressiveness and hostility toned down and he seemed both happy and improving. He was strongly attached to his instructor, who was firm, but also kind. In each group of rooms for the boys, there is a man instructor. The boy more than once remarked that his instructor was firm like his father. However, when the boy was separated from his instructor and sent to a kibbutz, he did not show the same improvement and development which he had been maintaining. He was unhappy and out of place. Sent back to Ramat Hadassah Szold, he did well. But the authorities were in a quandary. Where could they send him? What could they do with him since he was in an institution where his stay could only be temporary? In addition, this boy had sudden moods of great guilt and fear. He did not know what he was afraid of, but his fears made him distraught. When women had to deal with him, there was great trouble. He couldn't get along with them.

He was not a badly behaved boy. He kept his room in order, brushed his teeth and obeyed the rules of the institution. The man with whom I was talking emphasized this fact. In a superficial sense, the boy appeared to make progress and to adjust easily. It appeared as though he would remain happy if only he were under the guidance of his instructor at Ramat Hadassah Szold.

The pattern of the boy's behavior strongly suggests that of many orphans, who learn to obey the rules of an institution and who in this sense make a good adjustment. However, this social adjustment only seems to mask a deep-seated and sometimes dangerous emotional disturbance. The case of this boy points to some of the problems of the new immigrants' children; but many of these problems have parallels in America and other countries. We see here the roots of the problem of integrating the new immigrants, not only children, but also adults. There is no necessary correlation between social adjustment, in the sense of accepting the rules and fitting into the practices of a society or a group, and becoming internally secure. This is a problem which has engaged the attention of many psychiatrists and it is at the heart of the difficulties of integrating immigrants, not only in Israel, but anyplace in the world.

I saw the fourteen-year old Moroccan boy. He was a bit under-sized, but compactly built. He was busily engaged in arranging the cultural center for the Sabbath evening celebration, and paid no attention to me. Not only was he absorbed in his responsible work, but he was doing it conscientiously and well. We can describe this boy as being a little orphan. We can see that the integration and education of many of Israel's Oriental immigrant children is that of finding ways whereby little orphans—actual or emotional—will find a place and will feel that they belong, that they can grow, and that they can contribute to the society and the nation which is in the process of being built.

CHAPTER ELEVEN

I

A JEWISH AMERICAN GIRL, who was a trained psychiatric social worker, passionately gave me her impressions one afternoon in the Hotel Zion in Haifa. She said that she had seen the babies, foundlings' parentless children, in the WIZO (Women's International Zionist Organization) home at Jerusalem. Whenever she put her hand out, a baby would grasp and cling to it. She insisted the babies felt a need, even in infancy, for more individual affection and attention than they received. She became emotionally roused and angry. According to her view, the way the babies were being treated was all wrong, and she insisted that anyone with a psychiatric orientation and experience could quickly observe this. She had visited other institutions besides the WIZO hospital, and was critical also of them for the same reasons. She was convinced that there was an over-emphasis on organization, and that this was psychologically or psychiatrically of crucial importance.

She believed that nothing could be done to change the situation and that Israeli authorities are pursuing the wrong policy. Also, it was her conviction that they cannot be reached, convinced or changed. She feared the results in the future, when these children will have grown up, will expose the mistakes of the present, and that many of the children, especially those born to the new immigrants, will face severe psychological difficulties and emotional problems.

I have described a Moroccan boy at Ramat Hadassah Szold. He was, in effect, an orphan. Dr. Bruno Bettelheim, director of the Sonia Shankman Orthogenic School of the University of Chicago, author of *Love Is Not Enough* and *Truants From Life,* had written of orphans. He pointed out that it has been his observation, and that of his co-workers at the Orthogenic School, that orphans usually make a good superficial social adjustment. In institutions they depend on authorities for food and care. Their survival seems to them to be bound up with their good behavior. They are like little refugees and frequently, they develop a set of attitudes and habits which are similar or parallel to those of actual refugees. Dr. Bettelheim has not, at least to my knowledge, drawn this parallel, but I believe that it is valid. Refugees will often freeze themselves in their situation, losing initiative, a sense of responsibility, and the will to want to live again in circumstances where they will be more self-responsible and be required to make decisions. To orphan children, the asylum or institution is the world, and adults ruling and directing it are the authorities of that world. It is easiest to do what these authorities want. The orphan child quickly realizes this.

The care of the orphan, who, like other children, needs love, is impersonalized. The emotional life, the need for love, go unfulfilled. Children are conformists, but when they are placed into a system of institutional conformity, they lack the love they need. This seemed to me to be involved in the disturbance of the boy whose case I have already described briefly.

Reflecting on these matters, as a result of my own observations and of the criticism of the trained American-Jewish girl, I wonder about the method of the Israelis in their handling of the immigrant children. I am well aware that the procedures adopted were virtually unavoidable. Nevertheless, I think that if we put this question clearly, we might gain fresh insight into this problem and related problems in other countries. I discussed these questions with many Israelis, men and women in different lines of endeavor. Some of them worked directly with the new immigrants and their children. Others were removed from this work.

A number of Israelis are convinced that, next to the problem of peace and of peaceful relationships with the Arab neighbors, Israel's major problem is that of integration. To repeat—will Israel become a Levantine state or will it remain and develop as a Western democracy? Fundamentally, this is a question of mentality. It is to be observed in the difficulty which many Asians, including immigrants, encounter in grasping the abstractions of Western civilization. A nervous, brilliant and amazingly erudite Israeli official discussed this question with me all through the Galilee for two days. Over and over again, he stressed this same point. He was proud of Israel's achievements, but he insisted that Westernization is not a mere matter of technique, and of material progress. It involves changes in the mind and in habits of thought. Values can be superficially believed in and acted upon or they can be absorbed into the structure of the personality, into character, or the self. This suggests that adaptation is not sufficient in itself. The Moroccan boy adapted himself at Ramat Hadassah Szold, but he could not do so elsewhere. He had been fitted into the kind of institution where he could adapt himself. We cannot generalize on the basis of one or a few cases, but we can see aspects of a complicated problem. The success of Israel, both in material achievements and in the assimilation or ingathering of many of its Oriental immigrants, is quite amazing. However, it will require the experience of perhaps several generations before the real significance of this effort can be fully known and tested. Quite obviously, similar or parallel observations can be made concerning the under-industrialized countries of Asia as a whole, as they now move into the new world of industrialization.

It is relatively easy to teach simple habits, and this is done. Not only the children of the Oriental immigrants have to be taught elementary standards of hygiene. This must be done with all children. But some of the differences between Western and Eastern attitudes and habits have no significance of consequence, except possibly for those who are concerned with the smooth functioning and on-going of life in an institutional setup. Some of the Oriental immigrants believe that a person should bathe or take a shower outside the home rather than inside. Westerners take their showers in their own homes. Such differences are clearly unimportant. Adjustment and conformity on these elementary matters is obviously necessary, but it is dangerous to use this as a measure of success in education and integration.

In general, the Oriental immigrants adopt the superficial features of Western life first. An obvious example is the desire, which almost all of them have, to own a radio. But usually, they tend to feel inferior as compared to Westerners. This, needless to say, is not peculiar to the Jews who have come to Israel from Asia and North Africa. It seems to be fairly widespread in other under-industrialized countries. It is even apparent in intellectuals. History, with its many injustices and the vast and rich variety of cultures it has thrown up, has created differences and inequalities underlying these problems. But history, lest we forget, is not a force or law separate and distinct from the capacities and potentialities of human nature and of human beings living in history. History has thrown the men of our time and generation into this present hour, each carrying the individual chains of his past and the additional chains of his culture. Engels formulated the so-called law of uneven and unequal development. The Marxists saw the significance of this law, or this complicated and involved series of facts, well, but in an economic setting. Many people in America, without knowing the ideas of Marx and Engels and even abhoring them, think also in purely economic terms. Many of the meanings of this law or these facts are rooted in the thoughts, the habits, even the most elementary actions of human beings. Samuel Johnson remarked that "chains of habit are too weak to be felt until they are too strong to be broken." The chains of habits of centuries have been reforged in the lives of new immigrants. Many of their children have been affected by them. Habits are mental as well as physiological and social. Integration and change involves more than economic improvement and social adjustment. Furthermore, it is made more difficult because of the strangeness of difference which people feel. These are factors involved in the effort to change the mentality of the Orientals; even though the Oriental children are more malleable than the adults, the influence of the past and of their own culture is sometimes demonstrated to have been rather strongly fixed in them. Some of them become disturbed. Some do well in their studies until they reach the age of about fourteen, and then they are blocked and face serious learning difficulties in continuing a Western education. Obviously I, as a visitor, could not sense too much of this, but even to Israelis who work with them lovingly to help them, there is much that is unknown about the inner lives of new immigrants and their children. It is even questionable to what degree the psychiatric concepts developed in our Western culture are applicable to these children. The reports and case histories on them are written by persons with a Western orientation. We cannot be sure but that the effects of change and of the conflicts of culture disturb them, possibly even more than the conditions in their home. This is an open field in the clash of cultures. But to the Israelis, it is not merely one of study and observation; it is a practical problem of creating a nation and attempting to produce the new types of the future generations.

Differences are to be seen in a number of ways. These could be put together and classified under headings or within categories called understanding and habit. Understanding and habit are not separated in the human being when he functions. However, they are not the same, and cannot be absolutely equated. Concerning understanding, one very important difference should be stressed here. The capacity for abstraction is highly developed in the West. Without this capacity our civilization would not be as advanced and as developed at it is. Many Easterners and Orientals can think with abstractions, also, but it seems to me that the capacity and power to use abstractions flexibly are not as widely rooted in Oriental cultures as they are in our own. This suggests one of the most difficult roots of the problems of integration. It will take some years before definitive conclusions can be made concerning any success in changing the mentality of the immigrants, or even their children.

In my interviews with Oriental immigrants we can note that their responses at least indicate the vast cultural differences between many of us and them. These differences exist between the Western and Oriental Israelis. They are not merely the results of superior methods of formal education. We absorb many notions, conclusions and habits as a consequence of the fact that we have lived in a society which is technologically advanced, and which, by standards of freedom as we can now establish and define them, is a free society. We know that the earth is round before we go to school. We know that water running out of a faucet will not harm us. We are familiar with the telephone. Our own present generation of children accepts new inventions, machines and gadgets which are still confounding those of us who are, say, over thirty-five or forty. Even brain machines and Univac are being accepted as something natural by our youngest generation. The fund of facts acquired by Western children in their early years is more considerable as well as different from that acquired by the little Oriental immigrants who have come to Israel after having lived their first years in such a different culture. Furthermore, the facts about our society which we absorb from an early age onward add to and strengthen our feeling of being at home in the world, and, while children, we are flexible and adaptable to new conditions and societies. Anxiety is nevertheless a constant condition of children. The Oriental immigrant children, as well as their parents, must acquire more of the feeling of being at home in Israel, a world so new to them. Obviously, immigrant children cannot have the same feeling of sureness than do the Western children, many of whom they sit with in classrooms or live with in children's institutions. To integrate Oriental immigrants, and especially their children, to change their mentality, means to give them this feeling of greater ease in the culture of Israel. It involves more than teaching skills. Likewise, it involves more than the simple behavior adjustment.

You can understand how and why a conviction of progress develops among many working with new immigrant children when you see that the children fit into the life, the regimen, the way of doing things at an institution such as, say, Ramat Hadassah Szold. Most of the children there show improvement, and they go out to be educated in various other institutions, and then to enter the army. But deeper problems remain, at least for some of them, and on these judgment cannot now be passed. A process is in motion, a process that is highly experimental and new. An effort is being made to remold human nature. The effort at integration goes on with more consciousness and awareness than was the case with the immigration to America. Poor as Israel is, its curriculum is far superior to that which were fairly common in nineteenth century America. All we need to do to confirm this statement is to go back and look at McGuffey's Reader. Much more is now known about education than was a century ago. And I doubt, for instance, that you could find in Israel anything remotely similar to the conditions of education so clearly described by Edward Eggleston in *The Hoosier School-Master*. There is a greater feeling for and spirit of experimentation now, and the Israelis have learned from all this. Their educational efforts are largely directed towards developing children, Western and Oriental, into citizens of Israel. They seek to give the children a sense of participation in the culture of Israel and the life of a growing nation. Considering this, we must also recognize that the problems of integration are highly complicated and that it is most dangerous now for many to see these problems purely in psychological terms, from the standpoint of a psychological or Freudian orientation.

Basically, Israelis are attempting to educate the Oriental children and to integrate them into Western ways, attitudes, skills and techniques and mentality. Those who are in control are Westerners, imbued with the ideals and ideas of the West. They believe in science and in reason. Their political faith is democratic. They think of citizenship in a democratic sense. And while it is true that they must persuade the Orientals on many matters, including that of the value of education for their children, the whole mechanism of society assists them in their efforts at persuasion. The adjustments which the Orientals must make are major: those which the Westerners must make to the Orientals are minor.

The suspicion which the Oriental immigrants feel towards Westerners is much less acute than is apparently the suspicion of other Asians and Africans. This is due to the fact that both the Orientals and the Westerners in Israel are Jews. The sense of being a Jew and the teaching of Hebrew provide some cement for this new society which is so shot through with differences. Because they are not "observant," many of the sabras and Western Israelis disturb and shock the Orientals. But this seems to be a minor friction taken in the context of Israeli society. It is the Westerners who brought the Orientals to Israel. The latter do not appear to regard the Westerners as their exploiters, although many of them believe that they should get as much as they can out of the Jewish Agency. A number of them come to feel that the land is theirs as much as it is the land of the Western Jews.

Concerning the children, there appears to be a growing resignation among many of the adult Orientals, as well as an acknowledgement of the success and benefits of Western methods. One of the young teachers whom I have already mentioned told me that the Oriental parents would tell her:

"The children are yours."

There are, then, many difficulties which the Orientals face, and there are frictions of East and West. Immigration under any circumstances is fraught with pain, anguish and loneliness, with all kinds of confusion. These problems and difficulties perhaps weigh more on the child than on the adult. Integration, next to peace, is Israel's big problem.

II

In attempting to understand more of this problem of integration, certain considerations should be mentioned. It is easy for Americans to measure other countries by conditions which now prevail here in the United States. Often Americans abroad, or when they are reflecting about the problems of other nations and societies, tend to think only of what is best in American society, and, also, they mix up aims and ideals with realities to the point where the former become fixed in their mind as though they were realities instead of projections of what is wanted and desired. In other words, Americans tend to judge other countries not only in terms of facts, but also on the basis of idealized or sentimentalized images of American life. Then also, some Americans who have familiarity with or are engaged in social work, psychiatric social work and education, tend to be overly critical and to leap to conclusions about other societies with needless haste. This is perhaps especially the case with those whose orientation is Freudian. If we commit acts of intellectual impatience, judge in full speed and possibly with that conceit about insight which even a smattering of Freudianism so frequently induces, we will be wasting our time. This is not an attempt to explain away possible criticism of Israel or to excuse real or possible faults in Israeli procedures. Rather, it involves the question of how well we can understand ourselves. The present is more than cursed with judgmental people who consider themselves to be intellectuals, and who, in their excessive capacity to make quick judgments, only demonstrate their own sterility. Along with this demonstration, they produce needlessly irrelevant arguments and polemics. This has happened concerning Israel, and especially concerning Israel's policies of immigration and integration. But discussion on such a level is fruitless.

In Jerusalem, I discussed these matters with Dr. Hanokh Reinhold. He is a gentle man, originally from Germany, experienced in and familiar with contemporary ideas and practices in psychiatry and social work. He direct the work of Youth Aliyah, which cares for children such as those I saw at Ben Shemen or Ramat Hadassah Szold. We met at his office on a very hot morning. Like so many other responsible Israelis, he must spend a great deal of time, too much in fact, meeting foreigners and answering their questions. The circumstances of Israel's present life, its great dependency on outside funds, especially American, makes this a necessity. I was another visitor from abroad, come to ask questions and to talk with him in the heat. On his desk was a pile of folders. Each one was the case history of a child. Decisions about all these children, described in each of these folders, had to be made. And the man who had to do this was Dr. Reinhold.

At the time, there was great tension in Jerusalem and all along the borders. There had been an increasing number of border incidents. Feelings of uncertainty seemed to be spreading through Israel. These had lurked behind many conversations I had. All constructive efforts and thought—and from the Israeli standpoint the effort to integrate the immigrants irregarded as perhaps their main constructive effort—were continued with a shadow flung darkly across the thought of almost everyone with whom I spoke. The Israelis are racing against time to settle the country and to push integration. Most of them impressed me as believing that Israel will survive, even though miracles are essential for that survival. However, they wondered and were apprehensive about what would be the cost of survival if war came. And it did not seem, on this hot summer morning in July 1956, that war would be indefinitely avoided. Constructive thought went on in terms of the assumption of peace and development. And the apprehension of war was widespread. This contradiction, frequently inducing unstated moods, gave an air of unreality to many discussions I had in Israel. Such was the case when I spoke with Dr. Reinhold. This mood of uncertainty hung upon both of us. As I talked, I had flickering questions in my mind. How much did discussions such as this one mean? Wasn't it irrelevant? Were we not talking about a future which was impossible?

But this was all unstated. Dr. Reinhold and I spoke about the new immigrants.

Yes, he said, there might be too much institutionalization in the handling of the children and the other immigrants. But they had faced other problems. The state had been born in war, and in the aftermath, Israel had been flooded and almost overwhelmed by its new immigrants. Food had been short. Inflation had imposed added sufferings on the people. Housing facilities had been terribly inadequate. Merely to have taken in so many immigrants without going under from sheer weight had been, in itself, an achievement. They—men like himself and many others working with the new immigrants—had not been too experienced. The problems they faced had been new, and they had to work with insufficient facilities. Yes, they had made many mistakes. Only now were they learning, trying to correct mistakes and getting into a better situation so that they could handle and manage these problems more successfully than they had at the beginning.

The act of immigration, Dr. Reinhold stressed, is a tremendous one, calling for an effort, if the immigrant is to adjust to his new world. The changes are sharp, and can have the effect of a trauma. There is much maladjustment. Many personal problems develop, more than can be handled. Also he granted that there had been many cases of emotional disturbance, both among the children and the adults. He pointed out that the effort of adjustment was hard for both groups. But these problems could be handled and were being taken care of. He did not minimize them, but he was sure that there would be success. He is close to these problems.

Putting his hand on the folders stacked on the right side of his orderly desk, he said, very gently, that these were cases. Every day he had to make decisions about children. Should they be placed in institutions? Should it be recommended that they be separated from their parents? He shook his head sadly. These decisions were not easy ones. You did not always know what was best and wisest. You did what you could and you continued to learn.

Concerning emotional disturbances among the children, he further asserted that in such cases, one had to look at the family history and the family structure. It was his experience and his conclusion that families encountered serious, rancorous and destructive problems; and even sometimes broke up, and that children became disturbed, in cases where the familial structure and relationships had been weak and cracking prior to immigration. He repeated with emphasis what a tremendous act immigration is for these Orientals. Again and again, he had seen that families which were on the verge of breaking up before immigration did not survive and maintain their familial integrity in Israel. And it was from these families that the social cases, the disturbed parents, the emotionally ill or mentally troubled or delinquent children usually came. Families with a solid structure survived and made the adjustment.

These observations of Dr. Reinhold's bear on what we can designate as the phenomenon of change. Ours is a world of rampant change. The act of immigration is a most dramatic and definitive example of change, but in every country we see this type of phenomenon, and in its wake, a whole complicated series of psychological problems and manifestations. This is familiar to specialists and to trained people, but not to many others, including some who are intellectually alert and well-informed. It is a commonplace to state that with each vanishing second, life is flowing on in millions of channels. Each second of life is lived in the mind, in the inner being of people. The human being, even when he is a creature of habit and perhaps stupid, is a tremendous internal dynamism. And all the rocks and shelters of security and stability which man has constructed in this world, so basically alien to him, are much less firm than he believes. Society often seems to be built upon solid rock: it is erected on sands. The immobility of centuries has been shattered. The values and habits of the past have been cracked. The image of self which is created in society with its traditions is threatened in the swift pace of modern change. We are all adjusting or resisting adjustment more than we generally realize. Similarities to the problems which Dr. Reinhold spoke of are to be found everywhere, if we can only recognize the fact that with all our cultural differences, there is a common humanity.

The integration problem in Israel, if seen in such a context, can be related to many problems of our world. It provides almost a laboratory example of the problem of change, as focused in terms of the rubbing together of what we consider to be the values of the East and the West. The frictions between the Western and Eastern Jews are not totally unsimilar to those between Jews and Arabs, although in the latter case hatreds, differences of religion and memories of war exacerbate the friction. Further, all of Asia and Africa are moving into the Western orbit. This is a consequence of technology, of modern media of communication and of the problem of freedom which is being posed anew all over the world. Asia is more face-to-face with Europe and America than it ever was in the past. So is Africa. Western methods, know-how, values and attitudes are a daily challenge in Asia. Asians are meeting this challenge in many ways, accepting, resisting, fighting, absorbing or rejecting unconsciously as well as consciously. And all this is a stirring and unsettling psychological drama. It is churning the inner lives of millions. It must be stressed that the Oriental immigrants are not only Jews but also Asians and Africans. They are actors in this drama of world change. What we can see and learn from their adjustment to Israel can teach us lessons about the new and uncertain historic epoch into which we are moving.

Let me add that the questions and problems of change go beyond political issues. If we think of the entire East-West situation only within a political framework, we will miss much by way of insight and observation: we will see and grasp all too little; we will understand even less than we could understand.

It is well-known that there is much difference of opinion concerning Israel's policy of immigration. However, it has produced a series of facts. The population of Israel has now trebled since the state was founded, and the majority of the new immigrants have come from Asian countries or else from North Africa. In this way, hundreds of thousands of them have been jerked or pulled out of immobility into a dynamic world of change; this has happened to them almost overnight. They have gone to a new land with the hope of finding life better in some way. This hope and aspiration is basically no different from that of hundreds of millions in the world today. To expect a change of this character to happen without problems would be to think in a world of Utopia. The problems that have arisen also serve as graphic examples of what is going on in Asia. Modern technology and the theories of democracy have opened up new perspectives to men—even to men and women sunk in the squalor and poverty which runs across the continent of Asia like a great and festering social sore. If we think in terms of a perspective such as this one, we can perhaps see the problem of Israel's immigration in a more meaningful context. We can see that here is a living anthropology and a human laboratory of what can be the birthpangs of a new era.

CHAPTER TWELVE

I

Prior to my visit to Israel, I arrived in Beirut in June, 1956, to deliver a lecture. I found a letter from the United Nations Relief and Works Agency (UNRWA) requesting that I visit some camps of Palestinian refugees. Immediately I changed my travel plans and accepted this invitation. I was given an official report on the activities and disbursements of UNRWA and some pamphlet material which I looked at before visiting the camps and which I have since attempted to digest. I asked to see the best and the worst of the camps. I was treated with courtesy and I am convinced that my Arab interpreters were truthful and accurate in translating the answers to the questions I posed.

The worst of the two camps I visited was Muslim. The best, in the view of UNRWA officials, is Christian. This difference was a matter of accident, not of discrimination. UNRWA does not possess unlimited funds, and the Christian camp was built as an experiment and after some experience had been gained in the handling of the refugee problems.

It was a hot, sunny morning and I was driven in a

UNRWA car, accompanied by an English official and an Arab chauffeur who spoke sufficiently good, if not always grammatical, English.

The Muslim camp was in a flat and rocky area. It was a Sunday morning, and most of the refugees were away. Spread all over it were wretched, jerry-built little houses, most of them makeshift. In many, there was no floor but merely earth. Here and there from windows without glass a dark-skinned woman peered at me. The faces of the women bore an expression of resignation and suffering so common among women of the people the world over. It is an expression which suggests that misery has become a part of the character and of the physiognomy. Children ran about. They stared but usually did not smile. They appeared to me to be better nourished than I had anticipated, but I was later told that the problem of tuberculosis among these camp children is very serious. A few of these children were well dressed; others were shabby and barefooted and looked like urchins. I was impressed by the fact that I heard no happy ringing shouts of growing children at play. The way they stared at me suggested that they were more suspicious than curious.

I was introduced to the camp leader, a refugee from one of the country areas of Palestine. He did not tell me the name of his village, but I have since gathered that he must have come from the area near what is called the Arab Triangle. He was a small, thin man in his fifties, with dark intense eyes. Later, as we spoke, his eyes began to burn with anger. He wore a moustache, a good pair of Western trousers, a shirt without a tie, and a Bedouin cloak. We entered his office, a small brick house or compound. He offered me a Capstan cigarette as we sat at a table in this rather bare office. Children immediately gazed at us through the windows, their eyes lit with interest and curiosity.

I asked the man how he had become the camp leader. He answered in Arabic and the chauffeur translated.

"Allah decided. It's God's will."

What had he been and what had he done in Palestine before he had fled? He had been a merchant and a farmer and said that his life had been comfortable.

My next question was—whom did he think to be responsible for the condition of his people?

"The Anglo-Americans. They help the Jews by money."

He was an honest man and seemed to resent my questioning. With an angry flash, he asked me:

"Would you like someone to drive you out of your country?"

I said "No."

I told the translator to assure him I was asking questions in order to learn. And I asked what kind of settlement this camp leader would favor in order to end or resolve the refugee problem. Looking at the Arab chauffeur he spoke and then I was given his answer in English:

"He does not like any settlement, whatever it is."

He elaborated on this point and I learned quickly that he wanted me to know that all of the people in the camps feel the same as he does.

Then I said that I wanted to know about the children in the camps and what was said to them. The answer given to me was:

"Children, they think of their country [and are told] and to do everything possible to go back to Palestine. They [the parents in the camp] force their children to hate Anglo-Americans because they drove them out of their country. But not personally. They hate whatever they [the Anglo-Americans] have done to them."

Did this man hope and expect to go back to Palestine? The answer was confidently affirmative. The camp leader spoke further and the translator told me:

"If they don't go back peacefully, they'll go back by war. The Jews find Americans to give money. They [the Palestinian refugees] might find someone to give them help."

I next asked about Russia.

"They [his people] had never thought of Russia. But if they get no sympathy, they might ask Russia to help."

The camp leader spoke further. Here are the exact words of the translator:

"A day will come when they might go back to Palestine. We don't think we'll help the English or Americans. They'll have to kill the old Jews, and if the Anglo-Americans take their hands off, they [the Arabs and the Jews] will fight together."

The camp leader had more to say. His manner softened. He was speaking with emotion. What had he said?

"It's a pity. I'm living in my home and there's someone who drives me out with no rights to it—there's no one to be blamed. I think there's a good impression on the Jews from the Anglo-American policy by money. We didn't think that the Jews drove us out of Palestine; the Anglo-Americans did."

In consequence, it was his opinion that the Anglo-Americans should solve this problem.

"How?" I asked.

"It's up to them," was the reply.

I asked to be told more about the children in camp. I wondered how they were educated.

"Whenever a baby is born, she [the mother] feeds him the milk and he is Palestinian."

And he wanted me also to know that they told their children:

"Don't ever die somewhere else except Palestine."

His passion was rising, and his voice was a bit harsh. The children continued to stare through the door and the windows. He said that in 1914 when Turkey and England were fighting, the Palestinian Arabs had helped England. They had given the British the chance to conquer Palestine but he, and his people, had never thought that the English would drive them out of Palestine.

"Ask him, please," I said to the translator, "how he was driven out of Palestine?"

His reply was that the Arabs had had nothing to fight with and that the other people, the Jews, had had everything. He claimed that he had been shot at by tanks and guns. Also, he said that there had been many attacks between the Arabs and the Jews. And he repeated that he had had a good living in Palestine. They had all been prosperous and had had goats and cows.

I asked if there had been trade unions in Palestine prior to 1948, when the state of Israel was founded. Some, he answered. There were a few who had worked in the factories or at the railroad station. Obviously he was speaking only of Arab workers.

Prior to 1948, what had he thought of the Jews?

He hadn't given much thought to the Jews. At the time, he'd had nothing against them. But when the Arabs saw that the Jews wanted to build the Israeli government, they'd fought against that. Troubles started in 1936. And they had asked the English government to stop the Jews from coming, but the English hadn't listened. And then after hearing that an Israeli government was to be formed, he, and other Arabs in his region, said, "Don't sell to the

Jews." This boycott was kept, he declared, except that some Arabs on the frontier did sell to the Jews.

I next asked what he knew of the life of Arabs who were still living in Israel. He had no contacts with them, but he had heard that they weren't living well, wanted to come to Lebanon and to have the case settled.

My interview had gone as far as it seemed advisable. The camp leader himself rose to terminate it. I asked if I might speak to some of the people in the camp and see the inside of the huts, but he would not allow this. I was, however, permitted to see the camp mosque; walking the short distance to it, I was able to see through the entrance of a few huts. They were squalid, dark, and with little furniture inside.

The mosque was a small stone building which the refugees themselves had built. The roof was of tent material which had been provided by UNRWA. The interior was clean and there was straw matting on the floor. There were steps at one end. On the walls were Arabic scripts which were translated for me.

"Be all together and don't ever separate.

"We give you whatever you want."

After I left the mosque with the leader and the Muslim priest who had admitted us, the former spoke again. He gave the information that in all of the huts of this camp you can find a board on which is written in Arabic the question:

"Who drove you out of Palestine?"

We shook hands in parting and I expressed my thanks. The camp leader fixed, almost drilled me with his sharp and intense eyes. He asked if I thought that what had happened to him and his people was right? I could not give him a conclusive answer. I had been touched, hurt by the misery I had glimpsed. I said that I should probably have agreed with him prior to 1948, but that now the state of Israel was a fact. This could not be undone. I would, naturally, like to see a settlement.

As we walked to the UNRWA car, still more children stared at us. A naked little fellow, no more than a year and a half old, toddled and tottered about. A black-haired, barefooted girl of about four, who wore a dirty dress, picked up a baby. The baby was too heavy for her. She stumbled but did not fall. Several women in old black dresses stood around a fire. A mother sat just inside of a hut, holding a small baby, and staring as though she might be watching a sadness of eternity. A radio could be heard. The Arab singing sounded mournful. A child finally smiled. A few others ran about in aimless play. Then I heard a few shouts. The sun was burning on the camp with merciless inhumanity.

We entered the automobile. As we drove off, children waved to us. I was asked if I wanted to see more. Actually, I did not. I wanted to flee from such scenes of misery, mass tragedy and perhaps incurable hatred. I said, "Yes, I would like to see more." We drove to the next camp.

II

Among the Palestinian Arab refugees, probably fewer than 100,000 are Christians. The remainder of the 922,279 who are registered as refugees (according to the latest UNRWA figure), appear to be Moslem. The Christian camp near Beirut, which I visited, is one of the more recently built by UNRWA. Located on sandy, rocky ground, sloping in some places, there are stone huts or compounds set in rows and spread about. The yellow stone catches the glare of the sun. When we entered the camp, I saw many children, some running about and shouting. They were more active, and on the whole better dressed than those in the Muslim camp. But this is a relative statement, for in neither camp could I say that the children were playing like normal children in a healthy social environment.

With better camps, UNRWA officials state that there is a rise in the initiative of the camp inmates. They become more inclined to get jobs which permit them to supplement the rations they receive from UNRWA. Most certainly the atmosphere in the Christian camp was not quite as oppressive as that in the Muslim one. On the whole, the refugees seemed better dressed, and there was more movement among them. I saw several young girls in new dresses; they also used cosmetics. They were refugees who worked and were visiting people in the camp.

We were met by a tall, gray-haired man with a small protuberance of stomach. Clad in a soiled Arab robe, he looked as though he might just have gotten out of bed in an old-fashioned nightgown. There was a hard stubble of gray beard on his broad tan face. Friendly, ready to talk and to show off his English, he said that he was a Haifa man. Before 1948, he had managed a canteen. Also he said that about 85% of the 1,000 people in this camp were from Haifa.

He led us to an office in a stone building. As in the Muslim camp, children stared at us from the doorway.

I asked the ex-canteen manager why his people were here in the camp, and what did they want or seek?

"They want their country."

Who was responsible for the loss of their country?

"England and America . . ."

A moment later he said:

"America is responsible."

What does he think America should do to remedy or change this situation?

"She can cover the case if she wants to. . . . In five minutes she can do it. Every Arab in Palestine was depending on England, America who were taking justice in their hands."

Also, the United Nations could settle the case, and then he added:

"If not by U.N., by war."

At this point the camp leader joined us. He was a big, broad and taciturn man who could have been either in his forties or early fifties. He was cleanly dressed in dark trousers and a blue shirt, which was open at the neck. Like the Muslim camp leader, he was employed and paid by UNRWA. Because of this he was at first reluctant to speak. However, the UNRWA official assured him that he could say what he pleased with impunity. He spoke some English, and answered all of my questions. He had a better command of French, and when he shifted to this language, I asked for a translation when I was not absolutely certain of his meaning.

After saying that he did not think war necessary, he added:

"With one word, we can go back."

"Most Arabs," the ex-canteen manager intervened, "can join the Bolsheviks if we don't get help from America and England."

I asked the camp leader to tell me what he knew about the lives of Arabs who were still living in Israel.

"They are not living well. Every day, they are slaves. Our cemeteries and our churches are being schools for the Jews. Some people are coming to Lebanon. They say no food. They are killing donkeys. They sell donkey's milk."

What did he want in Palestine?

He wished the same for the Arab, the same for the Jew.

What, specifically, did he mean by this statement?

"We agree to that. Nil and nil the Jew and Arab made that. America and England made this trouble."

What he meant was that he favored equality for both Arabs and Jews, and that there would have been no trouble in Palestine but for the United States and Great Britain.

The gray-haired ex-canteen manager interrupted:

"Churchill makes friends with Russia to make war with Germany."

Thus, he believed that the Arabs would be justified in making friend with the Soviet Union.

But what did this man think of Russia?

"The same like Britain and wants to make peace by helping the Palestinian. We don't like to be under any government, America, or England, or Russia."

The ex-canteen manager held that England is more responsible than America, and he elaborated:

"Every child knows about it. We lived through them for about thirty years. Everybody knows that they are imperialists. They like to take other countries, India, Singapore—what they are doing in Cyprus? We fought the British 1921, 1929, 1936."

I then asked the camp leader how he had regarded the Jews in Palestine prior to 1948.

"Before that, they were poor, like the sheep, you know, how it goes to the slaughter."

The ex-canteen manager had not expressed himself fully about the British. He said:

"British governments, they make the rules all against the Arabs. They put too many taxes on their lands. At the end of the year, I mean, they [the Arabs] are forced to sell their lands."

"We left everything in our country," the camp leader said.

"England," the ex-canteen manager said with rising anger, "told the Arabs and the Jews the mandate would finish on the 15th of May. Until the last moment, we're fighting the Jews, and we have been always the winners. At midnight before this date, I don't remember clearly, the Brigadier of Haifa made a phone call to the Jewish Agency and he told them he is leaving. Of course, when the Jews knew that, they make advance by the British ammunition and equipment."

Both the UNRWA man and I asked—could not the Jews and Arabs live together?

"Why not?" the camp leader quickly answered.

He added that if something were to be done about partition, then both could live as citizens.

Would he be willing to live in Haifa under a Jewish government?

"Why not? If I were going to find anything extra [special privileges or considerations] for the Jews, I would leave Haifa."

Next, I attempted to get a clear account of their departure from Haifa. However, they were clearly confused about what had happened. The ex-canteen manager believed that the Arabs were in no way responsible for the failure of the partition resolution of 1947 of the United Nations General Assembly, and, at the same time, that partition would have avoided any refugee problem. But he also told me that when he left Haifa, he had been told that he would be back in fifteen days because Arab leaders had said that the Arab armies would take Palestine in about that period. After telling me this, he paused, almost visibly seeking to recall more of what had happened; and then he said:

"The King Abdullah said in fifteen days they would take Palestine. Everybody thought he was an English agent. That's why he was killed. Why the Jews in Lebanon, they are living with the Arabs. In Iran, I say there are Jews. In every country there is Jews. I blame the dictatorship of Hitler. It was in 1934 the immigrants came."

At this point another Arab in the room spoke; he was a refugee but well employed and was not a camp inmate.

"We are going to return to Palestine by war."

"If the Agency," the ex-canteen manager continued, "the United Nations Relief Agency, would stop giving us this ration, in two weeks we will be in Palestine."

The Arab who had just spoken of war disagreed:

"We'll stop it [the acceptance of rations] when we get money to buy revolvers. We are stronger. We have the right."

"America and England," declared the ex-canteen manager, "should press on the Israel government the partition of 1947."

I was unable to get any satisfactory answer as to why the 1947 partition had failed. They did not remember that Arab leaders had originally rejected the resolution.

But enough had already been said. Had I tried to pursue my questions further, I should have not only heard a repetition of what had been told me, but I would have engendered emotional strain. Hatred, misery, frustration, a hard exile stood behind their words.

We walked slowly about the camp. There were the compounds of yellow stone set on sandy, rocky land. On the left was a little cafe, painted blue and looking like a small bandstand. As when I entered, children played. A few of them passed us. A pretty adolescent girl also walked by us. I noticed that she was using lipstick.

The camp leader asked me if I wanted to see the inside of any of the compounds where the refugees lived. I did.

He led me to one of the yellow stone compounds and knocked before entering.

There was one large room with a cement floor. It was dark inside. There were a few pieces of non-descript furniture. By one wall there was a small stove and a few pots. Holy pictures were hung on the walls, including representations of Christ and the Blessed Virgin Mary. Also I saw a wash drawing of a symbolic Armenian design. The family living in this hut was Armenian.

A woman and five small children stared at me. A blond baby of about one year of age was perched on a sewing machine. The woman was small, plump, broad-hipped and her skin was quite dark. Her eyes and her face were inexpressibly sad, and her dress was very shabby. She continued to stare at me. The silence was almost awesome.

Then the woman spoke in Armenian and the camp leader translated for me. She was hungry. For ten days her husband had been ill and in order to illustrate what his affliction had been, she rubbed her left hand as though she had been scratching it. For a few seconds the camp leader sought the proper English word for her husband's illness.

"Eczema," I said.

He nodded and there was recognition on her face. She repeated the word.

She continued to stare at me, a poor women who was hurt with misery.

After we left, the big, gentle man took me to the camp church.

It was a clean little church with holy pictures and statues, and was dominated by a small wooden platform before the altar, over which lay a black cloth. The camp leader explained that this was in memory of a camp member who had died. It would be taken down now.

After this visit, we shook hands and said good-bye. People were moving about. Women, looking worn out with work, misery and child-bearing, stared at us. And as I was leaving, one man took me aside and said quietly:

"We'll never go back."

Driving along a road back to Beirut, I heard music. We came upon a small group in khaki marching to music and carrying flags.

"It's Syrian boy scouts."

We passed them as they marched in formation. Most of the boy scouts were men, not boys. They resembled a small army contingent. Arab villagers watched them. They marched along the road, silent and ominous, while the music blared.

We drove on. The threatening sense of possible war hung over my thoughts.

III

It is immoral to trifle with or to manipulate the misery of human beings. And when we see spectacles of collective misery and suffering, what are we to say? What is to be written?

I spoke with only a few of the refugees in these two camps. But I knew that they represented thousands, some hundreds of thousands, who live in a separated world of squalor. They live in hatred and dependency which day by day, and year after year, has slowly poisoned their lives, eaten away at the core of their humanity, and left them dumped and stranded on small and wretched little islands. They have become the rejected of history. They lack the concepts to understand what has happened to them. They cannot think and dispute with the objectivity which we can bring to bear on any study of them, of the causes of their plight, and of the question as to who is responsible for their condition. They are the objects of debates in the chambers of the United Nations. Also, they are used as illustrations of argument and counter-argument, polemics and counter-polemics. And around their passions of frustration, other passions of hatred are poured through the world. These passions have reached America. Because of a letter I contributed to an American newspaper stating my view that Israel's right to exist should be defended, I recieved a vituperative letter from a man with pro-Arab sympathies. He told me that I must have made a hop-skip-and-jump through Israel, that I was uniformed and asked me had I seen the plight of the refugees; obviously he was assuming that I had not. Also, he asked me if I were one of those who wants the Russians to take over the Western world for a handful of pioneering "Jewish dupes." He sent me provocative leaflets which came from Jordan, and which throb with phrases such as "Zionist gangsters," "murderers," "usurpers."

With these remarks in mind, I wish here to repeat a few pages of reflections which I wrote while still in Beirut. These represent a partial report of my first efforts to reach conclusions concerning my visit to those two camps.

Here is a portion of what I then wrote:

"My visit to the two Arab refugee camps was deeply depressing and has left me in a thoughtful but saddened mood for two days. As I sit now, writing . . . and gazing through an opened window at the blue Mediterranean, the sounds of hammering, the noises of automobiles, the voices of people on the streets of Beirut, my sadness of mood clings to me like something damp. Asians with whom I have spoken do not, as one would expect, react to their problems as might the white outsider from a faraway country. In meeting and dealing with their own problems, Asians do so out of their own past and their passions, not ours. The attempted objectivity of a foreigner might offend, or at the very least, bewilder them. Often their thoughts and passions are focused on their political problems and rivalries . . . as well as on an impatience to get ahead. In fifty years the face of Asia can be changed, and this continent can rise in economic power. Much of the bottom of poverty, misery and degrading squalor can be eliminated. But these are lessons of history which can be learned from other nations and other continents. And the lessons to be learned, the stimulations to be gained are not at all to be found in revolutions, technology or even in the democratic ideals of liberty, equality and fraternity. Asian intellectuals might well re-study the history of rivalries on the European continent. Bound up in these rivalries is the ideal, the factor, the phenomenon of nationalism. The historian, Carlton J. Hayes, described nationalism as the religion of the nineteenth century. And Eurpoe has had its nationalism, its wars, its dislocations, and its hordes of refugees. One might hope that a phrase of Rudyard Kipling be pondered—'*Lest we forget.*' "

These general remarks are included here because the Arab refugee question is one of the most sore, distressing and dangerous among those questions linked together in the nexus of danger which can end up in the tearing apart of the entire Middle East. . . .

The refugee problem ought not to be understood solely as a political issue but also as a human and moral one. In refugee camps the dignity of human beings is offended day after day. The camp is largely a world of its own, and in that world, people are dislocated and rendered dependent. The memories of the past are insufficient to give people the emotional sustenance they require in order to go on in a living sense. And this, I fear, is the case of the refugees. I also wrote at the time:

". . . the children. While they look healthy, I have been told that the incidence of tuberculosis among them is a grave question and a danger. Many were brought from Palestine when they were so young that all Palestinian memories will fade from their minds. Palestine will become only hearsay to them. Others have been born in the camps, nourished in an atmosphere of both squalor and dependency. Observers have already noticed a growing sense of dependency among a number of the adults and the parents. An intelligent, trained and perceptive Arab woman who has spoken to some camp children remarked to me on the danger to the future of the camp children.

"In the camps, there is hatred, bitterness and pride which has not only been wounded but in fact mangled. Let us leave aside here every claim made as to who is to blame in order to focus on this one feature or aspect of the situation. If necessary and for purposes of illustration, let us accept as grounded every Arab claim and contention concerning the refugee situation. Even . . . . within such a frame of reference, a most concise question should be posed. What is the future of these children to be? And the future is more complicated than can be assumed as an automatic development from ideals of national faith and religious acceptance. The inner equipment which the boy brings into manhood and the girl into womanhood will not only condition a life that is productive and stable in the personal and inner psychological sense, but also in the field of constructive social action. The concepts of nationalism and religion need to be sprayed through the life of a new nation if these are not to become negative and self-enclosing. In Asia, nationalism is knotted with anti-colonialism and anti-imperialism. The emotions behind anti-colonialism and anti-imperialism are aggressive."

Here I had to stop, and did not have the opportunity to continue my reflections. Had I, I should have attempted to show that politically, the Arab refugee camps reveal in a raw, naked, primitive and elementary manner problems in the Arab world, and problems, also, which have parallels and similarities with other ones in Southeast Asia.

The refugees are the political raw material of nationalism. The political statements made to me and quoted verbatim in this book are evidence of this. There are political factors mixed up here in the moral situation. On a dramatically sordid level and in a most tragic manner this is evident.

IV

In Beirut, I discussed the refugee question with various people including intellectuals and politicians. It was only to be expected that I would be asked what my impressions were. I sat at a restaurant table overlooking the Mediterranean. The night was splendid and clear but for a soft haze hanging over and falling into the water. The sea was calm. The wash against shore and rock was gentle and monotonous, filling me with a melancholy mood. Phoenicians, Greeks, Romans had heard the monotonous wash of the waters just as we had. Among our group was one of my friends, a man of deep sincerity, intelligence, and fine perceptivity, who had spoken with pride of the ancient Phoenicians. We had discussed much else, including the Israeli-Arab conflict. He had held to his views and I to mine, but our discussions had been serious, rational and civilized. He was as troubled as I because of this situation. We both felt an inner strain. We had much in common, and shared a similar outlook on many problems, social, political, literary and even philosophical. There was a moodiness and a feeling of unuttered regret hanging between us. Difference of view, situation, feeling and position on this one issue tainted our discussions with sadness.

To our left was a big, craggy and naked rock, dark in the night. It is a suicide rock from which some Lebanese, bent on self-destruction, have leaped.

We ate, listened to the recurrent music of the waves, and talked.

Questioned as to my impressions of the camps, I spoke of the children. I told an anecdote. Several years ago, I was making a purchase in a New York drugstore and a nineteen year old American boy, born of Armenian parents, had spoken to me.

"I don't hate the Turks," he had said spontaneously. "I don't hate the Turks. My parents tell me to hate the Turks. All my life, they told me to hate the Turks. I know the Turks killed Armenians. Maybe they killed a million Armenians. But I wasn't there. I never saw them. I don't want to hate the Turks. I want to live."

Using this story for purposes of illustration, I suggested that the refugee camp children had been very young when they were taken from Palestine and that some of them had been born in the camps. They probably could not remember ever having seen a Jew. They would have no clear and conscious memories of Palestine. They are growing up in a world of squalor, dependency and hatred. Soon they will want to leave the camps. Also, they are living in a kind of frustrating and limiting isolation. They are Arabs but are not fully of the Arab world. In Lebanon, neither they nor their parents have the rights of citizenship. And most important, their young emotions are being saturated in hatred. Hatred is very mobile. It can be turned onto other objects beside the original ones.

"It can be turned on you," I said.

"Yes," an intelligent Arab woman exclaimed. "They will become thieves, marauders, murderers."

We discussed the question in these terms, and my Arab friends said they had not thought of the refugee question in this context.

To a normally intelligent and serious American, and to anyone with any practical and somewhat serious psychological or psycho-analytical orientation, these observations are fairly obvious. They are not at all original. But to these intelligent Lebanese they were new and original. I offer my own guess as to why this was so. The Israeli-Arab issue distorts minds, locking them up in antipathies, passions and even barren polemics. Also, this issue is linked up with the use of anti-imperialism as a slogan.

Let me illustrate. I interviewed a promising, influential, sensitive, intelligent, well-educated and honest young Lebanese parliamentarian, professor and journalist. He is both pro-Western and anti-Communist. He has gone through various political peregrinations, but I found him frank, and completely unequivocal. He told me what he thought openly, and gave me permission to quote him.

When we discussed Israel, I asked him why the status quo in the Middle East could not be maintained. He answered that Arab opinion could not be gotten to accept it because of the past period of Western occupation. He declared that the fundamental need in the Arab world is that of preparing the future through pushing and aiding economic development and by the inculcation of civic spirit.

Then I asked him what was being done towards the achievement of such aims.

"Very little," he admitted, "because of the Arab concern over Palestine. It has become"—and here his emotion deepened and was expressed in the tense sincerity of his voice—"a hysteria, a complex, a bother, and finally a strain on our budgets. One third of our budgets go for puppet armies."

Continuing, he said that "even governments find the Palestinian question a reason for doing nothing else. We are living in a state of war which makes every one of us think of things as hypothetical. The very preparation of the future is undermined because we do not feel that we are secure enough." And lacking a sense of security, "there is none of the serenity necessary for the quiet profound thinking that building a state requires."

Alluding to the refugee problem immediately after having made the above statements, he asserted that the refugees constitute one tenth of the population of Lebanon. The official figures of the UNRWA are about 7.7%, but this inaccuracy was understandable; he spoke without having notes or figures at his command. The refugees are, for Lebanon, he said, "a tremendous burden and many-sided problem with implications for economic, social and political life." Also he stated that the refugee camps are excellent breeding grounds for all sorts of demonstrations, and anyone "can organize a demonstration [of Palestinian refugees] for ten thousand pounds [Lebanese]." He told me that, in fact, this had been done at least three times. And Charles Malik, in his article, *"Call to Action in the Near East," (Foreign Affairs,* July 1956) has written in a parallel vein. He wrote of "the Arab refugee camps serving as hotbeds of Communism." The press reports from the Middle East, the Middle Eastern crises and the subversion in both Jordan and Lebanon, and also civil war in Lebanon, have since confirmed what this Lebanese parliamentarian told me about the political use made of the refugees.

To return to our conversation in the restaurant, we fixed our attention on the human aspects of this problem rather than its political features. Regardless of who were right or wrong here, what could be done about those children? It was recognized that they need more attention from the Arabs than they are apparently getting. One of those present cited a study made of the children in the camps. I was told that this emphasized the dangers inherent in a condition of psychological dependency such as that which prevails in the two camps. The question was posed—how many of the adults are rehabilitable? It seemed that they, or at least that many of them are gone, gone and lost for future constructive effort. One of the Arabs said that he did not care much about the adults, but this was neither callousness nor lack of sympathy. What he meant was that possibly these adults, or at least a proportion of them, had sunk over the line of real return. But the children are different. And how to do something for them? This question was left unanswered, but it hung in everyone's thoughts. I would assume that it continues to haunt all of us who talked that night by the shores of the Mediterranean. That rugged suicide rock now rises in my memory. I see it, jagged and strong, standing like a lonely and dangerous sentinel with the waves of the sea washing, swirling, rushing and beating against it. Is the Middle East as sturdy and permanent as that rock and will the waves of passion, prejudice, division and hate beat in vain, or will they wear away and submerge the rock of Middle Eastern stability? Now, over two years later, the Middle East is no closer to an era of stability than it was on that June night of 1956.

V

Unlike Jordan, the refugees in Lebanon are not granted citizenship. There is a reason for this. The population of Lebanon is balanced between Muslim and Christian and were the refugees to be granted citizenship, the scale would be tipped too heavily on the Muslim side.

In 1956, it was no secret in Lebanon, in Israel or to informed persons elsewhere that the Lebanese Christians were worried. They belong to various churches and sects, but down the centuries they have retained their Christian faith in the face of Muslim rule. Through the centuries, also, there has been almost no intermarriage between Christians and Muslims. The Christians usually did not openly proclaim their concern and worry, but it definitely has colored their thinking. One Christian, a cultivated man, did speak to me in private, but he was not among the group I was with in the previous section.

"After the Israelis, it will be our turn," he said.

This pattern, however, was reversed. The attack on Lebanon, rather than on Israel, was made.

There were many evidences of Lebanese concern, even in June 1956, before the Suez crisis. The prospects of future dangers and war, including civil war, were then at least dimly apparent. For instance, the English-language press suggested that there were softer views prevalent in Lebanon than in other Arab countries. One can note other evidences of this fact also. Thus, there have been fewer incidents along the Israeli-Lebanese border than along the other borders. It is a well-known, openly admitted and much recognized fact that considerable smuggling goes on back and forth between Israel and the Arab countries. I saw no instances of this personally, but heard it spoken of frequently. Outside of Israel, an Israeli official told me how he had been on the Lebanese border during a vacation and had seen extensive and impressive smuggling operations. Israelis have a soft spot for Lebanon. Many of them state that the second peace will be signed with this country. Sabras and many Israelis who lived in Palestine prior to the War of 1948, will speak nostalgically of vacation trips to Beirut, of Lebanon's attractive mountains, of Baalbeck, a magnificent site of ancient ruins. They will talk of how short the trip by motor is from Haifa to Beirut, of the superiority of Lebanon to Israel as a place in which to spend vacations, of associations, holidays and trade relations which might be possible if peace could be achieved.

The Lebanese to whom I spoke, with one exception, defended the Arab position against Israel. Some are familiar with Israeli material and if I asked them to show me both positions on any questions, the documents were available. One Lebanese expressed admiration for Ambassador Abba Eban as a brilliant man, although he disagreed with him. In Beirut, I even heard one admission as to the stature of Prime Minister Ben-Gurion.

At the same time, the following views were expressed. The Jews of America support Israel with money, and there is a Jewish press in the United States. American papers, including *The New York Times,* will sometimes suppress statements of the Arab position or the case against Israel when it is presented in interviews by Arabs.

The proposition that if peace could be established, Israel would be in a position to help the Arab countries is one which does not appear to be attractive to many Arabs, especially the Lebanese. An intellectual flatly said that they had no need of Israeli or Jewish help. The West was the source of ideas, and of scientific and technological development. Some of the Arabs had studied in the West, at the London School of Economics and elsewhere. The idea of being helped by the Jews offends Arab pride. And the factor of Arab pride furnishes one of the psychological and emotional features of the explosive Middle Eastern situation.

Concerning the refugee problem, one common attitude expressed to me was that Israel should make a gesture. This same attitude has been expressed by many Westerners, including anti-Zionist American Jews. Well over two years ago, the Cairo correspondent of *The Manchester Guardian* wrote: "Acceptance by Israel of a limited number [of refugees] might be invaluable as a gesture. . . . Israel could still do an incalculable amount for her own eventual benefit and for the world by yielding some of the border territory she seized outside the United Nations partition line. She could therefore make possible a return to normal life in numerous border villages." Charles Malik made a similar proposal in his *Foreign Affairs* article: he suggested that as part of a settlement, Israel cede part of Western Galilee for the repatriation of refugees.

While in Beirut, I interviewed Mr. Selim Lahoud, then Foreign Minister of Lebanon. By profession an engineer, he three times occupied that position. He spoke frankly. On the refugee problem, he began by stating that it is abnormal and irregular that there should be refugees anywhere in the world. Of Jewish refugees, he asserted that they would not be happy anywhere; nor could any country be happy with them. Further, we cannot solve one problem of refugees by creating another one.

"Maybe when there have been Jewish refugees, the mistake might have been their own or of the government of the land" from which they fled.

"Here," he went on, "we have refugees who left their country against their will."

To the contrary, he asserted, the Jewish refugees wanted to leave Germany. And he said that the Arab refugees who flooded into Lebanon drove Lebanese people out of the country: some of the latter went abroad. He was referring to those refugees who had found work, and who, in the main, do not live in refugee camps. Such refugees, he said, do not want to stay in Lebanon, but they are working.

By statute, refugees in Lebanon are prohibited from getting employment. But Mr. Lahoud told me that the Lebanese government took a humane view of the refugees and allowed them to work.

This, he went on, is however most unfortunate for Lebanon. For, he claimed, the refugees will accept lower wages, and business firms, because of this as well as of human feelings, will hire them. Thus Lebanese lost their jobs. He next told the story of a Palestinian girl, a refugee, who had been employed by a Beirut firm for four years. When this firm closed down, she demanded four years' indemnity money, for the time which she had worked. The significance of this case is not clear to me, but Mr. Lahoud emphasized it as an illustration of the economic difficulties which he contends Lebanon must encounter because of the refugees to which it is host.

Had the refugees, I asked, contributed to the growth and development of Lebanon? His answer was unqualifiedly negative. Most of them, in his view, do not measure up to the skill and standards of the Lebanese in workmanship. Other Lebanese made the same claim.

A Yemenite Jew, Captain Yeruham Cohen, was the adjutant to the victorious General Yigal Allon against the Egyptians in 1948. In February 1953, Captain Cohen wrote an article in *The Jewish Observer and Middle East Review,* and described the secret Negev talks. Besides much interesting information about Nasser and the Egyptians, he pointed out that prior to the Palestinian war, the ". . . Egyptians had scarcely ever met Palestinian Arabs. Moreover, they had difficulty in understanding the Palestinians because of the great difference in dialect." But while they considered it their duty to help the Arabs in Palestine, the Egyptians "wanted to know why the Palestine Arabs did not cooperate more in the fight against the common enemy. The Egyptians blamed them for cowardice and laziness." There was tension between the two groups. Cohen thought that Nasser was too harsh in his judgment of the Palestinian Arabs, "who had, at first, fought well, but had afterwards lost their fighting ability, mainly because of the contempt with which the Egyptians treated them." The Israelis dispute such estimates of the Palestinian Arabs, and contend that they are the most skilled and best workmen and farmers in the Arab world.

To continue, pro-Western Lebanese intellectuals appeared to consider the Arab-Israeli conflict as a barrier which thwarts and restricts the spread of Western influence, and which helped the Communists to penetrate into the Middle East.

Thus, a parliamentarian declared to me that "although Moscow and Washington share the same views on Israel and are equally responsible for Israel and maintain with Israel the same relations, Moscow has succeeded in appearing to be entirely pro-Arab whereas the United States has given the impression that it is entirely pro-Israel." Since this statement was made to me, of course the Soviet Union has come out quite explicitly in favor of the Arabs.

But distorting as the Arab-Israeli conflict is to the thinking of those with whom I spoke, their minds did focus on and were concerned with other issues and problems. They expressed the desire to see Lebanon develop, and to witness a movement towards greater freedom and justice in the Arab world. At times some of those with whom I spoke wanted to forget Israel and to think of growth and progress in Lebanon itself. And they pondered and wondered as to how bonds with the West could be strengthened.

At the time of my brief visit, there was much complaint and even disillusionment because of the differences among the Western powers, the United States, Great Britain and France, which were a source of concern in Beirut even prior to the Western split over the Suez situation. "Western embassies," said one Lebanese, "seem to be fighting one another more than they do the Russians. There is no common line of thought among them. Each is conducting its own propaganda in its own way." This Arab complained of backbiting and incidents of petty rivalries and declared that, lacking a psychological understanding of the Arabs, Western leaders and governments do not "know how to make a gesture nor what type of gesture can be made."

Despite the changed situation of the present, attitudes such as this should be recorded for America. They are bound up with all Middle Eastern problems, as well as with the Arab-Israeli conflict.

Quite obviously, I have not given a full account of Arab views. Rather, I present what was said to me directly in one Arab country. The refugee problem cannot be separated or isolated from the other features of the Arab-Israeli conflict.

CHAPTER THIRTEEN

I

THE ARAB REFUGEES are cared for by the United Nations Relief and Works Agency for Palestine Refugees in the Near East. This organization has a mandate from the United Nations to continue its functions of relief and rehabilitation until 1960. UNRWA is concerned with medical care and the education of the camp children as well as with direct relief. According to the Report issued by the Director of UNRWA for the period covering July 1, 1955, to June 30, 1956, there were 922,279 refugees registered with the Agency and receiving rations or some form of relief. This marked an increase from 905,986 during the previous year. UNRWA also has stated that the original number of refugees, following the Arab-Israel truce agreement of 1948, was 800,000. Of the number of refugees listed on the rolls two years ago, 333,487 live in camps. Others have found accommodation elsewhere, sometimes with friends and relatives, usually in overcrowded conditions. Also, UNRWA has estimated that there is an annual increase among the refugees of about 25,000 per year because of new births.

Eligibility for status as a refugee is described as "the

person whose normal residence was Palestine for a minimum period of two years preceding the outbreak of the Palestinian conflict and as a result of which he lost both his house and his means of livelihood."

There is no absolute certainty as to the exact number of qualified refugees and Israelis dispute the present figures. *The Arabs in Israel,* a booklet published in English by the Government of Israel in 1953, would set the figures of the Arabs who left as approximately 530,000; other Israelis calculate that the number of refugees runs from 550,000 to 600,000. Many Israelis claim that the rolls, especially in Jordan, include non-Palestinian Arabs as well as refugees. The 1955 Report of the Director of UNRWA reported some progress in "the matter of improper registration." Also, it stated that "Although the situation in Jordan showed no real improvement during the period under review [1954–1955], there were indications at the end of the period that the [Jordanian] Government would be prepared to cooperate in measures which the Agency had proposed. The lack of co-operation from the Government in the past and the active opposition of the refugees for several years made it impossible to operate in Jordan any system to determine the *bona fide* [italics in original] of ration recipients and to delete from the ration rolls the names of persons not entitled to relief." The 1956 Report stated: "Although agreement was reached between the Government and the Agency, in October 1955, on procedures for rectification of the relief rolls through a jointly administered system of additions and deletions, it has unfortunately not proved possible to put those procedures into effect. This has been mainly due to the troubled political situation in Jordan, which apparently has made the Government unwilling to embark on any new action that might be opposed by refugee leaders. The distribution of relief therefore remains inequitable in Jordan, to the detriment of many refugee children and much against the wishes of the Agency."

Another but minor aspect of this situation is that of Arab immigration into Palestine in the last twenty-five or so years. After 1920, when there was a new Jewish immigration and Histadrut, The General Federation of Jewish Workers, had been founded, there was some Arab immigration into Palestine because there was a gradual improvement of conditions. There can be no doubt that the Jewish immigrants did contribute to an economic improvement in Palestine. These are facts which should be fitted into any assessment of the total question.

According to the 1955 Report of the UNRWA Director (and this seems to have remained unchanged in 1956), the Agency gives rations to those on the rolls, provides camps, medical services and educational facilities for the children. Roughly about half or almost half of those listed as refugees were under 16. The rations provide for a calorie intake to children over 1 year of age of 1,600 in summer and 1,700 in winter. Children between 1 and 15 years of age receive a daily issue of skim milk. Pregnant women and nursing mothers receive a daily ration of milk and extra basic rations "when they report for medical supervision." But, the 1955 Report states, "In spite of the above considerations [such as those I have cited], the margin of safety provided by the present basic distribution of foodstuffs is small, particularly in areas where work, and therefore earnings, is almost unobtainable."

There are a number of projects calculated to rehabilitate refugees and make them self-supporting, but these have, in part at least, been stalled by various of the host governments. "Progress," again to quote the 1955 report, "toward the General Assembly's goal of making the refugees self-supporting is necessarily slow." The reasons cited for this are the absence of a solution of the Palestinian refugee question along the lines of a resolution of the General Assembly calling for the compensation and repatriation, "the meagreness of the physical resources, made available for development," and in some cases, the attitude of the refugees themselves. The 1956 Report states on this subject: ". . . the work opportunities are especially scarce in the areas in which most of the refugees live—Jordan and the Gaza strip.

"One should not, therefore, draw the conclusion that the willingness of individuals to work will permit substantial progress towards making the mass of the refugees self-supporting and independent of outside support."

The 1955 Report speaks of "the strong desire of the refugees to return to their homeland. This feeling has not diminished . . . and its strength should not be underestimated. The demand for repatriation springs mainly from the natural longing of the people for their old homes, strengthened and encouraged by the resolution [of December 11, 1948] of the General Assembly to the effect that 'refugees wishing to return to their homes and live in peace with their neighbors should be permitted to do so at the earliest possible practicable date, and that compensation should be paid for the property of those not choosing to return."

This view of the situation is attributed to the former Director of UNRWA, Henry R. Labouisse of the United States. And another paragraph of this same 1955 Report, which has frequently been quoted in and outside of the United Nations, should here be cited.

"For the majority of the refugees, repatriation means a return to the conditions they knew in Palestine prior to 1948. It is not possible to know how many of them would in fact accept an opportunity to be repatriated if that repatriation would mean something different from returning to their old homes and to their former ways of life. No prediction can be made until the refugees have been given the opportunity of choosing between distinguishable alternatives, namely on the one hand, repatriation the true nature of which is clearly understood at the time of the choice and, on the other, the amount and form of compensation that would be offered instead. It must be strongly emphasized that unless opportunity is given to the refugees to make their choice, or unless some other political settlement can be reached, the unrequited demand for repatriation will continue to be an obstacle to the settlement of the problem as proposed by the United Nations."

From July 1st, 1955, to June 30th, 1956, the total income of UNRWA was $23 million. Expenditures in this period for the relief program totaled $23.4 million against an approved budget of $26.8 million. The facts that is was not necessary to use operational and other reserves, that certain construction and the purchase of equipment were deferred, and that commodity costs were lower than anticipated accounted for the differences in the amount of the approved budget and the expenditures. The Agency ended the year with a deficit. Also, the host government, in the main, provided services rather than cash. These included transport, offices and warehouses for supplies.

Other parts of the Reports deal with the legal status of the Agency and legal problems. Efforts were made to tax the agency with stamp taxes on documents, and to control employees through national labor laws. There were difficulties and complications concerning transportation costs from country to country, and the Agency was attempting to get intergovernmental agreements between Syria, Jordan and Lebanon on this matter. There have been difficulties in getting diplomatic immunity for employees and there have been court cases on claims. Briefly, the Arab governments have not made it easy for the Agency to work in caring for the refugees. At one point, the Syrian government, arbitrarily refused entry to some officials and attempted to levy income taxes by deduction at sources on non-Syrian and Syrian employees of the Agency. These are examples cited of the legal difficulties which UNRWA encountered.

When all this is boiled down to results, UNRWA is able to spend something like $27 a year for rations for each refugee. There appears to be increasing poverty, and spending year after year of exile is quite apparently a very demoralizing way of life. My direct account of my visits to the two camps might give the reader some sense of the misery and bitterness which is the lot of these people. The fact that about half of the refugees are now under 16 adds to the urgency of the problem.

Why does it continue?

II

I have just posed the question—why does the refugee situation continue? I cannot give a definitive and final answer to this question. And also it is not my purpose to stand as a kind of Olympian moral judge or censor. But I do want to discuss it.

I have presented direct quotations from refugees themselves and have also written what some Arabs have said, as well as presenting the views of Mr. Labouisse, who recently retired as Director of UNRWA.

But what about the Israelis? What do they say? What is the view of some of the Israelis?

It is no secret that many Jews, both inside of Israel and

in America are troubled by the refugee question. Some of them bitterly criticized the government, both on the refugee question and on the treatment of Arabs in Israel.

Immediately after my arrival in Israel, I asked questions about the refugees.

"Believe me, Mr. Farrell," said one official, "we want to settle this question."

But how?

The official Israeli position concerning the Arab refugee question has been stated by Mr. Abba Eban, Israeli Ambassador to the United States and his government's Permanent Representative to the United Nations. In speeches delivered before the Ad Hoc Committee of the General Assembly of the United Nations on October 30, 1952, and November 18, 1955, he has spoken on this question.

"Today," he said in his November 18th speech, "we confront a somber picture of misery and deadlock. The number of those receiving relief has increased, not diminished. Arab governments hold all of the major rehabilitation projects at a standstill or in suspense."

A basic assumption of the official Israeli position resides in the question of original responsibility. And Mr. Eban spoke on the question as follows, again in his November 18th speech:

"The problem of the Arab refugees was caused by a war of aggression launched by the Arab states against Israel in 1948."

The state of Israel was proclaimed on May 14th, 1948. The British Mandate ended and the British forces were withdrawing from Palestine. There had previously been fighting between the Arabs and Jews there. War between the Arab nations and the Jews broke out on May 15, 1948. One of the original actions leading to war occurred in the

Jerusalem section. One of the first actions was that of blowing up the Jewish quarter of the Old City of Jerusalem. The Secretary-General of the Arab League at the time, Azzam Pasha is reported in an Israeli government pamphlet, *The Arabs in Israel* (Tel Aviv, 1955) as having stated:

"This will be a war of extermination and a momentous massacre that will be spoken of like the Mongolian massacre and the Crusades." Arab armies moved into Israel and there are many quotations from Arab leaders which indicate that the Arabs expected to attain a quick victory. An Israeli told me that a British General on leaving Haifa, also expected the Arabs to win very quickly and said to his Jewish friends on departing: 'I'll meet you in Hell.'"

As I reported above, the former canteen manager from Haifa, now in a refugee camp, told me that he had left Palestine because he had been told that he would be back in 15 days.

It is a historic fact that the Arab states refused to accept the United Nations resolution which established the partition of Palestine, providing for both a Jewish state and an Arab state which would live together in peace and in an economic union. A United Nations Commission, reporting on this question in 1948, declared:

"The Commission has had to report to the Security Council that powerful Arab interests, both inside and outside Palestine, are defying the resolution of the General Assembly and are engaged in a deliberate effort to alter by force the settlements envisaged thereto."

Along with the argument that they are not responsible for the problem since they did not cause it, the Israelis contend that they tried to persuade the Arabs not to leave Palestine.

Mr. Jacob Solomon, a practicing lawyer in Haifa, represented many Arabs and knew Arab leaders. He went to them and urged, argued and pleaded with them not to leave. In an interview with me, he asserted that privately some of the Arabs were inclined to agree with him but that the appeals and urgings of Arab leaders were stronger and there was a vast exodus. Mrs. Golda Meir, present Foreign Minister of Israel, journeyed from Jerusalem to Haifa and pleaded with the refugees not to leave. Mr. Abba Hushi, present mayor of Haifa, also urged the Arabs to remain. He and Mrs. Meir were ready to give them guarantees as to their safety. Undoubtedly, fear and confusion on the part of many Arabs were important factors here. About a month before the establishment of the State of Israel, a Jewish terrorist organization wiped out the population of the Palestinian Arab village, Deir Yassin. Jewish national leaders denounced this action, but to this day, Israel suffers as a consequence of Deir Yassin. At the time, it added to the fright of the Arabs, especially due to the fact that prior to the establishment of the Jewish State, most of the Arab leaders had already left Palestine.

Abba Eban in speeches at the United Nations, and other Israel officials of the Israeli government, have rejected the proposal of Mr. Labouisse. The Israeli contention is that Israel cannot take back the number of Arab refugees, especially in the light of the fact that they have now been educated for years in hatred of Israel. To take them back under such conditions would endanger the security of Israel and breed even more conflict in Palestine. Life has changed since the mass exodus of the refugees, and they could not return to live under conditions like those which prevailed before their departure. A state cannot take in hundreds of thousands who will hate it, who will be disloyal to it, possibly destroy it. This is a basic Israeli point concerning the refugee problem.

Thus in his November 18th speech, Mr. Eban said:

"Here then is our country with its embattled frontiers, the cherished sanctuary of the Hebrew spirit, the focus of so many deep universal sentiments, the product of infinite patience and toil. This small domain of sovereignty is savagely begrudged by a people whose territorial possession stretches out over a whole continent. Cut off from all land contacts, intercepted illicitly in two of its three maritime channels,[1] subjected to blockade and boycott, to siege and encroachment, to infiltration and commando raids; the object of an officially proclaimed state of war and the target of a monstrous rearmament campaign—this is the picture of Israel's security. . . . Can the mind conceive anything more fantastic than the idea that we can add to the perils by the influx from hostile territory of any number, small or large, of people steeped in the hatred of our very statehood? I do not believe that any responsible conscience will sustain such an idea. There could be no greater unkindness to an Arab refugee than to expose him to such an invidious role, perhaps reproducing the very circumstances which first made him a refugee. . . . On the one hand, Arab representatives tell you that it is intolerable for Arabs to live in Israel. On the other hand, they suggest that thousands of others should be driven back into this intolerable and explosive tension."

Mr. Eban rejected the proposal of Mr. Labouisse. He additionally stressed that Israeli representatives could not gain admittance to Arab camps and have a fair opportunity to present the situation of repatriation or compensation in terms of the changed situation in Israeli Palestine since

---

[1] At the time of this speech, the Gulf of Aqaba was not open to Israeli shipping.

1948. Mr. Walter Eytan, Director-General of the Foreign Ministry of Israel, took the same view in his recently published book, *The First Ten Years: A Diplomatic History of Israel*.

As I have indicated, Arabs and others have proposed that Israel should make a gesture. I put this question to Mrs. Meir in the course of a personal interview in Jerusalem.

"Yes," she answered, "make a gesture and die."

Mr. Ben-Gurion's response to the same question, when I asked it of him, was:

"Why should we make a gesture? Things wouldn't be better. We gave up part of Lebanon."

Along with her rejection of the idea of making a gesture, Mrs. Meir responded negatively to any ideas of a token return of some of the refugees. Her reason was that if Israel did this, then it would be faced with demands for taking in additional refugees and Israel would be trapped into a position of increasing danger to herself.

Various Israelis have pointed out, further, that Israel has in recent years taken in several hundreds of thousands of new immigrants, including Jews from Arab countries. Including Arab sections of North Africa, Israelis estimate that they have taken in up to 470,000 new immigrants from the Muslim world. This total has been increased by the more recent influx of Jews from Egypt. Israelis point out how much they, and also how much world Jewry has given and done for Jewish immigrants, and contrast these actions with their contention that Arabs neglect the refugees.

Furthermore, they point out that they have taken back some Arab refugees in cases where families would have been split, and that some millions of blocked funds for compensation have been paid already. The entire question of compensation is highly complicated and technical. Before any just and final compensation could be settled upon, a serious investigation would have to be made concerning titles, value of property, and so on. Israelis insist that they do not refuse to negotiate some settlement of the refugee problem, but refuse to accept proposals which they view as virtually menacing their very existence.

The Israeli counter-proposal to repatriation is resettlement, and Israelis insist that the Arab countries have the land and resources to make resettlement of the refugees feasible. They charge that the Arabs have delayed rehabilitation projects for refugees, and that the Arab refusal to allow work to go ahead on the project of diverting the water of the Jordan River in accordance with the Eric Johnston Plan is preventing the resettlement of 200,000 or more refugees in Jordan. Also, UNRWA has $200 million to be used for rehabilitation and resettlement projects, but only a small portion of this has been used because the Arab position is one rejecting resettlement.

Again and again Israelis, both highly placed and ordinary citizens, expressed a desire to have the refugee problem settled; they believe that it is now only being worsened. This, they are convinced, is done by Arab leaders for political reasons. They are informed enough about conditions in the camps to be convinced that the refugees are being continually inflamed against Israel. This, plus the fact that there are continuous voices of hate and even calls for the destruction of Israel, causes them to be resistant about repatriation.

Mr. Eban has pointed out, also, that if Israel is willing to give compensation to the refugees, the blockade of Israel should be broken. Quite obviously, Israel cannot give compensation and resettle the refugees at a time when the Arab nations are attempting to strangle her economically and are interfering with its commerce with other nations. There are further problems connected with this. Besides the problems of fighting, animosity, hostility; there are those of housing for the resettled Arabs, building of schools, providing doctors, as well as finding the personnel necessary for any rehabilitation program. This latter task in itself would be more stupendous than might seem to those who write lightly about this question.

Most Israelis with whom I spoke or questioned on this problem regard it as a major obstacle to peace and a settlement of the conflict. And they speak constantly of peace. The refugee problem in Israeli minds is bound up with the other issues. They see it as part of the bigger and overall question of peace.

III

On many occasions, Israeli officials have proclaimed their desire and willingness to conduct negotiations with the Arab nations. Mrs. Golda Meir made such a statement in the United Nations, following the Sinai campaign. In Jerusalem, she also stated to me the willingness of her government to negotiate with Arab leaders any time and any place.

On the question of peace, Mrs. Meir stated that Israeli officials are willing to meet and negotiate with Arab leaders at any time. Then she laid down only one condition—that the agenda for discussion not be laid down in advance. She stated that, if such negotiations were to be held, any issue could and would be discussed. But most firmly, she said that Israel would not allow the agenda to be controlled and set in advance. Later, at the United Nations, her call for peace negotiations was more unconditional than this.

In an interview I had with Prime Minister Ben-Gurion,

he said that for Israel, "the big problem is the building of the nation. This depends on us. Include also the country, the desert." This future depends on peace.

"But peace," he stated, "is the big problem."

At the time of the interview, tension along the Jordanian border was mounting. The situation vis-a-vis the Arab countries had already deteriorated recognizably.

Despite this, he said:

"I think we can get peace. I am certain of it. But peace depends on two preliminary things. So long as the Arab rulers believe that they can destroy Israel, they will not make peace!"

But:

"Israel is here to stay."

He insisted that the Arab rulers must accept this before there can be peace. Further, he believes that among the Arab people, leaders must arise whose main concern will be the welfare of their own people. He spoke of health and a rise in the standard of living.

"What is Nasser doing?" Ben-Gurion asked. "He is spending the whole wealth of Egypt for Soviet arms. You cannot educate by planes and tanks." Egypt lost much of the equipment she received by mortgaging her cotton crop. However, she is now reported to be getting a replacement of her lost equipment. Also, Mr. Ben-Gurion stressed that the health of the Arab people cannot be improved and disease cannot be eliminated by buying military equipment.

The essential need of the Arab people, of all people, he declared, is that of understanding the blessings of peace.

"Peace cannot come by compulsion. Peace is a state of mind. Here [in Israel] this state exists. A small section of the people don't have it. Our people do. One of the sure ways of bringing peace and strengthening Israel, he is convinced, is by developing the will to peace. "You cannot compel them [the Arabs], not even America can."

Despite the Israeli invasion of Egypt, Ben-Gurion and other Israeli leaders have continued to maintain the same attitude. I might add that some Israelis believed, as early as June 1956, that by September of that year Egypt would have attained arms superiority to such a degree that war could result at any time. They were not only concerned because of the border situation and the constant infiltration and raids, but also by Egypt's build-up with Soviet arms. Various foreign observers, journalists and others, believe that Israel is sometimes provocative. While not asserting that Ben-Gurion is for preventive war, they think that if the policy of the Israeli government were softer and more conciliatory, tension would be reduced. The policy of retaliation is cited in this context. Prior to the invasion of Sinai, there was a period of almost daily infiltration. Some of this was for purposes of smuggling, or for robbery. Cattle, sections of irrigation pipe and equipment and the like were stolen. Also, Arabs sometimes crossed over back and forth to see their relatives. In other cases, the infiltration was military, and Israelis were killed.

Even though we must see the refugee question as a moral and humanitarian one, it is apparent, especially in a situation as tense and dangerous as that between the Arabs and the Israelis, that moral and humanitarian problems have political consequences. A moral and humanitarian solution, separate from the political implications, is obviously illusory.

And underlying all of the questions dividing Israel and its Arab neighbors, one issue is central:

Does Israel have a right to exist?

If one answers this question positively rather than negatively, then it appears that repatriation of all the refugees is an impossibility. Not only they suffered from the war. So did the Jews. Not only was Arab property destroyed. So was Jewish property. Almost every sabra family lost a son or daughter or else has close friends who suffered such a loss. The war and the continuing conflict since the armistice agreements were signed has set back the development of Palestine. And not only Palestine, but the entire Near or Middle East needs, and needs crucially, to develop. The cost of the conflict is a burden both on the Israelis and the Arabs.

"It will take another generation and perhaps twenty years before things can get better," one intelligent Arab said to me.

I will not try predicting. But at present solution seems to be far off, perhaps farther away than it was in 1956 when I was in Israel.

"These problems will be here when your grandchildren and mine are grown up," a neutral military man observed when he and I discussed the question.

CHAPTER FOURTEEN

I

THE READER will recall that I asked refugees in the Lebanese camps how they thought the Arabs in Israel were living. Their view was that these Arabs were living badly, that they had to kill and eat donkeys, and that Arab mosques and churches had been turned into schools for the Jews. In passing, I might remark that while I was having a cup of coffee in Nazareth, I struck up a conversation with the waiter. Immediately he tried to sell me a donkey to bring back to the United States as a souvenir. He was willing to sell me various donkeys for different prices, but I could not get a clear statement as to the actual value of donkeys. Along the roads, and in Nazareth particularly, you see many donkeys. There can be no doubt but that the Arab refugees are misinformed on this as well as on many other points of Arab life in Israel. The fact that the living conditions of Israeli Arabs had been falsely presented to the Arab world was discovered by many Egyptians when, after being captured in the Sinai fighting, they were taken through Israel on tours. A visit to Arab villages and a drive through the Arab sections of Israel when you see the land under cultivation and the crops coming up, is more than sufficient to demonstrate how much the refugees have been misinformed.

With the mass exodus of Arabs from Palestine as a consequence of the war, Arab life was thrown into chaos and confusion. Among the first to leave, as I have already indicated, were most of the leaders of the Arab community. This left the Arabs in confusion and fright. Many of them could not have known what to do. The fact that they resisted the appeal of Jewish leaders to remain and that they fled is humanly more than understandable. Also, some of them had engaged in the fighting. Quite definitely, most of the Arabs must have wanted the Jews to lose, and the Israeli victory not only wounded Arab pride, but has left the Arab world itself in a state of confusion. It has not digested the facts of the Israeli victory and of the establishment and success of the Jewish State.

The war came last to Galilee and by the time it reached that area of Palestine, the Israelis were winning. In consequence, many Galilean Arabs remained; there was virtually no alternative for them.

Today, about 120,500 Arabs live in villages in Israel. 51,000 or so live in towns and about 20,000 are nomads. 102 Arab villages cover an area of 1,250,000 dunams. 550,000 dunams are under cultivation, and the remainder of these dunams is pasture land. The Land Authority of the Ministry of Agriculture has leased 80,000 to 100,000 dunams to Arab peasants, and Bedouins in the Negev cultivate about 300,000 dunams every year. The Israelis, however, have been subjected to much criticism from abroad, as well as from the Arab world, in connection with their land policy. It is claimed that many Arabs had been dispossessed. One contention is that the Arabs should have more land. The Israelis maintain that the land previously held under the title of the British Mandate Government now belongs to the State of Israel, which is the successor to that government. This question is a technical one which I cannot enter into. However, it is necessary to indicate that it exists. The charges against the Israeli government concerning its land policy towards the Israeli Arabs do not refute the fact that the majority of the Arabs in Israel are living relatively well, perhaps better than they ever did in the past. Until very recently there were at least 20,000 Arabs who were internal refugees. They had fled from their homes during the war in 1948 but did not leave the boundaries of what is now Israel. It is doubtful if many of these Arabs were better off than they had been before the war. However, this last year, the Israeli government has taken action to resettle these internal refugee Arabs.

Agricultural produce is in great demand in Israel. This has led to an increase in the volume and value of Arab production. According to the Government of Israel, the value of Arab farm produce in 1954 was 20,000,000 Israeli pounds. Arab farmers are encouraged to use chemical fertilizers and all other advances in scientific farming are available to them. Tractor stations have been set up and Arabs can get tractors on lease. Also according to Israeli Government figures, loans up to 400,000 pounds have been granted Arabs for seed and fertilizers. At least 150,000 animals are owned by Arab farmers and they can get the services of Government veterinarians to care for them. Arab fishermen can get government loans for cleaning and repairing boats. Health services are being improved and the same is true for school facilities.

Economically, the mass of Arabs in Israel then are doing well, and it is the policy of the Government to give aid and encouragement in the economic field. This of course is especially true in agriculture because of Israel's need to expand its food supply for a swelling population.

However, the Arab problem in Israel can only be a most painful one, marked by confusion, distrust, misunderstanding and suspicion. As long as the conflict with the Arab world continues, the Israelis cannot be certain of their own Arab population. Arabs can and do hear the Egyptian radio daily as well as the broadcasts from other Arab countries. Those along the borders, as I have indicated, have some contact with their relatives because it is easy to step back and forth across the borders at night. They are divided from their own kin, and they constitute a minority in a country where, once, they were a majority. They have political rights and in Arab towns their own elected officials. The Mayor of Nazareth is a Christian Arab. There are seven or eight Arabs in the Knesset, the Israeli Parliament, and the Arabs have their own political parties or else are linked up with the Jewish parties. In Acre I saw a political poster on a wall, depicting an Arab behind barbed wire. I asked what it meant, and was told that it was an election poster of the General Zionist Party, calling for an end of military government. The left wing parties also urge the end of military government.

Military Government is in operation in three districts, along the borders and around Nazareth in Galilee. The main aim of the military governors is that of controlling movement. Any Arab, seeking to leave the district, must get a pass. Passes are given when there is a purpose for travel such as business or work. For instance, a number of Nazareth Arabs work in Haifa. In cases like these, the passes are good for about a year. Those who must travel regularly for business reasons get long term passes also.

However, Arabs considered dangerous to the security of Israel do not receive passes. If Arabs are caught shielding infiltrators, they are likely to receive harsh treatment in the courts. Judging by visits to Arab villages and to

Nazareth, the policy of the Military Government sounds harsher than it is. At least, this was the way things appeared before Sinai.

In America, Israel has been criticized because it has applied military government in three districts. A number of the critics are American Jews. The position of the Israeli Government is that this constitutes a necessary security measure. Surrounded by hostile Arab states with a population far outnumbering its own, Israel is definitely in danger. The Arabs in Israel have ties of blood, language and a common cultural past with their brother Arabs across the border. Many of them cannot help but resent Jewish rule, and it is reasonably certain that they do. They remember the Arab defeat in the war. They hear, daily if they wish, anti-Israel broadcasts from the Arab countries. They see all around them the energy and enthusiasm with which the Jews are building the country. The Arabs are slower to adopt Western methods, and are quite individualistic. They do not accept ideas of cooperatives as readily as have the Jews. And with cooperative methods and the application of science, the Jews are making tremendous strides in agriculture and otherwise.

The enmity between the Jews and Arabs precedes 1948. There were clashes, shootings, and the Jews had to have watchmen to protect the workers in the fields and guard their settlements and colonies at night. Some of the Israelis blame the English for this enmity, just as many in the refugee camps blamed Britain and America for partition and for their present plight. Also, it is clear that a large number of Arabs did not take the Jews quite seriously prior to 1948. Their pride has been wounded not only by their military defeat, but also by the fact that they more or less stood by and saw the Jews reconquer the desert and turn malaria-infested swamps into fertile fields.

It is difficult to get Arabs in Israel to tell you of their real feelings. The Israelis themselves meet with and are consequently aware of these difficulties. Besides this fact, besides all other sources of enmity and exacerbation of feeling, a number of Israelis believe that there is a difference in mentality between Jews and Arabs. This, they believe, is not only along religious lines, but is at the crux of the difference between the West and the East.

I found that a number of Israelis will speak objectively or at least with sympathy of the Arabs. Either because of principle or for reasons of political expediency, some of the parties, especially left wing, defend the Arabs. I met and spoke with officials who have something to do with Arab problems, and one of them in particular mentioned the tragic dilemma in which the Arabs find themselves. In the present situation, how can they know what to do? If there is a full scale war, the Jews will be forced to take strong security measures. Should the Arabs fight and win "the third round," how would the returning and victorious Arabs treat their fellow Arabs who had not gone into exile? Will the latter be considered traitors? Will they lose their prosperity and will some of them be damned as collaborators?

The Israeli Government seeks to win at least a passive loyalty from the Arabs by encouraging their economic development, improving the facilities of health and welfare, developing and expanding the school system for Arabs, and, generally speaking, providing for them the same opportunities as it does for Jews. Progress is slow and difficult, because Jews and Arabs live separately. Except in universities, to which I shall refer later, they usually go to separate schools. They live side by side, and there is no intermarriage. In fact, in Israel there is no civil marriage. Jews are married by a rabbi, Christians by a priest or clergyman, and Muslims by their clergy according to Muslim ceremony.

It would be difficult to prove that the Arabs have not benefited materially and economically from this policy, despite any criticism which may be made of it. The economic improvement is insufficient. In passing, this situation proves that certain notions of progress and its consequences, and also ideas of Marx, may be handled by easy over-simplification but they can be refuted by reality. Material progress and economic advance do not necessarily win loyalty. A policy of internationalism and of class loyalty does not necessarily win allegiance along class and political lines; by attempting to create conditions which result in a rise in the standard of living, it does not follow that you can eliminate the causes for disaffection, especially in small countries, where disaffection lies outside its own borders. It is a safe assumption to assert that there are many dissatisfied Arabs in Israel.

Arabs are not subject to military conscription. If a young Arab volunteers for service in the Army, he might be accepted. As of a year or two ago, I believe that about forty had volunteered and were accepted. However, in Arab towns like Nazareth, you will find Arab policemen. The Arabs receive a proportionate share of the benefits of progress in Israel but are not asked to bear the burdens of responsibility.

In explaining and defending their policies in the present situation, Israelis state that they do not want to deepen the moral and emotional dilemma in which the Israeli Arabs find themselves. To conscript them would put the young Arab soldiers face-to-face with the possibility of having to shoot at their own kith and kin. It would also create new security problems for the government and the army. They also declare that it is most difficult of all to get the Arabs to grasp concepts commonly understood in the West. Here, of course, they speak principally of the Arab peasants and workmen, not of advanced and educated Arabs.

The Israelis hope that with material improvements and education, a new generation of young Arabs will emerge and that they will be the carriers of Westernism to their fellow Arabs and the leaders of the Arab community in Israel. Also, they hope that if peace eventually comes and with the establishment of peaceful and commercial relationships between Israel and the Arab countries, tension will be reduced and the Israeli Arabs will be released from the painful and seemingly hopeless contradiction in which they now find themselves.

Personal attitudes towards the Arabs vary just as do personal attitudes towards Jews, Negroes, Catholics, Italians and others in the United States. For instance, I met a newspaper man, a Sephardic Jew whose forebears had returned to Israel from Spain in the 16th century. Sitting with me in a Tel Aviv cafe, he burst out with the statement that he liked Arabs, had always had good associations with them, and missed the Arabs and his Arab friends who have gone into exile. He insisted that Arabs could be trusted and that the government should do all it could to understand the Arabs and work for peace. There was a definitely implied criticism in his remarks.

I met the heroic Yemenite officer, Captain Yeruham Cohen, whom I mentioned before.

"Nasser," he said, "is an honest man."

But, he went on, Colonel Nasser is politically inexperienced. He came to politics late and with little background for it. Captain Cohen asserted that Nasser had grown too big for his boots. He also stated that Nasser's support is not as strong as is believed, and that at the present time, the Egyptian government is the victim of the military. In July 1956, Captain Cohen shook his head and said that the only way for Nasser to stay in power was by war.

Israelis would speak of Arab friends and then mostly would remark that they varied, as do all people. But many also used the phrase, "The Arab mentality." They argued that they, the Israelis, being closer to the Arab world and having dealt with the Arabs, can understand the Arab mentality better than Western statesmen in Washington and London. A number of them also stated that one cannot rely on the word of the Arabs.

On the whole, the Israelis I spoke with did not seem afraid of the Arabs as such, but only of the superior military equipment which they were getting, thanks to the Egyptian-Czechoslovakian arms deal.

In the foregoing chapter, I have observed that one Arab stated that the Arabs did not want Israeli help, nor did they need it. However, I put to many Israelis the question—what can or might Israel do to lift the level of life in the East, provided there is peace?

Most Israelis asserted that they think Israel would have a contribution to make and that they want to make it. When I put this question to Prime Minister Ben-Gurion, he said:

"Very important," and he meant that he thinks Israel definitely can help in a major way.

"People," he went on, "may be always inclined to exaggerate their importance and ability." Perhaps he implied that the Israelis do the same when they speak of the contribution they can make in the Middle East. Nevertheless, he is positive that Israel can make a substantial contribution because of its "real experience in developing industry," and in improving the health of its people. Both of these are, he thinks, necessary for the Arabs. In addition, he thinks that Israel could become a scientific center for the Middle East.

"We can give our neighbors, when friendly, technical and scientific knowledge. We can help them develop the natural resources of their country by our experience and by sending them technicians. We wouldn't mind helping Nasser to develop his country."

Israel, he also stated, would have an important psychological contribution to make. No other Israeli stressed this point in such a context in conversations with me on the problem.

"They [the Arabs] have a complex of inferiority," and people with this psychological trait "like to boast. We can help them get out of that complex. Jews, always in the Diaspora, have such complexes. They need to apologize. They would like to show reason for their existence. Here we have got rid of that complex. We can help the Arab."

Continuing, he emphasized that the feeling of inferiority begets a false sense of superiority, and that "people ought to appear just as equals. Both complexes are a sign of abnormality."

But he also said:

"We must do things for ourselves. Our main task is to build a civilization in this country."

Mrs. Golda Meir, in speaking of this same question, stressed that Israel with its now considerable experience in handling new immigrants from North Africa and Asian countries, would have valuable knowledge in helping the refugees to be resettled, if such a solution to the refugee problem could be agreed upon.

One young newspaper man who has been on both sides and was only beginning to have experience in the problems of the Middle East, stated that a basic reason for the conflict is Arab fear of Israel's progress. He specifically mentioned Solel Boneh, which handles the industrial enterprises of Histadrut. He said that the owners of infant textile factories in the Arab world and other such enterprises were fearful that in the event of peace, Israel would prove itself industrially and economically too superior to the Arabs. This is a very important and perhaps fundamental question. Arab leaders constantly criticize Zionism and assert that because of this movement, Israel will expand. They usually do not make statements about industrial and social progress in Israel. As we have seen, the refugees are completely misinformed about the situation of Arabs in Israel. It is now quite generally recognized that in terms of health and welfare, in organizing workers, in the effort to spread out the fruits of progress, Israel has positive achievements to her credit. What is or what can be the meaning of such achievements in the Near East?

Concluding a report on a visit he paid to Israel with a delegation of C.I.O. trade unionists, Walter P. Reuther wrote warmly of Histadrut. He stated:

"We in C.I.O. share the hope . . . . of Histadrut . . . . that the day will not be far off when in every country . . . . of the Middle East . . . . the city and farm workers will build strong and free democratic trade unions. When that day comes the people will not only refuse to permit any colonialist expansion, but will also reject any demagogic attempts to lead them away from their struggle for social progress by pushing them into a mad attempt to invade and destroy the State of Israel and its democratic institutions."

And W. D. Kennedy, President of the Brotherhood of Railroad Trainmen, in a report on a visit he paid to Israel, observed in his concluding summation:

"Israel could be used as a pilot plant for trade union movements in the underdeveloped countries . . . . Israel and Histadrut have much to contribute . . . . which will greatly strengthen the free world against the forces which threaten it."

An Arab parliamentarian in Beirut stated to me when I interviewed him that "our socio-economic and political structures in the Middle East are not, in themselves, very democratic. Our people, in most of the Asian countries, struggled against governments that have been the tools of ruling classes which the democratic powers have supported."

He also said:

"But the Western powers do not look upon us as human beings possessing human rights, possessing will, having intelligence, and also being entitled to the same dignity with a decent standard of living as Western man is entitled to."

I have already asserted my view that Israel has made strides to approach giving the Arabs in Israel something of what they, and a great many of us in the West, feel and believe that the Arab is entitled to—dignity and a decent standard of living. But the problem is complex and dangerous. And whatever final conclusions we do reach on these explosive questions, we cannot honestly avoid recognizing that the social question here is of primary importance. It has been mostly ignored in Arab polemics and by many Americans when they consider the Middle East and the Arab-Israeli question; they do not see and think of this social question with sufficient clarity—in particular, they do not think of the overwhelming importance of trade unions in the Middle East and of the necessity of developing strong trade unions there. With the United States backing Arab monarchs our Government apparently does not seem to have given much attention to this problem. As a result, the possible role which Histadrut can play in any Middle East settlement or developmental plan is largely ignored. This is a grievous omission. We cannot think of Israel without thinking of Histadrut, and we cannot think of a Middle Eastern settlement without thinking of the role which Histadrut can play.

II

Most of the Israeli Arabs live in villages and a large proportion of them own and work their small plots. But there are Arab workers. And Histadrut has an Arab Department, and is organizing it. Seeking information and a statement of Histadrut policy towards the Arab workers, I interviewed Mr. Eliyahu Agassi, one of the officials in this department. He is an Iraqi-born Jew, slender and balding. His mind is precise, he has a clear and extensive knowledge of working conditions in the Arab world, and he made an effort to give accurate and well-phrased answers to my questions.

The Arab Department handles all the trade union and working problems of about 16,000 Arab wage-earners who have been taken into Histadrut. When I was in Israel, the number was almost 11,000. They receive all of the benefits of any Histadrut worker, and can vote for local officers but not for national officers of the Executive Board. I questioned another Histadrut official on this point, and his explanation was that Histadrut must develop the Arab workers to the point where they can assume full responsibility. One need in the fulfillment of this task is that of training and bringing along new Arab trade unionists who will become the leaders, the conveyor belts of trade union consciousness to their fellow Arabs. Israelis who are not officially deeply involved in Histadrut activities and policy-making criticized this explanation. Here, let me stress, we have another fundamental question concerning the under-developed countries and people who live in backward conditions: how much responsibility are they to be given? And in Israel this is all a facet of the security problem. Histadrut policies towards the Arabs will be bound up in this security problem as long as the Arab-Israeli conflict continues.[1]

Of the Arabs in Histadrut, about 3,000 own land but their plots do not exceed 25 dunams. They also hire out as agricultural workers to other Arab landowners, and thus receive wages. This makes them eligible for admission to Histadrut. Arabs who own more than 25 dunams of land are not eligible to became members of Histadrut, but they may become members of cooperative societies. In total, there are about 18,000 Arab wage-earners in Israel.

Before the establishment of the State of Israel, that is, during the period of the British Mandate, Histadrut attempted to help the Arab workers to organize themselves in unions which would have some degree of autonomy from Histadrut. This policy was considered to be wiser and more advisable because of racial and political considerations. In the beginning (Histadrut was founded in

---

[1] According to both American newspapers and the *Jerusalem Post,* a Communist-led riot took place in Nazareth on May Day, May 1st, 1958. As a result of this, Mapai leaders in Histadrut proposed the expulsion of Communists from the Executive of Histadrut, but not from Histadrut itself. The Communists are likely to be a continuously disturbing influence among Israeli Arabs. And recently, the Communist line seems to have changed. They now seem to be demanding a separate Arab state in Galilee.

1920) there had been efforts to bring Arab and Jewish workers together in one union: Arab leaders strongly opposed this. Arab workers were incited against cooperation; hence the decision to try and help establish separate unions. Also, Mr. Agassi said that Arab capitalists and Arab leaders, in an effort to thwart organization, formed "yellow unions," a parallel or virtual equivalent to the company union. He said that as a result of this, Arab workers were confused. Trade union issues and problems were mixed up with politics and political antagonisms. He also said that this confusion has not been dispelled to the present day. Histadrut must cope with this in everything it does to raise wage levels and win improvements in working conditions for Arab wage-earners.

Membership in the autonomous Arab unions was never high, but Mr. Agassi stressed that they were, nevertheless, more effective than their actual members might have suggested. These unions were originally named the Palestine Labor League, and later the Israel Labor League. Finally, it was decided that the Arabs should join Histadrut, although in some Arab villages there are still branches of the older organization which functions in social and cultural activities. Since the State of Israel was founded, Arab workers are receiving higher wages and better protection than they used to.

In the National Union of Teachers there are about 14,000 Jews and 700 Arabs. During the Mandatory period, there were many Arab teachers in government schools, but, said Mr. Agassi, they were unorganized. Jewish teachers in Jewish schools were, to the contrary, organized. They received better salaries than did the Arab teachers.

Following the proclamation of the State of Israel, most of the Arab teachers left Palestine. The new government faced a serious problem in finding teachers with qualifications for the Arab schools. Many Jews from Iraq had to be used because they could speak Arabic. This shortage of qualified Arab teachers has not yet been fully overcome.

The Ministry of Education does not train teachers for secondary schools, but it does aid in the establishment of seminars for teacher training. Arabs as well as Jews are helped in this way.

Also, with the establishment of the State, salary differentials between Jewish and Arab teachers were eliminated. In addition, intimidation concerning organizing any union was ended. Since 1948, teachers' salaries have, according to Histadrut, been increased by about 200%. Even though there has been inflation, this figure would suggest a rise in the real salary. Arab citrus pickers used to earn about 100 pounds for a season which lasted from four to five months. When I was in Israel, they were earning between 650 to 750 pounds a season. Previously the Jaffa dock workers earned about one pound a day for nine hours work. This rose at least to $6\frac{1}{2}$ to $8\frac{1}{2}$ pounds for an eight-hour day of work. In addition, they get what we now call fringe benefits.

Mr. Agassi stated that in representing Arab workers, Histadrut meets with greater difficulties from Arab than from Jewish employers. This is most notably so in the instance of agricultural workers because of the prevalence of clan spirit and clan feelings. Even though Jewish employers frequently oppose Histadrut, they understand it better than Arabs. Hence, Histadrut usually finds it easier to reach agreements with Jewish employers.

He gave an instance of how Histadrut defends Arab workers. Early in 1956, about 400 Arab workers were locked out by the Arab owner of a quarry in Nazareth. The point of dispute involved social or fringe benefits;

the quarry owner resisted paying his share of the cost of these benefits. Pressed by Histadrut to do so, the owner locked his workers out. But during the lockout he failed in an effort to employ "blacklegs" or scabs. Histadrut finally managed to get the issue settled and the owner agreed to pay his contribution.

But wages at this particular quarry were sub-standard. The workers were earning 4½ pounds a day, and the general rate in Israel was between 5 and 6 pounds. The level of wages in Arab areas is another problem Histadrut must take into account in representing Arab workers and in its dealing with Arab employers.

But the Arab problem in the ranks of the workers is similar to the Arab problem elsewhere. Suspicion keeps rising or ebbing with the oscillations in the general political situation. To some degree at least his suspicion fluctuates according to the headlines and the radio broadcasts. Histadrut's policies are not likely to cause any significant change in this situation, at least for some time. Histadrut leaders believe that trade union concepts have not as yet been fully or even adequately grasped and assimilated by a sufficient mass of the Arabs. Along with the deeper assimilation of trade union concepts there is a need for some development of international consciousness. During the Mandatory period there was, apparently, no international consciousness felt by most Arab workers. A simpler fact to mention is that Arab workers have not yet come around to an acceptance of the idea of paying dues; they resist doing so. Histadrut's task of organizing the Arab workers is obviously difficult. These are the problems it faces.

But despite these, and despite the complicating and negative factors in the situation, Histadrut is known throughout the Arab world, and, were peace to prevail, its influence would be felt positively and even widely. Prior to the present period, many workers' groups in Lebanon, Egypt and Iraq sought the aid and advice of Histadrut in matters of organization. As late as 1946, Histadrut received a letter from workers in Amman, the capital of Jordan, in which there was a request for guidance in organizing. This was politically naive and Mr. Agassi stated that Arab authorities quickly put an end to such naiveté. But clearly, Histadrut stands as an example of trade unionism for workers of the Middle East. It has acquired a most valuable fund of experience which can be drawn upon if peace and stability in this area ever are attained. The existence of Histadrut is a factor which must be assessed and estimated in coming to conclusions about the Middle East.

III

A vast majority of Israelis place great faith in education and many of them hope that through education the problems relating to the Arab minority will be at least partially eased. They count on and hope that a new generation of Arab youth will emerge, Westernized and imbued with modern and progressive ideas.

As I have already noted, the founding of the State, the war and the mass exodus of Arabs had a demoralizing effect on the Arabs in Israel and on the education of Arab children. The absence of teachers constitutes a serious problem. For a period, teachers lacking in sufficient education and pedagogical qualifications had to be hired. The process of weeding out some of these and of training more competent teachers continues but the situation is admittedly unsatisfactory.

In Arab villages bordering on the Triangle, I spoke with Arab teachers both at Tayibeh and Tira. The Arabs are noted for their hospitality and, invariably, they invite you into their homes, offer you coffee, sweets, water and cigarettes. One of the teachers, a youngish looking man, invited me to his home. He had already had fifteen years experience in education. Several of his friends were with him. We sat around talking and smoking. An official who speaks Arabic was with me and acted as translator.

I asked my host what was the difference in teaching at the present time as compared with the past when he, himself, was a school boy. He admitted that it was different. Then, the pupil had no freedom and the teacher would strike and hit the pupil with a stick. The child then went to school at eight but now he starts at seven. And in his boyhood, no girls went to school. Now the girls also go, but there are problems here concerning the girls I shall touch on presently. New subjects are taught, among them Hebrew and music. Hebrew is a compulsory subject and is taught to Arab children as a second language. This teacher also spoke of history, and said that it is taught better now than it was in his day. Then, he said, ancient history was the main subject and nothing of the history of Palestine was given to pupils. Now they learn much about the history of Palestine. Also games are part of the educational system and he thinks that that is good.

On the same day and in a nearby village, I also spoke with three Arab women, all of whom were progressive. One of the three was a young teacher. Her observations and conclusions were similar to those of the man. Concerning present methods as contrasted with earlier ones, those of today are better. Children do not only learn from books. They see, they do, they learn. This was the way she put it. The fact is that both of these Arab teachers hold what we call progressive ideas and one of them recognized the name of John Dewey and knew that he had been a great educator.

I asked the Arab teacher did he think that the quality of teaching and of education in Arab schools was as good as that in Jewish ones? This, he answered, depended on the teacher. The question of a shortage of Arab teachers came up. I have already mentioned this. Personally, he hoped to see better Arab teachers developing in the future.

Good work is necessary, he said, and part of this depends on the effort of the children. But also he thinks that discipline in the Arab schools is much better than in the Jewish schools. He mentioned fear as a factor in education. In his day, he said, the child had greater fear both of parents and of teachers. Then, if the teacher beat a boy, it was likely that the father would administer a second beating as added punishment.

Boys, he said, were stronger in studies than girls. But the Arab women were not sure of this. The Arab young woman teacher saw no difference between them, and insisted that it always depended on the individual pupil.

But among the Arabs, and especially in the villages, there is opposition to the education of girls. When the girl reaches the age of ten, the parents want to keep her home because she has reached what they consider a dangerous age for girls and also because she is needed in the home to do work and to act as a baby-keeper and sitter. The Arab families are usually big. Among the poorer people, the women work, doing hard labor in the fields. Girls are needed to help take care of the home and the younger children. Thus, one finds in the villages that the attendance of girls at schools declines from the age of ten on, even though there is a law making education compulsory for primary grades. This law is not easily enforced in the villages. The Arab teacher told me that about fifty per cent of the parents in his area would oppose education of girls. And even when the girls do attend school they are often under pressure from home. However, he said that there is less opposition concerning the education of boys; they are wanted in the fields for work at harvest time and on special occasions. We have already noted that these attitudes correspond with those of the newer immigrants.

What he told me was only part of the story, of course. But it is clear that there are contradictory and conflicting elements in this situation. Thus, the teachers all told me that now more is known about the children and their home life than was the case in the past. And the Arab man spoke of fathers wanting to have their sons educated, and taking an interest in the progress their boys make in school. Further, he said that now if a boy is hit, the father will even come to the school and protest. Also the children speak of their parents, of conditions at home. But at one point, the teacher broke out with the statement that the new generation is being spoiled.

This conversation with the Arab teacher took place in a border village of about 150 families. The average plots owned by the Arabs run about 10 dunams, although some own larger plots. There was no electricity in the village. The sun burned down almost mercilessly on the stone huts and houses. The streets were unpaved, stony and bumpy. Clearly, it was not a rich village. Entering it, looking at barefoot Arab children, watching a little girl in a dirty dress taking care of a toddler, passing an Arab here or there, you think of how near the frontier is, how close you are to danger. You feel not only the strangeness of primitive and backward people, but also an added strangeness of modern political conflict which distorts the life of this village.

To continue, the Arab man answered more of my questions. In their local school, they suffer from a lack of facilities. Since it is an agricultural community, agriculture is also taught. And they want to teach carpentry, but must wait because at present facilities for this are lacking. In addition, he spoke of the shortage of books in Arabic. This complaint I heard elsewhere. Israel is a poor country. In poor countries, much that we, with our wealth and productivity take for granted, is the source of problems and difficulties. The textbook problem is but one of the minor but harassing difficulties in countries whose economy is poor.

The problem of education shades into many other problems. A number of these can be classified under the heading of West versus East, Westernism and Levantinism. The new awakening in Asia is a product of the impact of the West upon the East. Even the sources of ideas underlying this awakening are Western. But what we mean by Westernism here is complicated and involved. We should not see it in an over-simplified manner. Slowly, gradually changes are taking place in the patterns of feeling and in the mentality of people. Education is one of the means, one of the major instruments of change in this process. And concerning the Arab minority as well as the new Oriental immigrants, the Israelis hope that education will serve effectively to help them ease and solve this problem of transformation.

There are signs of stir and change among the Arabs of Israel just as there are in the Arab world and in all of Asia. Change is welcomed as well as resisted. These thoughts ran through my mind frequently when I was in Asia; they did when I visited Arab villages. When we came to

Tayibeh, a prosperous or relatively prosperous Arab town, electricity was being introduced. The mosque was being repaired and re-done, with aid from the government. We visited the home of an advanced and progressive Arab family. The husband, a local leader, was away but I spoke with his wife and two daughters, one of them the teacher whom I have mentioned.

Besides education, other subjects came up in the discussion. We spoke of Arab women and how they feel. Shortly before the time of my visit there had been a suicide attempt by an Arab girl which had received wide publicity in Israel. This girl's father had demanded that she marry the man he had selected for her, and in protest against the father's insistence, she had taken a poison and almost killed herself. I was told that Arab girls can now, at least occasionally, refuse to marry the man whom their father selected as a husband; they cannot, generally speaking, select their own mate. There is a beginning of Westernization among the women. They want the change and liberation. This is as true of the Arab women as it is of the new Oriental Jewish immigrant women. It is even possible that this will play an important role in future developments of the Arab-Israel conflict. New methods of education, the effort to educate girls and women, and progress towards the liberation of women are likely to rouse resistance on the part of many Arab men. I have already noted that it has raised resistance among Oriental immigrant men.

It is a commonplace to stress and insist that Arabs are human beings. But just as we often object to foreigners seeing Americans *en bloc* or monolithically, so must we keep our guard up so that we do not do the same thing about others. We must be careful not to see all Arabs *en masse* and to deduce from this an Arab mentality which we apply to every individual Arab. We should remember that this is not merely a mass, but a large number of human beings who are living out their life span in a world tormented with problems and confusions. The pace of change is gradually being accelerated in the Near East. Change for the Arabs, and most especially for the Arabs who live in Israel, has come rapidly, decisively. It has forced upon them many adjustments. They have much to assimilate, much to comprehend. And in the face of this, they have all the entanglements of their personal and individual lives. They live in an undecided world. Much that has happened seems to be or can seem temporary.

Both the social and physical landscape is being altered, and with this there is an alteration in the inner landscape of the feelings and emotions. Much of this is invisible, but we do catch glimpses of it.

Health is a big concern of the Israelis, and they are proud of all their achievements in this field. It is the policy of the government and also of Histadrut, to expand health services and facilities for all of the people. This includes the Arabs in Israel. In the romantic conception of exotic peoples, formed from movies, novels, fancy and ignorance, the matter of health rarely enters the picture. The Bedouins are romantic in this sense, and highly picturesque. Their cloak and head-cloth, their freedom to roam the desert, make them into romantic images against the sky of a fading day. But health was and is a problem among the Bedouins. This is not solely the consequence of poverty. Their dietary customs are responsible for digestive illness such as pellagra. Also, the conditions of childbirth and child care have been such as to raise the level of infant mortality.

In order to deal with these problems, health clinics and dispensaries have been established, and mobile X-ray units have gone into the Negev. I visited a new dispensary but recently opened near the Triangle frontier. It was clean and well equipped. Most of those working in it were Arabs, although the doctor is Jewish. Besides outpatient service, there were rooms for emergency cases and also for child deliveries. The first two Arab women to deliver children in the dispensary were still there as patients. One, a young girl, was deeply depressed. Her child, a first born, had been a girl not a boy. Sitting in bed, she was sad and uncommunicative, and her face reflected her dispiritedness. It was as though she felt that she was a failure in life. Beside her was a gay and happy Arab wife who had given birth to her sixth child. She had boys.

With an Arab interpreter I attempted to talk with the two Arab women; they resented my questions and wanted me out of the ward. In fact, they asked me to get out. The doctor and nurses spoke of them and of pregnant Arab women. At first, there was resistance to the idea of Arab women not delivering their babies at home, and even more, the Arab husbands were adamant in their opposition to the idea that a male physician attend the delivery. They wanted a midwife from the locality, and only when this was agreed to, did the husbands consent to allowing their wives to deliver at the dispensary rather than at home. The doctor immediately agreed. Besides the local midwife, however, he also had in attendance a trained midwife. He used this as an opportunity to try and educate the local midwife in hygiene and more advanced medical procedures.

When I asked the doctor about the Arabs, their psychology and attitudes, he answered that he knew little of these matters, and that he was new in the vicinity. He insisted that his interest and concern were health, health services and preventive medicine. He was a doctor and would only talk of his own professional work. He was more than hopeful that progress would be made in medical fields. Perhaps in time statistics will provide a more concrete picture of the health question concerning the Arabs. Infant mortality among the Arab population in Israel was 66.7 per thousand in 1952; among the Jews it was 38.7. By 1954, the figure had changed to 61.2 among the Arabs. A United Nations statistic on infant mortality in Egypt for 1947 gave the figure 208.4 per thousand.

The dispensary in Tira which I have mentioned here was built in one year. Plans were afoot to use it for community purposes and to show motion pictures on its roof. The need for community centers in the rural areas is obviously great and important. Karl Marx coined the phrase, "the idiocy of rural life." There can be more than idiocy to rural life in poor, under-industrialized countries. Besides isolation and limitedness of perspective, there is disease, poor health, and a lack of hygiene. One might say that the peculiar and fascinating developments in the rural areas of Israel can be interpreted as a conscious and rational effort to end this "idiocy of rural life." And the Arabs are not being neglected in this matter.

I might add here a few odd impressions and bits of information. Arab youths and others often cross over to the other side, that is, to the Arab countries. Undoubtedly anti-Israel feelings motivate some of the Arabs who take this course of action. In the light of the present situation, this is a serious offense in Israel. But in the Arab villages I learned that sometimes there are also other motivations. I was told of the cases of three Arab boys who had gone over because of family reasons. They were mad at their fathers or sisters. Arab boys, in family conflict, can easily run across the frontier to an uncle in Lebanon or a relative in Syria. Family and clan feelings are central with the Arabs. With progress and Westernization proceeding as rapidly as the economy and defense needs of Israel permit, there is likely to be an increase in family tensions among the Arabs in Israel. These can and undoubtedly will become involved in political attitudes and possibly, they will even find use in political exchanges, arguments and propaganda. The education of girls, the desires which Arab girls may and are likely to have for more liberation, conflicts over marriage and the selection of a mate, the new ideas and attitudes which both boys and girls will learn in school, all of these are possible sources of personal and family conflict. For a period they may even exacerbate the Arab-Israeli conflict. I have already observed that something parallel has happened among the Oriental Jewish immigrants in Israel. We can also find parallels to this in our own social history; we have had our conflicts between generations, particularly in immigrant families.

What will safer and more hygienic deliveries in dispensaries or hospitals come to mean for Arab women? What will improved hygienic methods and an expanding practice of preventive medicine mean? On the other side of the ledger, progress and advance produce dislocation. The crusts and layers of custom are being broken. This is a problem which extends through the entire underdeveloped world. Despite the fact of intense conflicts and hatreds in the Arab-Israeli situation, we must not fail to recognize that some of the happenings there are only a part of the general process of our changing technological age.

It has often been asserted that the Arab world is a fertile planting ground for Communism and that sympathy for Communism is growing. In fact, this has even been used as a virtual political blackmail to gain acceptance of Arab demands. Among the Arabs in Israel, I was told, there is sympathy for Communism, and the Communists do work among them.

I have already quoted what was said to me concerning the Soviet Union, Britain and America in the two refugee camps I visited. In an Arab village, I asked such questions as—"What do you think of Russia?" "What do you think America is like?"

An Arab teacher said that Russia is a place where there is Communist power. "Land and jobs are distributed. It is socialist. Everybody is happy, no rich, no poor. Many wouldn't believe this."

And America?

"It is the richest country in the world. It knows how to play the game of politics."

Had he met many Americans or Russians? Yes for Americans, but no concerning the Russians.

A few odd complaints were expressed to me. I was told by one Arab that he would like to see Arabic films, and that he did not like or enjoy Western music which can be heard over the radio. In Tira, they want electricity, but had not raised enough money for its installation. They hoped to. Also there is some progressive thought about finding means for the material improvement of the community. During the days of the British Mandate, there were three tractors in the area: in 1956, there were twenty. Today, prices are higher and so is productivity. Some of the Arabs lost land because of partition and war. They could not get the land back, but only compensation. Marketing is organized on an individualistic basis, in contradistinction to most of the marketing done by Jews. In some other areas, the Arabs market collectively. A merchant goes to the villages and fields, buys the produce and moves it away. But in answer to my question about economic improvement or the lack of it since the establishment of the State of Israel, the answer was a "Yes," there was improvement.

CHAPTER FIFTEEN

I

ACRE (Acco in Hebrew) is one of the oldest cities in the world. To visit it as a tourist is one of the most rewarding experiences one can have on a trip to Israel. I shall not treat the history of Acre here because I have not studied it sufficiently to say anything which is not already familiar. In this book, I do not wish to paraphrase the guide books or do a hasty job of quick reading and then give a summary of overnight homework. But a few facts are relevant. Acre was a Crusader's town. In 1799, Napoleon Bonaparte invaded Palestine and invested the city. There is a mound or hill near the city where the French guns were mounted. But Napoleon failed. At one time, Acre was a more prosperous city than it is today, and was a major outlet for produce from the Palestinian hinterland. The camel caravans came to it in profusion. Its history goes back to Roman and Biblical times. Its buildings are among the most picturesque in Israel. During the Mandatory period, Haifa was made the administrative headquarters of the district and Acre declined in commercial importance. It was captured by Jewish forces during the War of 1948. Its population of something like 16,900 is largely composed of newcomers, although a small percentage of Arabs, both Muslim and Christian, remained. In the main, they live in the old town, where there are so many picturesque sights, including a citadel which juts into the Mediterranean, and a beautiful mosque. The mosque was being repaired when I visited Acre.

I visited Acre with a group of four including a young Arab who teaches Hebrew in a private school. It was during the time of a Muslim festival commemorating the journey to Mecca. Arriving at the end of the day, we first visited a new naval school for young Jewish boys. This visit once again impressed into my mind the conflict which so maims the life of Israel and the Middle East.

We visited this naval school because one of our group, a Jewish woman, was so proud of it and hoped that her own son would quickly become a student there. Missing the commander, we were shown around the various rooms, the dormitories where the boys sleep, the library and reading rooms. As we were leaving the school, a group of fifteen or sixteen year old boys was returning from an expedition or drill outside of the school grounds. Marching in formation, with rifles over their shoulders and knapsacks and field equipment on their backs, they were singing lustily and like healthy boys. Then they broke ranks and passed us. Their faces were dirty from sand and dust. They were blond and dark, and the down was on their faces. And the rifles, which they had used for drilling, seemed to be so much a part of their lives. I had already been in Israel long enough so that the surprise of seeing many with rifles or revolvers had worn off. Yet I looked at these boys carrying rifles and then at the young Arab with us.

What were his thoughts? His branch of the family was the only one which had not left in the mass exodus of

Arabs from Haifa. He said that he and other members of his family were out of contact with their relatives who were now on the other side. Beyond the gates of the school, the street was full of Arabs who were celebrating the three-day festival. Children were laughing and eating ice cream. The Arab women were congregated together talking, holding their babies, watching their children. Yes, I kept thinking, what was in this young Arab's mind?

He was educated, intelligent and most obliging. His grasp of languages was excellent. He spoke good English, and his command of Hebrew is such that he teaches the language. He answered questions about himself, his work and his family. He made no political statements. But now and then, I sensed an undercurrent of dissatisfaction, even of bitterness. He had spoken of teaching. Though Muslim, he teaches in a private Christian school. He was not satisfied with his salary, and stated that he was not allowed to become a member of Histadrut, although he did say that he had been a member of the Palestinian Labor League. On this point, I could not get clear answers. The Arab teacher in the Triangle area had confirmed that he and other Arab teachers were members of Histadrut. But more significantly, this young Arab spoke of a lack of prospects for the future among Arabs. This was perhaps his main complaint.

When we left the school, dirty-faced little Arab girls of three and four in soiled dresses and bare feet stood holding out their hands, and saying:

"Shalom, shalom."

I could not be sure whether this was in simple play or mimicry. We walked by the celebrating crowds, visited sites, the mosque, and a smaller mosque of a dissident Muslim sect. Then we paid a visit to the Cadi of Acre to congratulate him on the success of the Festival.

In most Arab homes there is one room set aside to receive guests. The room in the Cadi's home was richly furnished with a table in the center and upholstered chairs around the walls. The Cadi, Egyptian born, is tall, gray-bearded and carries himself with dignity. I was told that he was over sixty, but he appeared young and vigorous for his age, and during the course of a talk lasting at least an hour, two young children entered the room and shook hands with us and with other guests. A girl of about five passed a plate of sweets. A boy of about seven shook hands politely with every one and the Cadi held him for a moment with affectionate pride. They were his children.

He sat in a big chair at the opposite end of the rectangular room from me. He was dressed in Arab costume. He spoke Arabic. He does not speak English. The Arab school teacher translated, saying that the Cadi was pleased to receive us and he was also ready to answer any question I would ask.

Having already visited Arab villages in the Triangle and talked of education with teachers, I raised the question of co-education and asked for the Cadi's opinion.

Co-education, he said, represents a current that nobody can stop.

"It's good to educate the other half of the man," the Arab teacher translated the Cadi's remark; he meant that woman is the other half of man.

Girls should go to elementary schools, but after that, it is not important to educate them. Up to the age of ten, it is proper for the boys and girls to be educated together. The girls "are still innocent."

At that time the first Arab girl had already entered the Hebrew University in Jerusalem and she was reported to be a fine student. I cited this case and asked his opinion. The Cadi did not oppose that either, and would allow girls of 18, 19 or 20 and of high mentaltiy to sit with boys. For by then they could judge the good and the bad. But time is also required and it is necessary to prepare or educate girls so that they will accept education in the next generation. He thought also that Jewish girls in the villages would be against education, and further, he said that a budget does not exist for expanding the schools.

Next, I asked if changes in education since the establishment of the State of Israel were better or worse than educational conditions and circumstances in the Mandatory period.

Without hesitation, he declared that they were worse.

At this point his daughter, with a ribbon in her hair, appeared and silently served sweets. The Cadi leaned forward and spoke, gesturing gracefully, sometimes raising a finger in an expository gesture and then bringing his hand down in a movement of confidence and emphasis. I listened to his easy flow of Arabic and waited for the translation.

Why is it worse now?

There is "a kind of liberty for the pupils not liked by the parents." When Palestine was under Turkish rule and also in the period of the Mandate, there was punishment, severe punishment. This helped to educate the boys and made good citizens out of them.

But "now, the pupil's behavior is not good at all. The boy is spoiled."

The boys are, the translator continued, not receiving enough education from the teacher, and they feel stronger than the teacher. They "feel free."

I asked about the parents. The Cadi answered that they "can't have anything to say."

Then I asked for more comment on punishment.

"In punishment, there is hope."

And he repeated:

"The education does not help the boy to become a good citizen." It produces guilty feelings and "the boy does not see a future in the school."

Then he went on to state that the pressures and conditions in Israel are different from what they were in the past. He spoke of good food, good water, music and of more people reading newspapers.

But:

"If we have a good education, a severe education, the boy will respect the teacher, the director of the school."

Other Acre Arabs arrived to pay their respects to the Cadi. They wore Western dress and greeted and congratulated the Cadi with signal respect. This he accepted with simplicity, but accepting it as his due. One of the visitors, a gray-haired man, spoke English. He was a member of the Acre Chamber of Commerce and Rotary Club. The visitors joined in our conversation. The talk was in Arabic and English, but occasionally, the Arab teacher spoke in Hebrew to the two Jewish women who were with us.

I asked if the Cadi would clarify what he meant by "a good citizen."

"The pupil who will be a studious boy, an educated boy, will not get a good future." He cannot get a good job. "He feels from the beginning to have a trade. This situation begins in childhood and as an apprentice, the boy or young man does not get a good enough salary." This was not a clear answer, but I am putting down precisely what was translated to me. After this, the conversation became more general and dealt with conditions in Acre. One of the Arabs said that fifty-two languages were spoken in the town, and another stated that they wanted an improvement of business and economic conditions. Business had all gone to Haifa. Acre, they said nostalgically, had once been the center of the district. But with commerce shifting to Haifa, they had empty stores. At one time, 2,000 camels' loads had come to Acre. But this is no more. And they seemed to believe that this was a result of recent years, since the state was founded. Actually, the commercial decline of Acre began under the Mandate.

Concerning the population, I was told that there are Persians, Arabs and Jews in Acre. But many Arabs left and the Arab visitors at the Cadi's home spoke of the present population. Many of them are Ghawarneh, dark-skinned as are the Sudanese. The Arabs looked down on them and one said they are "like serfs."

And then there was more discussion of education.

Some feeling was expressed against co-education. Education should be based on their "own old belief."

"Two sexes should not mix," said the gray-haired Arab who spoke English. Then, because he was possibly sensitive about his remark and the interpretation I might make of it, he leaned towards me and slowly enunciated: "We Arabs are fastidious about our ladies." He meant that they are concerned about preserving the virtue and the role which the woman now plays in Arab life.

The conversation had reached the point where the Arabs were willing to express more of their dissatisfaction.

The teacher, as well as others present, strongly asserted that the opportunities for Arab students were utterly insufficient. He declared that there was a 1% to 5% opportunity for Arab children. Citing the number of Arabs in Israel, he stated, and with discontent in his voice, that there are only 67 Arab students in the Hebrew University. (This was in July 1956.) Out of 204 who had wanted to matriculate, he said, only 4 had been successful.

"It is a lottery," he said.

Here the two Jewish women intervened to point out that students are not accepted for the Hebrew University by any form of lottery but rather on the basis of competitive examinations. These are stiff and many Jewish students also fail to pass.

"If they (meaning matriculation candidates) can't pass the examinations, no one can help them," one of the Jewish women said.

"We don't have enough textbooks," the Arab teacher declared.

Then there were further statements about the Ghawarneh, and their alleged inferiority. The Cadi cut in to state that there is not much opportunity for Arab boys to become lawyers.

"The best an Arab boy gets to be is a policeman."

The teacher turned the subject to textbooks. In government schools, there are old books. New books are needed. This was agreed upon as fact, but the Jewish women stated that the same problem existed concerning Hebrew books. Under present conditions, enough new books cannot be printed. I asked what the situation was in non-governmental or private books. The teacher answered that the books were old.

The Cadi then stated that the low number of Arab students at the Hebrew University involved a question of language. Examinations for the University are in Hebrew. The Cadi said that boys, especially from the villages, don't master Hebrew. One of the Jewish women remarked to the Arab teacher that he spoke excellent Hebrew, and that now Hebrew is taught Arabs as a second language. Also many of the Jewish immigrants must learn Hebrew and that they face this same linguistic problem. A number of them are from Arabic countries and they grew up learning Arabic as their natural or native tongue. The

Cadi remained in disagreement. He said Arab boys do not speak Hebrew at home or where they play.

"I have seen Iraqi boys. They come and speak to me Hebrew," he said.

"Why don't the Arab boys speak Hebrew?" one of the Jewish women asked.

"The mother speaks Arabic, the boys speak Hebrew," the Cadi said.

The discussion ended amicably but with no resolution of the problems raised.

The next day I visited the Technion at Haifa. Here, technical and mechanical training is received. Experiments are carried on and students learn both simple mechanical processes and scientific technique. One of the first questions I asked was how many Arabs were in the school. The number was then twenty-one. But everything possible was being done to increase the number of Arabs. Admission is through competitive examinations. In the last two years, there were 1,000 applicants, and of this number 300 were admitted. The examination papers are arranged in alphabetical lists at the Technion and also at the Hebrew University. I learned nothing to convince me that discrimination was practiced. The situation, in part at least, flows out of the problems of Israel, the economy of the country, and the fact that it is still not rich enough to provide more textbooks or to give more aid to students of secondary schools and the University. For instance, I spoke with a doctor in Jerusalem where medical students are trained and educated. They only have the facilities to handle sixty new students a year, he said.

Worthy students do get help, but the relative lack of facilities means that the situation is far, far different from what it is in a rich country like America.

What do Israelis say and think concerning the problem of the Arab minority as this concerns education? I questioned a number of Israelis and here summarize their views.

This, as all other problems concerning the Arab minority, requires time for a solution. Every problem of this kind was worsened by the war and the mass exodus, and it is daily distorted because of the Arab-Israeli conflict, the absence of peace and of peaceful relationships with Israel's neighbors. The Arab community was demoralized with the flight and departure of the Arabs. Most of the leaders of the Arab community left. New ones had to be developed.

Concerning language, Hebrew is the language cementing the Jews in their homeland. Arabic, as has been indicated, is taught in the Arab schools. In time, the Arabs will learn Hebrew and with the new generation the language question concerning examinations will not be so difficult. At the moment, Israel does not have the funds and there would not be enough students to establish a separate Arab university. Improvements can be made in this matter in present institutions. These will be done as rapidly as possible. Also, if there were peace, everything would be different.

And further, the educational situation as well as that of health and welfare is related to the economic conditions in the country. The two big drains on Israel's economy are the costs of security and of the new immigration.

Thinking of these problems and talking to various people I would put the question—is the Arab minority problem insoluble? Many of the answers to this question were uncertain. But to repeat, its solution depends on peace. This was one of the most common remarks which I heard.

II

After we left the Cadi's home we walked through the old city of Acre. Lights were dim. Some of the narrow and very ancient streets were deserted, dark except for occasional lamps and lighted windows. From an open window, I heard an Arab girl singing. I passed a coffee house. The Egyptian radio was on inside. I asked what was being said, and the Arab teacher told me that the broadcast dealt with news of the Muslim festival in Egypt. We went to a restaurant on the shores of the Mediterranean. You could see the lights of Haifa across the water like many jewels, just as you can see the lights of Acre from Mount Carmel on a clear night. The waves gently hit the shore with fascinating monotony. Near our table, two young Arabs sat having soft drinks with Jewish girls. One of the Arabs spoke in English about going out again with the girl. I thought of this and we spoke of how Arab girls are guarded. Jewish girls of Western origin are more emancipated, more like American women. This fact in itself bears on the Arab problem. Also there were a few remarks on education. The Arab teacher said he has to punish the boys at his school. He defended this practice.

We ate Arab food and sat listening to the waters, then drove back to Haifa.

III

There are 17,000 to 18,000 Druses in Israel. They are classified as Arabs, but have been traditionally hostile to Muslims. They trace their religion back to the father-in-law of Moses, the Prophet Jethro. Recently, they were given full rights in Israel. The Druses live mostly in villages, although there are some in Haifa. Under the Mandate, they did not possess separate status as a religious community but were considered Arabs. With the establishment of the State of Israel, they were granted a separate status as a religious community. During the War of 1948 the Druses sided with the Jews, and some of them fought with the Israelis against the Arabs. The young Druse men are conscripted into the Israeli army. Two Druses are members of the Knesset.

I was one of a party of tourists—one of the few occasions in Israel when I went with a group of tourists—which visited the village of Isfiya, which is near Haifa. The population is Christian and Druse. Isfiya resembles many Palestinian Arab villages. It is located in hilly country, and the houses are small and built of stones. The streets are mainly rocky and unpaved, and a number of them are narrow. The village grew and is unplanned in contrast to newer Jewish settlements. The women are dressed colorfully in native costume. The older men are in Arab dress. The younger men look like young Arabs and wear trousers and shirts open at the neck. Children are everywhere, a number of them barefoot. A sense of poverty or at least poorness and backwardness permeates the atmosphere. The women stare at you dark-eyed. The men are friendly and you will receive more smiles than in an Arab village.

We met one of the elders, a grandfather, who proudly pointed to pictures of him taken with his family and government dignitaries, and then, with refreshments, we were addressed by an educated young Druse who speaks English. Afterwards, he answered questions and I had a private interview with him. Because we were coming, he had gotten out of a sick bed to receive us.

He explained that the Druses were a minority and that the rites of their religion are secret. Thirty Druses had married Hebrew girls. The Druses can live together with Christians or Jews but not alone in a Muslim community. There are about 150,000 Druses in Syria and "the Syrian government does not want to help the Druses." He further said that the Druses are an individualistic people who believe in freedom and have fought for it. One of the last times they did was when they sided with Israel against the Arabs.

"We believe," he said, "that if there are any people all over the world to be establishing world's minorities, it is the Jews. If there is anyone to understand the word freedom, it is the Jews."

And he claimed that the Druses are related to the Jews through their prophet Jethro.

He continued:

"We believe that this state is our state, our home. The State of Israel is paying the bills of freedom for all the minorities of the Middle East."

He further described the life of his people. Women pray separately from men, set apart from them by a partition. Cigarette smoking is against the code of the Druse religion but many of the young Druses smoke. If they do, they are not considered pure and cannot pray. He does not conform to all of the practices of his religion, but he stays with his people and wants to see the conditions of their life improved. A new road had been built to their village, but they still needed electricity, and, also, better schools and school facilities.

There are, he asserted, 50,000 Druses in America, and he stated that Danny Thomas is a Druse. He described his plan to visit America with the hope of raising money among Druses there. He wants to launch a bond drive, selling bonds just as there are Israel bonds sold here. He has since done this and appeared on television in this country. The money thus raised could, he said, be used to aid in the economic improvement of the life of the Druses. And he said:

"It's our dream to have our own state."

Many questions were asked of him, religious, political, social.

He said that while there was much to be done and achieved, the Druses were not satisfied with material conditions of the present even though there has been much improvement in these respects since the founding of the State of Israel.

Also he referred to the secondary schools, a problem in all Israel. The government cannot afford as yet to give free secondary school education, although there are indirect aids. This situation is not at all satisfying, and it is hard for the Druses because of the cost of education.

A new thing, though, in the life of the Druses is that they are serving in the Army. The Israeli Army, as is well known, is used as a means of education and of integrating new young immigrants. The Druses, according to this young man who is one of their leaders and spokesmen, consider that by being allowed to serve in the Army, they have gained a right.

Most of them work in agriculture, raising cotton. Some are skilled workmen, or are policemen or soldiers. They are getting some new machines and tractors. In his area, they had one tractor in the Mandate period, but in 1956, they had ten.

Speaking further, he said:

"Revolution is our life. Our youth go to kibbutzim and feel themselves sabras."

By revolution he appeared to mean change, progress.

But these changes have produced conflict among the Druses. The old people and the young do not see with the same eyes or hopes. Thus, he said, 90% of the old are religious; 90% of the young are unorthodox. As another instance of change and conflict, he referred to a Druse woman who is married. She threatened to leave home if she had to vote as her husband told her to. This Druse woman is not as singular as she may seem. During the last Indian elections, there was a dispatch in the *New York Times* telling of an Indian Rani who was running against her husband. The women in the district told their husbands that unless they voted for the Rani, they would not cook their supper. The Rani defeated her husband and took her seat in the Indian Parliament.

The young Druse leader kept stressing and coming back to the assertion that "We feel we are citizens."

On further questioning concerning the economic conditions of the Druses, he estimated that there had been about a 30% improvement for them since the establishment of the State. Also they now have farming co-operatives, but not on a large scale.

I asked him how did he know, what information he had that his fellow Druses were suffering in Syria. He stated that because of the Arab-Israeli conflict, they had no contact with their fellow Druses in Syria or other parts of the Arab world. But he cited an instance, then recent, of a Druse who, as Syrian Chief of Staff, had been dismissed from the Army and had fled. And he insisted that in Syria, Druses do not have equal rights.

In another context, he had said:

"With Muslims alone, we don't live."

There were more questions on education and he spoke of the lack of funds, but added that this is a problem of all Israel.

He also stated that he favored girls going to school, *up to 15*. He stressed this age. Prior to the founding of the State of Israel, Druse girls didn't attend school.

Peace was also on his mind: "Fanatic Arabs could not understand they could live peacefully with the Jews." And the only chance of peace is to be seen in socialist movements in the Middle East.

"A new socialism and democracy would remove them [the Arabs] from their chains."

But there are Druses on the other side who would support the Arabs in war. This is painful to him. And he insisted again on his friendship for the Jews. One of the last things he said was:

"If you have now Jews willing to build the State of Israel, this proves that you have freedom, democracy here."

Peace, progress and material improvements, these were what concerned him. Even little improvements are significant to him.

Also, he stressed all that is yet to be done, the need for more advances. He said that a particular problem is that of finding work for returned soldiers:

"I would like to do everything for them. I have done nothing" for there is "nothing on hand."

There were dances by the young Druses and when we left many waved good-bye. A number of the young men were smoking cigarettes.

Among the Druses as among the Arabs and others in Israel you see the stirrings of progress, the effect of technology entering the lives of people and also the impact of Western ideas. You are aware that there is a multitude of problems and the rising of hopes. With this, there is the tension of old and new. And some of the things which are new are to us so familiar that we take them for granted. Thus, it has been an important fact that now there were five telephones in Isfiya, and that there is a better bus service to and from this little village. When we consider what is going on in Israel and the Middle East, we must understand that there are clusters of problems. All of the other problems of change, progress, education, the development and deepening of democracy, are distorted by the Arab-Israeli conflict. The other problems exist. They seem clearly to be inducing changes in the mind and heart and attitude. In Israel, you see these problems with perhaps added sharpness because of the essentially Western ideals of its founders and leaders. Ben-Gurion, when interviewed by me, asserted that while they based themselves on the prophets, they believed in science and the development of rational techniques. The effort to apply science and technology, the attempt to build a prosperous state in what was once a desert—this is where the sharp contrast between East and West exists. There were similarities between some of the problems of the Arab minority and some of those faced by the new immigrants. There are cultural clashes between generations, between old customs and new ways. If we constrain and confine our conception of Israel to the issues, often so polemically presented, of the Arab-Israeli conflict, we will deceive ourselves into understanding less than we might of what is happening. We can generalize by stating that the problems of Israel are those of peace, progress and integration of its population. In the foregoing pages, I have concerned myself largely with representing these problems in terms of what some of the people themselves say and think. I have attempted to give some picture of what it is like to them and what they are like.

CHAPTER SIXTEEN

I

M^Y TRIP to Israel was part of a journey around the world. I happened to stay longer in Israel than in other countries because my schedule permitted me to do this. In the other Asian countries I visited, all too briefly, I did meet a variety of people. I asked questions, interviewed as much as I was interviewed, spoke with writers and intellectuals, statesmen and parliamentarians, airplane stewardesses and officials, union leaders, journalists, businessmen and others.

There were times when I seemed to have lost my perspective. Thinking and consuming impressions on the run, learning how many of my views and assumptions were not fully grounded in fact, my thoughts fluctuated; at times, it seemed as though I were in contradiction with myself. I was received with a kindness I shall always remember, cherish and regard as a demonstration of the potential goodness and generosity of human beings and of their capacity to gain some understanding of one another, even though they are from different cultures and live at opposite ends of the earth. In spite of this, I sensed the potential, if somewhat generalized, hatred which many Asians bear toward white men, Americans included. In some instances at least, this is superficial, and due to the fact that Asians must digest so much which is new to their experience and they must adapt to so many changes in their world. In Karachi, at a group luncheon, a gifted, well-read and fine looking girl broke out in bitter anger and berated an American official; she proclaimed that she hated white men. Also in Karachi, a woman, gifted, talented, a fine writer, with acute sensibility, said:

"I hate white men."

This was not a total statement of their feelings, but rather an expression of mood. In many instances, this hatred should be analyzed as such an expression of mood rather than a full expression of the feelings of Asian people.

In Bombay, I rode through police lines to interview Prime Minister Nehru. Within two hours, the crowds behind the police lining the Marine Drive were rioting violently. Attending a session of the All India Committee of the Congress Party, I missed another riot by the skin of my nose. In Karachi, the director of a big textile factory criticized me bitterly because I was an American and he held me responsible for various American policies to which he objected. To the contrary, I must add that I met others who were friendly to America and Americans.

On the whole, I can only be impressed by the number of people I met who discussed questions with me frankly, intelligently and openly. Various of the people I met had little in common. Some of the Pakistanis felt bitter about Nehru and India. Others did not. There were Indians who reciprocated the Pakistani feelings of bitterness. The Arabs were anti-Israel. Some looked to America; others were confused about it, or even resentful. But from all this welter of experience and impressions, I carried away with me a feeling of the number of serious, kind and hospitable persons there are in this world.

I can perhaps never forget the poverty I saw, the people sleeping almost like flies in the streets of Bombay, some because of the heat, but others because they were homeless. The crowded streets of Bombay at night, girls in their little cubicles, boys on the street, simple Indians, some of them from the country, visiting the simple and beautifully arranged grave of Gandhi. A wretched refugee camp in Karachi, workers in Karachi. Hindus on a Sunday at Raj-Ghat in New Delhi, burning or cremating their dead, the smoldering ashes of burned corpses. I saw a world of hope, fear and hatred, a world in torment, a world of startling contrasts.

Considering all this varied experience, why did I concentrate on Israel and devote this book to some of my impressions of that country? If my sympathy and desire to understand something of these other countries means anything, let me say that it is not that I love Israel more or prefer it. I did, however, on arriving in Israel, find myself more at home because it is Western. Among Western Israelis I was able to talk with less of a sense of strain, the strain you feel when you want to be frank, clear, and when you are talking with sensitive people from another culture whose frame of references is so different from your own. Furthermore, in Israel I had a better opportunity to meet with many who come from the simple humanity of Asia. I refer to the Oriental immigrants whom I have described in this book.

Much time will be required before East is not East and West is not West. Effort as well as time will be necessary before the emotions of people of different cultures settle and they feel a stronger sense of identity or, even though the word be sentimental, of brotherhood. And an effort to attain this ideal must be made on both sides of invisible bridges of misunderstanding. A Swedish journalist and teacher visited my home after spending a year in the American Midwest. She was returning to her home in Stockholm.

"Perhaps we Europeans and you Americans can be cousins," she said.

Perhaps many of us from different cultures must first become cousins before we can attain brotherhood.

This book is but a beginning for me, not a final statement. We Americans are but beginning to learn of the world. And abroad, they are but beginning to learn of us. In this present world, we cannot escape politics if we seriously seek to understand others and to participate, however little, in the many types of constructive effort which are now called for. We cannot honestly be continuously neutral and cautious. We are cowards if because of the dread of mistakes, we attempt no conclusions or risk no generalizations; we are cowards if we sink ourselves into endless ambiguities, avoid discussion and fear to think aloud.

II

Among Jewish people, the establishment of the State of Israel, the winning of a Jewish homeland, has created many crises and an upsurge of much feeling. It is an oversimplification to classify American or other Jews as Zionists, anti-Zionists, or neutral. The State of Israel has many meanings for Jewish people, involving emotions of pride, hope, guilt, opposition and antipathy. It is my impression that there are Jews who are both Zionist and anti-Zionist, who are against one another and who have a strong and apparent sense of guilt. One sensitive, intelligent and extremely well-informed Jewish intellectual openly revealed this to me. Recalling his boyhood in Russia, he described how the Jewish children were poor, excluded, on the outside. Now in Israel, he observed, the Jews are the majority, and it is their country. The Arabs are in the minority and in many ways they are excluded. In this new situation, one so totally strange and seemingly miraculous for the Jews, are they doing right? Are they being moral? Does Israel have a moral case? Is Israel acting fairly to the Arabs? Should not Israel and its leaders be more moral, even more moral than leaders of any other country? Questions like these are a source not only of doubt but also of torment.

The establishment of a State of Israel after centuries of dispersion is an extraordinary fact in history. It is all the more extraordinary after the scourge of Hitlerism. An American-born girl, now working in Israel and a citizen of that country, remarked to me:

"When we saw the Jewish policemen, we didn't believe it."

Only the day before, the police were British, regarded as the enemy, the force of imperialism. And then the British were gone. The new police were Jews. It did not seem believable.

A couple of Israelis, Western-born but raised as Zionists, laughed and one of them joked:

"I believed it was true when there was the first rape case; then I knew it was our state."

The sense of this remark was that now the Jews had their own land; they could be themselves. Not all of them were good. They were human. Some were even evil. But they had something of their own.

Another Israeli, Viennese-born, explained to me the moment when he knew that they would win the war in 1948.

"There were the four corners and the Arabs were shooting and sniping from every one of them. I saw a man of forty-five with a hat on. He walked across the street, reading his newspaper. The shots were flying . . . This way, that way, every way. And he walked on through them. He kept reading his paper. He didn't look up. Then I knew that we would win."

If Israelis, either sabras or immigrants, who have staked their life on a future in Palestine, could feel bewilderment, then many Jews in other parts of the world would feel likewise; perhaps their feelings would even be more pronounced. It seems to me that many Jews abroad should not or could not react to the news of the new state casually, as though to another item of information from afar, or, let us say, as though they had just heard on the radio that the New York Yankees had won another World Series. The assimilation of the fact that a collective dream had come true—and for some Jews *Eretz Israel* was precisely this—produced an intensification of emotions and attitudes. Elation, joy, disillusionment, guilt, confusion. The State of Israel has stimulated passions, in the Jewish world as well as in the Arab world.

Because Palestine is located in a strategic area of the world which has become the political battleground between the two giant powers, the Arab-Israeli conflict has become a world issue and its meaning in America should not be underestimated. While many of the points of bitter issue, and many of the thoughts, feelings and passions bound up in this conflict are local in character, the significance of this same conflict is recognizably international.

In the debates, the unleashing of charges and countercharges, blasts and counterblasts, facts and polemical points are mixed together as though they were the same thing. Behind the conflict, in addition to its passions and feelings, there are many disputed points of history. Who is responsible for the conflict? Who is responsible for the mass flight or exodus of the Arab refugees? Who is responsible for the continuance of their miserable plight? Who should pay for them? Morality is involved in the answer to these questions, but fundamentally, they pose issues of fact. There are additional questions of importance even though these be secondary to the ones I have just posed. Thus, is the Government of Israel fair in its treatment of the Israeli Arabs, and are its laws, especially its regulations about absentee Arabs, just? An ordinance permits the government to take the land of Arabs who were absent from their villages and homes in 1948.

But all of these questions can be centered around one which is basic. Does Israel have the right to exist? Should it be destroyed? There is no doubt that many Arabs desire its destruction. In New York, I discussed these questions with three Egyptian officials. One said:

"I wish for Israel to cease to exist."

The two others concurred. So do many other Arabs.

In considering the question of Israel's right to existence, are we going to answer this in the affirmative and offer as our reason the fact that Israel is a *fait accompli?* Or do we think that there are facts and moral reasons to warrant the assertion that Israel has earned its right to remain a sovereign nation? It is a creation of the U.N. But U.N. resolutions are not always universally accepted as binding international law, and the policy of Arab nations has generally been that of accepting U.N. decisions and resolutions which the Arabs consider favorable to them. India on Kashmir and the Soviet Union on Hungary have flouted U.N. resolutions.

Concerning these questions, I did not, by direct experience and by reading, uncover or find what I could consider sufficient evidence to conclude that all the blame, that full responsibility, morally and historically, can be laid at the door of Israel and its national leaders. This is all that is necessary and sufficient to take a position other than one demanding of Israel that she make all of the gestures, compromises, sacrifices and concessions. Such a demand is, in essence, what many Arab leaders and some who defend the Arab position want.

A further set of questions is involved in this very complicated and dangerous conflict. When the U.N. partition resolution was passed, the Arab nations refused to accept it. Now the Arabs demand that Israel abide by this resolution, as well as by a U.N. resolution calling for it to permit either repatriation or the payment of compensation to the Arab refugees. Conditions in Israel have changed since 1947. For Israel now to abide by the 1947 resolution would mean to give up land taken in war after the Arab armies had marched into Palestine rather than accept the partition resolution.

The Arabs contend that Israel is expansionist and that it will seek to establish as its borders the ancient territory of Zion. Selim Lahoud, then the Lebanese Foreign Minister, made this contention to me in an interview. The same assertion has been made by others. Also, Israel is described as a nation of Western imperialists and it is stated that it will destroy the Arab world. It is probably or at best possibly true that the right wing Herut Party, if it should win power with strong enough popular support, might try to launch an expansionist war. But Herut is not all of Israel. We make distinctions in our judgment of other countries. We do not equate the Pujadists with all of the French. We do not attribute to all of Great Britain the views of Aneurin Bevan. During the height of the McCarthy furor, we ourselves often argued with Europeans and Asians that the late Senator McCarthy did not represent all of us. Are we reasonable and fair in attributing to all of the Israelis the views and position of an extremist party?

The immigration policies of Israel are often criticized. It is claimed that by its policies of unlimited immigration, Israel is preparing to expand and that it will even have to do so. What I have already written in this book about the new immigrants is, I believe, adequate evidence to indicate that such criticisms are, at best, oversimplified. The new immigrants are needed as part of the defense of the country. This is clear. But that is not the only reason why they are admitted to Israel. And a *few* of them, the old, the lame, the blind, the helpless who are admitted are of no military or economic value whatsoever to Israel. Many Israelis welcome the new immigrants and do not see them as dupes or cannon fodder. This is fact. The idea that the new immigrants are being brought into Israel merely to serve as soldiers is false. The greater proportion of Israelis to whom I have talked have as their main hope the building of the little portion of land which they now occupy.

In any consideration of Israel's policies of immigration, there is a further point which must be stressed—that of national sovereignty. Israel is a nation, recognized by many other sovereign nations. If in addition to recognition of this fact, you also assume that Israel has the right to exist, then it can be more strongly emphasized that Israel has the right to determine its own immigration policies. If France or Switzerland take in an unlimited number of immigrants, would it be demanded that the U.N. act to force them to abandon such a policy? If the Government of Pakistan admitted Muslims now living in India, would the same demand be made? Or if the Nasser government admitted a number of Sudanese, would the U.N. be called upon to stop Egypt from doing this?

The Arab nations, now in the fevers of a fierce nationalism, are constantly asserting their independence. Many who write on the Arab-Israeli conflict demand that the U.N., the United States, or both, require that Israel make a number of concessions to the Arabs, restrict its immigration policy, sacrifice sovereign national rights; they even propose that a form of economic sanctions be imposed on Israel if these demands should be rejected by the Israeli Government. Thus it is proposed that the United States end all aid to Israel and by government action prevent American Jews or others from sending private aid and capital to Israel if they so desire. Would the same demand be made concerning Pakistan which could not subsist without American aid? The case is somewhat cognate.

The reader will note that in the refugee camps, I was told that if the United States does not help the refugees, they will take aid elsewhere, that is from Russia. Arab leaders and many others have spoken this same language. President Nasser has already done precisely that. Others, like Charles Malik, have warned of the Communist danger, especially among the refugees, and are of the opinion that unless the United States adopts an understanding position towards the Arabs, the Communists will gain. These statements, often verbally similar, must be differently interpreted according to who makes them. The refugees speak out of confusion, frustration, misery. Malik, pro-Western, a democrat, a man of ability, was issuing warnings, warnings which, clearly, were also related to the fate and future of Lebanon. Since he made such statements, Lebanon has known civil war. Others are speaking this language in what amounts to virtual international blackmail.

It is argued that the Israelis are 2,000,000; the Arabs are 45,000,000. The course of *realpolitik* would call for America to support the Arabs. Besides oil, there are 45,000,000 to fight Communists. But there are about 90,000,000 Pakistanis and about 370,000,000 in India. Nehru and the overwhelming number of Hindus resent American military aid to Pakistan. This even includes pro-Western Hindus who are friendly to the United States. If the argument is here applicable to the Israeli-Arab conflict, it is equally relevant to the Pakistani-Indian dispute over Kashmir which is almost as bitter.

This argument is also based on the assumption that there is unity among the Arabs and that they can be organized into a political and potential military force which can oppose the Russians if and when necessary. Events since the Suez crisis should have dispelled these illusions.

Furthermore, the advice to back the Arabs lest they sell out to the Soviet Union could well put American Middle Eastern policy at the mercy not only of blackmail but of street mobs. It was street mobs which forced General Glubb Pasha out of his position as head of the Arab Legion in Jordan. The American flag in Amman was torn down by a mob. Street mobs were called out in the effort to force Hussein into an anti-Western, anti-Eisenhower Doctrine position, but the young King won that round. If the United States bases its Middle Eastern policies on this kind of reasoning, the State Department and the President will be at the mercy of any ruler with an unstable government who can threaten us. President Sukarno of Indonesia can tell us that he'll go over to Khrushchev, too, unless we give him what he wants. In New Delhi a successful journalist, a man who knows the West and is sympathetic to it, said to me:

"You Americans are afraid of the Communists. If we

insult you and flirt with the Communists, we can get more aid."

I have no evidence that this is Nehru's view. But the fact that this statement was made by a man known to hold pro-Western sympathies, is illustrative of the possibilities in store for this country if it adopts the caricature of a policy of *realpolitik* and gives aid and unqualified support to any nation on the ground that otherwise that nation will go to Moscow.

Concerning Israel's policies, it should be recognized that Israel's situation is extreme, not normal. The relationships between Belgium, France and the Netherlands are normal. Israel is blockaded economically. Arab leaders have threatened its destruction. The Arab League even attempts to force various private companies not to do business with Israel. Infiltrators do go into Israel to steal, maraud, kill. Civilians and children have been killed, and even foreigners are not always safe. Every time you drive in a taxi on the frontier, your taxi driver carries a gun to protect you and himself. In most instances you are safe, but you never can know. In this situation, Israel has pursued a policy of retaliation. Mostly the retaliations are military commando attacks, aimed at a police post or military objective. But Arab civilians, too, have been killed, for instance in Kibya in October 1953 when 66 Jordanians were reported to have died from Israeli bullets. It is claimed that the Arabs have been forced to arm, to infiltrate, and that Nasser was driven into the lap of Moscow because of Israel's attacks. There is not and cannot be all right and justice on one side in the kind of situation which prevails along the Israeli-Arab borders. There cannot be one-sided provocation. It is not my aim here to take a one-sided pro-Israel position. Rather, I want to describe the situation as I see it. It is important to recognize that the majority of the Israelis fear that if they are weak, they will be killed and driven into the sea. They build up their military strength consciously and at the expense of a more rapidly paced development of the country. This and the other facts cited here are a result of an extreme situation.

If the following propositions are true, then they have bearing on the moral judgments made concerning Israeli policies. To repeat—the situation is extreme. Israel has the right to exist as a nation. The Arab leaders refuse to recognize that right and some of them have plainly declared that they want Israel obliterated. The United Arab Republic claims the rights of belligerency in refusing the passage of Israeli ships through the Suez Canal. In such a situation, a government does and must act differently from, say, the way the governments of Switzerland or Denmark would. In connection with all of these points, propositions, contentions, one more significant question is relevant. Do the Arab leaders bear any responsibility for the situation, and especially for the outbreak of war in 1948? If so, and clearly they do because they ordered the march of their armies, then any moral case against Israel, especially since the situation is extreme, must be based on an acceptance of responsibility for that war. We know Nasser and other Egyptian officers who fought in the war were bitter, felt betrayed and believed that the real enemy was at home. For instance, Captain Yeruham Cohen has indicated this in a most interesting article, "The Secret Negev Talks," published in *The Jewish Observer and Middle East Review* (London) for February 18, 1953.

To an outsider, such as myself, it would seem that none of the evils and the claims of injustice can be as threatening and as unbearable as the situation of running conflict and continuous deterioration which exists in the Middle East. How can the "evils" of peace be worse? Peace must be negotiated, not imposed. It will not be peace if the big powers force Israel to concede to Arab claims in advance. This is especially so because the bases for these claims concerning the war, the development of the refugee problem, and the recurrent fighting are not firm and clear. The evidence does not point one way and directly at Ben-Gurion and the other Israeli leaders.

It seems impossible now to expect negotiations. But even so, why cannot there be negotiations in a neutral capital? Why cannot this be a central aim, one around which world opinion would be organized? And if we should stress negotiations for peace as our main aim, does it do any good for us, especially private citizens, to sit on another continent and to outline what the peace conditions should be and who should give up what, even in advance of negotiations? If, for instance, Charles Malik lays out conditions, this is different, regardless as to whether we may agree or disagree with him. He is involved in the conflict in a responsible manner. But for us whose responsibility is nil to say that Israel should give up Western Galilee or to make other concrete demands—this is irresponsible. What is responsible conduct is to emphasize that the road to a solution is that of direct negotiations. The festering hatreds of defeat in the past cannot produce anything but more pus and bloodshed. Russian submarines sold for Egyptian cotton will feed no fellaheen. For the Arabs as well as the Israelis, this situation and conflict can in the long run be maiming and destructive. Even during years of tension, Israel has progressed, developed, and is growing stronger economically. The Arab nations are underdeveloped, and there is admitted poverty and misery in their lands. The governments are unstable. They must turn to the United States or the Soviet Union to continue any struggle. They cannot open a full attack on their own problems, problems which not only press upon the mass of the Arabs but also cause a shortening of the lives of many of them. It is inconceivable that a nation of less than 2,000,000 can rule 45,000,000. With peace, it is safe to assume that the extremist right in Israel will decline rapidly in any influence it possesses. It is not the government. The Israelis I have described in this book, often presenting the exact words I got in the translations, clearly are not thirsting to march to Saudi Arabia and to rule all the land in between. With peace, most of them will try to do what we and our forbears have tried to do—live a little better, with a little more security and happiness, and to grow a little more. They deserve that much. And the Arab peoples deserve no less.

III

It is always more comfortable to observe the faults of others rather than one's own. It is easier for Americans to criticize the practices, policies and customs of another country rather than those which prevail here in the United States. Especially since the onset of the cold war and the continuing Russian hate-America campaign, a number of Americans have attempted to defend and uphold the institutions of this country and, at the same time, to explain that while we have problems and serious evils to eradicate, there are nonetheless many positive features in the American way of life. They have attempted to convince foreigners that a black and white picture of the United States is not only false, but is even a gross distortion. They have objected to and opposed those who would hold a monolithic view of the United States. It is well for us to remember this when we look abroad, and especially in all instances when we are describing the conditions, the problems, and the evils in any democratic society. For in a democratic society, there is a free play of groups and an open conflict of interests. Many people can talk and write. Parties can be organized. We even have the Ku Klux Klan in America. In considering some of the problems of Israel, then, let us keep considerations like these in mind. For regardless of any rationalizations, charges and accusations, Israel is a democratic society. The rights of opposition, association, free speech and assembly exist. During the recent period of pressure on Israel, when there was a dangerous threat of the imposition of sanctions, Prime Minister Ben-Gurion won support for the decision to withdraw Israeli forces from the Egyptian territory by democratic means.

I have expressed my own view that Israel's two big problems are peace and integration. In the United States, this may evoke surprise because so many influential Americans think too exclusively in terms of technological and economic concepts and believe that given the conditions of technological advance and economic rise, the good society will almost automatically develop. This is a kind of vulgar Marxism and vulgar faith in progress which does not use what is best, suggestive, provocative and still valid in Marx and in the ideas of progress. Economic determinism is, especially in our day, crude and dangerous. If on the basis of a crude economic determinism we assume that with the American check book alone we can save the free world and assure progress, we risk making a mistake so grave that the free world can be lost. Economic determinism will only make all the more likely the chances of Communist success because of the manner in which they manipulate the hopes and the hatreds born of frustration; they also inculcate a crude oversimplification of Marxism, which in itself is a form of vulgar economic determinism.

In addition to the need for material and technological

progress in the underindustrialized countries, there is also the need for freedom. These countries must not only breach the barrier of poverty and raise the standard of living of the people, but they must do this while they are developing a democratic society. The alternative to progress under conditions of freedom is authoritarianism and totalitarianism. In our day, this means the kind of society which now exists in the Soviet Union.

The democratic freedoms which we now enjoy have been paid for at the cost of blood, thought, feeling and work. First conceived in ancient Athens, democracy as a system still only prevails for a minority of the world's population. And the price which mankind pays for tyrants has always been tragically high. Today, it can even be totally catastrophic. We are still paying the price for such tyrants of our own era as Stalin and Hitler. Despite all of the other factors involved, despite the clusters or networks of problems which are connected with and part of the East-West rivalry and the hydrogen stalemate, the basic issue today is that of freedom or slavery.

Ortega y Gassett observed in *The Revolt of the Masses* that the state is a creation. The state and society are both creations of the mental and physical efforts of many men over the long course of the generations. And democracy, with its ideals, its hopes, its institutions and its way of life is such a product. It literally represents the hope of mankind to end the long period in which history has been a nightmare tale of "blood, sweat and tears." Democracy represents a spiritual investment, the basic capital of the West at the present time, when the survival of mankind itself can hang in the balance. Squander and waste that spiritual investment in democracy which should be our heritage, and all of our wealth and know-how can only give us and our heirs a life of continued and perhaps exacerbated torments. Dissipate this investment of the generations and we can become a new Rome, a technological Rome. For our own security, for the preservation of a great heritage, and with this, in order to make of our democratic tradition something living, we need to stand by those countries which are free.

In his article, *Seven Great Errors in United States Foreign Policy* (*The New Leader,* December 24-31, 1956), Reinhold Niebuhr remarked that America cannot let Israel go down. If for no other reason, this cannot be done because of the spiritual investment of the West which it represents. Niebuhr was thinking of the Judeo-Christian religious tradition which is also a motivating factor in the background of all Western society, including modern Israel. Niebuhr's remarks represent my own attitude towards Israel.

As I see this little country, the question is more than Zionism and anti-Zionist: it is that of a free society struggling to survive and to grow. Israel is a democracy and represents something of the best of Western tradition. To many Arabs also, Israel represents the West. But the West is not solely the inventor and practitioner of imperialism. The West has been and is the repository of freedom. The West of the ideas of freedom and democracy is also part of what Israel represents. The leaders and founders of Israel did not only read the Bible. They were products of the West in a period of hope, of faith in progress. I refer to Ben-Gurion's generation. Prior to World War I, socialism was a profound and healthy moral force in Europe. The Russian revolutionary movement was saturated with moral fervor, faith, hope in the Westernization of Russia after the Tsar should have been overthrown. In those days, fascism had not been conceived, and antirational philosophies had not captured many sensitive minds as it now has. Young Jews like Ben-Gurion absorbed the ideas of freedom and progress which nourished the cultural and political climate prevailing prior to the onset of World War I. Nevertheless, the ideas of progress, democracy and socialism were often linked together in the early years of this century, and these constituted the great hope of a future in which there would be peace, security and a chance for everyone to develop in accordance with his capacities.

Nationalist movements against a foreign oppressor acquire characteristics different from the nationalism of, say, the French. Religion and socialism, Karl Marx and God, are sometimes mixed in the nationalism of subjugated peoples. They sometimes rely on the ideas of an ancient past as a source not only of argument but also of confidence and emotional strength. After the Parnell defeat and fiasco, the Gaelic past was rediscovered and became an inspiration for the Irish literary renaissance. The Jews are peculiar here because they did not live together in their own land. But with Zionism, the hunger of many Jews for *Eretz Israel* was stimulated. They became profoundly anxious to return to Palestine, which they considered their homeland. As is known, Theodor Herzl, founder of Zionism, projected the idea of a Jewish State. In Palestine during the first two decades of this century, Zionist or national consciousness, if you will, acquired new roots and added depth of emotion. In the 1930's, the Jews fought the British, who were then the rulers of Palestine. Many of them attacked British imperialism. During the course of the secret armistice talks in the Negev, when General Yigal Allon's army had encircled the Egyptian army, Captain Yeruham Cohen, Allon's adjutant, spoke at length with Colonel Nasser about the Jewish struggle against British imperialism. Nasser listened and asked many questions. At that time, Nasser's nationalist feelings were directed much more against England than Israel. The change in Nasser from 1948 to the present indicates how the Arabs, whose nationalism is intense, but often negative and destructive, have fastened on Israel as a representative of Westernism. It is a mistake to see nationalism *en bloc*. It can be progressive or reactionary. Within any nationalist movement there are always antagonistic forces. But nationalism, in order to be progressive, must have a social content. The significance of the generation of Ben-Gurion is that their Zionism possessed a positive, a progressive social content. They were Labor Zionists. Factors like these have important bearing on our interpretation of the Arab-Israeli conflict.

Israelis often say that if they did not have many problems, they probably would miss them. One of Israel's problems is religious. In America, a number of liberal Jews fear that Israel will become a theocracy; others declare that it already is one. Israel is not a secular state such as is ours. Asia, let me add, is the continent of religions. Pakistan is an Islamic state. The secular state is a product of the Enlightenment and one of the first such states was the United States. Americans may or may not like it or admire it, but there are many states which are not secular. Some, even though we find grounds to criticize, are democratic. Israel is such a state.

I did not pay much attention to the religious problems in Israel, but such problems exist. They are quite in the open and are discussed. The Rabbinate is an important institution. There is no civil marriage in Israel. Israeli citizens, to be able to marry in the country, must belong to the same faith. A French writer, André Chouraqui, who is very favorably inclined to Israel, observes in his book, *L'État d'Israel,* that with the establishment of the state, marriage was liberalized as contrasted with the Mosaic code. The fact that there is no civil marriage works less hardship than it would seem to, because members of the major religions in Israel rarely intermarry. In Lebanon it is exceedingly rare for Christian and Muslim Arabs to marry. There was one case in Israel which gained considerable publicity. However, in the future, the absence of civil marriage may cause personal pain and agony, and it may in time work as a factor against the full integration of the Arab minority. It is well possible, especially as Arabs are being admitted to institutions of higher learning in Israel, that Arabs will feel more deeply that they are second class citizens.

On certain matters, food and the observance of the Sabbath, observant views prevail. Many restaurants are kosher. In a restaurant in Afulah I asked for milk in my coffee after having had meat. It was refused until my Jewish guide explained that I was a *goy*. In my hotel in Jerusalem, one side of the hotel restaurant was for meat meals, the other for dairy meals. I had to go to the lobby for coffee after a meat meal, and was asked not to smoke in the hotel restaurant on the Sabbath, but some Jews, as well as I, would smoke in the lobby. The army kitchen is kosher. If it were not, then two kitchens and two sets of dishes would be required. Many of the new immigrants, as the reader knows, are strictly observant. Originally, it was a jolt for them to see their daughters go into the army. They feared this, but now many of them accept it. However, an abandonment of kosher food in the army would be too much for them. As it is, they are sometimes shocked by girls in shorts and by the general conduct of the non-observant.

You can get bacon in some places in Israel. But in the midst of a crisis, with infiltration increasing, tension mounting, and the Israeli-Jordanian situation deteriorating, the Knesset took time off to discuss a restriction on the raising of pigs. Some of the observant would ban all pigs from Israel. There is one story of a festival on a kibbutz. Images of all the animals raised on the kibbutz were painted on placards. Among them was the image of a bear. This was supposed to represent pigs. Most of the kibbutzniks are, let me add, non-observant.

Economically, the quite widespread practice of serving kosher food tends to raise prices, and affects the economy of the country. The *shohet*, ritual slaughters, must be paid. Non-kosher food for the non-observant would be cheaper. If Israel raised pigs in quantity, it would be required to import less meat, and would thereby save foreign currency. There is one substitute for this in the increasing amount of poultry raised.

Sabbath in Israel is very restful, and you do find yourself falling into a mood of inner peace. The troubles of the world, your own problems and guilts, the sense of pressure in you, all dissolve in the absorbing quiet which takes hold of you. To experience Sabbath in Israel, even for a gentile, is to know an experience which is rare. On Friday afternoon, you begin to anticipate it, and your expectations rise. Soon the sun will go down and you know that then, some atoms of that refreshing inner peacefulness which we all seek and rarely know will slip inside of you. The buses do not run on Sabbath, except in Haifa. Taxis are operated but in fewer numbers and the rates of the sherut service are higher. But you can travel on Sabbath. Nonetheless, the strictness with which Sabbath is observed produces a rise in the cost of living. For instance, girls in stores or working for the government usually receive salaries which only permit them to get along; they must pay more if they wish to travel on Sabbath, to leave Tel Aviv, which is hot, for a beach or to go somewhere in the country. This constitutes a hardship on some of them.

In Jerusalem, the fanatics of the Neturu Karta sect in the Mea Shearim section will, on occasion, stone you in a car on Sabbath. Now and then, if you walk along the street smoking, you might be insulted, and in a rare instance, a fanatic might even spit in your face. But most of the Israelis are tolerant, including many who are orthodox and strictly observant.

Concerning the question of the Reform Jews, this is an issue which I shall not discuss. It excites some American Jews, and they are even bitter in their criticism. Jewish people themselves can deal with this question. For me to become involved in it would be as exhausting and time-wasting as it would be to get in the middle of a quarrel between a husband and wife. However, I might add that since I began this book, I have learned that a new institution in Jerusalem will include a Reform Synagogue.

Here, at all events, are aspects of the religious problem of the Israelis. The Muslims and Christians are not directly involved in it, and they, like the Druses, have freedom to worship according to their beliefs and conscience. The Rabbinate is not the only factor in this situation. To repeat, the mass of the new Oriental immigrants are strict. They will probably play a strong role in any effort to restrict the power of the rabbis and to relax observance as it is now practiced. Politically, observant Jews have power, mainly through the right wing parties, and they can also gain some support among elements of American Jewry, on whom Israel remains so dependent. More important is the need of unity in Israel in the face of a dangerous foe from without. For Israel now to engage in a full-fledged fight on religious issues could tear the country apart. This issue in the face of a common danger becomes secondary. Whether measures be good or bad, brave or cowardly, principled or opportunistic, an extreme situation produces compromise and causes a postponement of some struggles. At least in part this is true of the religious issue in Israel. However, if and when Israel attains a secure peace, the fight over religion is likely to break out with much bitterness. It cannot, in my opinion, destroy the country, but it well can produce a divisive struggle of a serious character.

Another problem awaiting Israel on the dreamed-of day when she may have security and peace is of a political and structural character. The state was made possible and could immediately function with at least relative harmoniousness because, prior to 1948, a shadow government existed throughout the Jewish community in Palestine. The Jews were highly organized. Histadrut, the kibbutzim, the moshavim, and of course the Jewish Agency, are examples. These organizations remain powerful. Some of the kibbutzim, for instance, are an integral component of political life. Mapam, left wing and somewhat comparable to the Bevanite wing of the British Labor Party, runs its own kibbutzim, as does Mapai, the major party. Because of these organizations, there still remains something of a shadow government in Israel today.

The Israeli Constitution is unwritten and in a process of evolution. It has been strongly influenced by the British Constitution. But there remain unresolved questions. How much power should the government wield, and how much should remain in the hands of these other organizations? In Histadrut, this question has already been discussed. And it is at least my view that one day, the structural and political problems will have to be openly faced and settled. But again peace is necessary before this can be done. From the standpoint of political theory and the evolution of democracy, this problem is a fascinating one. The variety of democratic institutions, the ingenuity and imagination of man are revealed in the peculiar Israeli institutions, which proved themselves to be so adaptable and valuable to the Jews in Palestine.

Not only in Israel, but all through Asia and the under-industrialized world, the institutional problem in relationship to democracy is fascinating. We will be foolish and unimaginative if we assume that any of these countries can literally take over institutions such as exist in America and make them function as they do in this country. A further development and deepening of democracy in the entire under-industrialized world and also in Israel will call for imagination and ingenuity in devising new institutions and changing old ones to meet problems as they arise.

Economically and technologically, Israel should be able to solve its problems and even one day become self-sufficient—always provided that there is real peace. The population problem with the steady influx of new immigrants is not as acute as that of, say, India. But with skill and know-how, work, and especially with capital released for investment as a result of peace, there should be no doubt of Israel's ability to progress economically. As it is, Israel has, because of the Arab blockade, had to buy above world prices and sell below them, carrying on much of its trade, as for instance with Turkey, on the basis of barter. And because of the conflict, Israel's economy can be thrown out of gear with an increasing emphasis on agriculture. Were there peace and economic relationships, Israel could buy some of its needed agricultural products from Arab countries and develop its manufacturing more than is now possible. Peace also would result in more revenue from the tourist trade, and neighboring Arab countries, Jordan and Lebanon, definitely would similarly profit.

These, then, are some of Israel's problems. The country is not Utopia. Politically it has about twelve parties and the main ones correspond to political groupings in the West. Political life is intense and competitive. In Israel, there is a saying: "Ten Jews and you have twelve political parties." Ben-Gurion and the Mapai Party must struggle to retain influence and leadership. Mapai faces continuous pressure from both right and left. This produces a major danger. If tension continues, if Israel lives on year after year in the present situation of uneasy armistice, with recurrent violence, Mapai can either be forced towards an extremist position or may even lose out to the right. We should not exclude this from the realm of possibility.

Many Israelis believe the nation will survive, even if by miracles. And while idealism runs high, there are dissatisfied people. The other coin of immigration is counter-immigration. This is not too easy, once you have immigrated, because there are restrictions on what can be taken out; but the counter-immigration is a fact, it might run as high as five percent of the number of immigrants who arrive annually. I met dissatisfied new Israelis, among them a Moroccan born and a Rumanian born waiter. They want to get out; they want to come to America. A dream is more attractive than the reality which that dream becomes. When life is hard and demands much work as well as facing danger, the human psyche can take only so much. Israelis are no different in this respect from others.

There are rivalries and dislikes on a group or nationality basis. For long, the German Jews, called "yekkes," were disliked. At present, many Israelis dislike the Rumanians. In turn, I spoke with a cultivated Rumanian

Jewish woman, who had been educated in a Catholic convent; she said that for years, like non-Jewish Rumanians, she had strongly disliked the Hungarians. It took her five years to lose this bias, which obviously stemmed from the rivalries between Hungarians and Rumanians in Europe. And a number of Western Israelis or sabras are dissatisfied about, and even in a generalized way dislike, the new Oriental immigrants. They are, however, a minority. This is not, except in perhaps unusual instances, based on differences in skin color. Rather, it appears to be cultural in origin. The new Oriental immigrants are culturally different, and since they must fit into and adjust to Western conditions, this difference appears as inferiority. There are Westerners who are concerned lest their children be held back when they sit in classrooms with Oriental children, who do not always learn as rapidly as those of Western and sabra parents. Some established Israelis fear that the new Oriental immigrants will overturn their lives and become the power in Israel. In perhaps a few cases, at least, it is not simply Zionism which motivates them in wanting more European and American Jews to immigrate. The relative question of numbers, especially since Orientals have big families, is a factor for their harboring this wish. They fear that their developing way of life will be washed out in a Levantine flood. At the same time, I saw many mixed couples and it appears that intermarriage is on the increase.

These observations point to a danger I sensed in Israel, that of cultural conceit. Occasionally, people revealed this attitude without being aware of it. Among Rumanians and Balkans, you will find a fair number of instances of this. To us in the West, the Balkans have always been regarded as a backward area. Cultivated Balkans usually seem French, or in some instances German, in their culture and sensibility. But in Israel, the Balkan immigrants are Westerners. They are sometimes inclined to over-compensate and act more Western than other Westerners. In addition, you have the factor of small nation psychology affecting these individuals. We Americans have not as yet begun to appreciate the many involutions, the indirect effects and imprints, the stamps on personality and psyche, and the sense of inferiority which winds through the character of many citizens of small nations. I have encountered this in Sweden, Denmark, Holland. Among some of the Israeli immigrants from small nations, and especially from the Balkans, this is apparent. The problem of integration, or at least of welding a national culture, are not limited to Asians and North Africans. Many Europeans must fit more comfortably into Israel also.

As in any other country, you encounter various attitudes. In Jerusalem, I was in a bar with a Viennese girl and her husband, both of them in business. She was in her late twenties, and he in his thirties. A shell wound in the head, received during the fighting, had affected his speech. Strongly in revolt against his father, with whom he had even become a business rival, he does not really like Jews.

"I like Arabs," he said again and again.

Both he and his wife seem to want to make money even to the point of compulsion. She was dissatisfied with the life in Israel.

"I can't tell you. You aren't a Jew," she said.

I strongly objected to this.

To the contrary, a woman I knew said:

"I can tell you this. You'll understand."

She had a good position, was most capable in her work, and could go higher. But even so, and in Israel where women have opportunities and are treated so often as equals, she told me that her advancement was slow and was being hindered because she was a woman.

There are many problems of personal frustration which are individual in character. A beautiful and charming young woman from a small Middle European country, a refugee from the Nazis, like her husband, she was deeply frustrated. She was a singer of folksongs. But she could not learn Hebrew well enough to continue her profession in Israel. To sing in her own language would not win anything but a small audience. Other work did not enlist her deepest emotions. She could not follow the career of which she had dreamed for years. This is not a peculiarly Israeli problem, and, in the main, it is felt by artists. The language problem is a serious one for actors, singers and writers. Anyone who has had contact and experience with writers-in-exile, especially those from small countries, is aware of this problem.

At the Gat Rimmon Hotel, I spoke with a French engineer who was in Israel for professional reasons. I asked him what he thought of Israel.

"It's artificial."

What is and what is not artifical among the nations? The answer to this question depends on what point of history you take as a starting point. America could have been called artificial in the initial period of its history. More important is the fact that people need a home, not only in a personal sense, but also in history and tradition. In a letter to Louis Adamic, Harlan Fiske Stone, the late Chief Justice of the Supreme Court, wrote:

"I never could see any good reason why a former citizen of Yugoslavia or even of Germany should be expected not to cherish the folkways of his native land, any more than I, born in New Hampshire, should not continue to take delight in the traditions which are unknown to most others. . . . A native born American citizen may have a special place in his heart for New Hampshire from which all others are excluded, even Vermont."

Israel is Chief Justice Stone's New Hampshire for many Jews. Without this emotion, this transmuted historic memory, this need, Zionism never could have attained the successes it had. This emotion and not the desire to be a pawn and agent of Western imperialism is, in my view, one of the heart-beats of the Zionists. Like or dislike it, but this seems to me to be the fact. All Jews, including some in Israel, do not feel it. Some feel it without articulating the emotion. But a sufficient number did to create a movement, to return to the ancient land of the Jews, to work as most of us never have, to fight, to risk their life, to lose limb and life in order to realize this emotion, and to win a home in history for themselves and for those whom they consider their kind and kin. In some instances, they were educated in Zionism. But we are all educated and our emotions find channels and outlets accordingly. Not only Hitler and persecution produced Israel. This need, an understandably human one, became part of the spiritual and emotional drive of the Zionists and of others who wanted to go to Palestine.

In addition, there is the phenomenon of the Ghetto. Israel represents a tremendous protest against the Ghetto, and the Israelis, or at least an amazing number of them, seem determined to refute all stereotypes about the Jew in the Ghetto, as well as all other stereotypes about and prejudices against the Jew. This is especially so in the case of the sabras and the new generation. They are becoming a new type. And as they grow, a new Israeli is emerging. In a sense, in this sense, you can say—the Israelis are not Jews.

Today, there are many able and even brilliant men in

Israel. In the struggles of the Israelis against the Arabs, the former have frequently profited by their leadership. But what of the future? Writing in *Commentary* of July 1957, Walter Z. Laquer remarked on the desire of the Israelis to travel, to visit Western Europe, even if for a brief period. He also spoke of a hunger for contact and news from the civilized centers of the West and of the impressive sale of foreign books in Israel as indicative of this hunger. But at the same time, there is much and sometimes intense concentration on Israel's own problems and affairs. That is principally what you talk about in Israel. This suggests the possibility that in the future, if there is peace, a majority of Israelis may develop a parochial, small nation psychology. When the present leaders are gone, and the experience in the West, the absorption of the ideas of the West, sink into the past, this can happen. In a way, the same possibility, and often in a dangerous sense, exists in other new countries. There is a need, not always fully conscious, to find the roots of being and growth in their own country and its culture. The superiority of the West, plus the overwhelming power of America, plus the power of the Soviet Union, plus dependency, are producing confusion, division of spirit, conflicts in mind and emotion, and a need to be proud of one's own country. In Israel, this is peculiar, different from the more homogeneous new countries, but it is there, a psychological factor which should not be overlooked or underestimated.

With success, a rising standard of living, peace if it be achieved, many of the pressures of the technological revolution in Western civilization will be felt more strongly in Israel. Already there is a drift to and yearning for the city. There are rich and poor, but not too many rich. While there are people in Israel from about seventy countries, Western ideas, patterns, ways of doing things, are dominant. As and if these succeed, the same kind of problems felt all over the West will probably be aggravated, ever exacerbated in Israel. But this, while relevant to the situation of modern Israel, is for the future, and at present the future remains somewhat dark and uncertain. However, dark and uncertain as it be, hope and the courage to face the future still are to be found in Israel and in abundance. Ironically, the Arab danger nourishes that hope.

Barring ruthless Russian military attack or total American sanctions, Israel has a strong potential of survival and growth. And if there be war, full-scale war, Israel could only go down if its people are killed or literally driven into the sea. War would be punishing to the Arabs, possibly more so than to the Israelis. It would produce violent crises in the Arab world. The Arabs could either be set back for decades or almost permanently, or else they could become dependent on help from without to a degree greater than that which has existed in the past. If sanity and reason could prevail, then there are prospects for the Middle East. In Averroes' *Commentary on Plato's Republic,* the great Arab medieval philosopher wrote that "man is in need of others in acquiring his virtue." So it is with states. Israel and the Arab states could acquire more of their virtues in neighborly relationships. But today, this seems remote, perhaps impossible. The alternative is, however, war. War would really mean that the Four Horsemen rode in tank and plane over and above the Arab sub-continent. An American can see this more clearly, perhaps, than some of those involved. The seeds of this dangerous and bitter conflict are not only political and economic: they are cultural and emotional, also. And they reveal in the sharpest outline, differences of

East and West. We should see here not only issues and oil, strategy and policy, but also people. A few of these people I have briefly introduced in the foregoing pages. There are many things for them to do besides fight. Conflict is grossly distorting life in the Middle East.

IV

On a hot Sunday morning, I drove with a few newly acquired friends from Tel Aviv to Lydda airport. An El Al plane took me off for Paris. On a sunny afternoon I looked down on Italy, glimpsing from on high what I had seen on the ground. Italy looked so big. And then France was so fertile, the garden of Europe. Flying over these countries, I realized how tiny Israel is. The Suez crisis had broken. Nasser had already nationalized the canal. The French press printed pages of news about the crisis and the Middle East. But the references to Israel were scanty. Just as Israel seemed so small to me when I flew over Italy, so was it secondary in the news about Suez.

Months later, when I was flying from Cincinnati to Chicago, I struck up a conversation with a Christian architect. Speaking of traveling, I mentioned that I had been to Israel; he thought for a moment, and then he said:

"As time goes on, Israel will be more highly regarded for what it is doing."

And in *Freedom and Culture,* John Dewey wrote:

"If there is one conclusion to which human experience points, it is that democratic ends demand democratic methods. . . . Our first defense is to realize that democracy can be served only by the slow day by day adaptations and courageous diffusion in every phase of our common life of methods that are identical with the ends to be reached and the recourse to monistic wholesale procedures is a betrayal of human freedom. . . ."

Day by day, Israel is trying to build towards this end. This is my conclusion now, two years after my visit, as it was when I left Israel, and after experiences and impressions such as I have recorded in these pages.

During the United Nations debates on the Israeli-Arab struggle, the proposal to impose sanctions on Israel, and the question of the final Israeli troop withdrawal from Egyptian territory, an Israeli official spoke privately with a statesman and a U.N. representative from Southeast Asia. The Israeli official said:

"I want to talk to you as a socialist. We're socialists, too. Why are you against us?"

"We envy you the luxury of an opportunity to develop," answered the Southeast Asian diplomat and socialist.

The need for development in Asia is so urgent, the frustration and misery of the masses is so profound and so evocative of sympathy, that one can understand envy, envy of the West, envy of what is dynamic and developing. But envy can bind Asian and Arab minds with an invisible iron band. To the contrary, any spot of Asia which is developed to raise the level of life of the people can be a gain for that entire continent. Any rise in productivity can stimulate a rise elsewhere. Any example of democracy can nourish the feeling for freedom across frontiers. The gains that Israel makes could be meaningful, stimulating even in the lands of its enemies. Again, and despite the seeming hopelessness of the present situation, the best, the most conscionable action we can take is to try to help create a world opinion which will cause a pressure for peace by direct negotiations. In this way, we can perhaps think and act constructively both in terms of policies and peoples.